# THE DEVIL I KNEW

## UNMASKING A SERIAL KILLER

THE INVESTIGATION BY FBI AGENT JONNY GRUSING
INTO THE SCOTT KIMBALL MURDERS

# JONNY GRUSING

# ENDORSEMENTS FOR *THE DEVIL I KNEW: UNMASKING A SERIAL KILLER*

"Over the course of my career, I have produced many true crime shows that feature the most diabolical murderers in the last fifty years. It was not until I covered the Scott Lee Kimball story that I realized, if there was an accolade for the 'most evil,' without a doubt, Scott would receive it. Scott Lee Kimball isn't just a serial killer—he's a haunting embodiment of manipulation, deception, and betrayal from within the very system meant to stop men like him. No one is more qualified to unravel this stranger-than-fiction story than Ret. FBI Agent Jon Grusing, the lead investigator who stared into Kimball's lies, untangled the truth, and brought him to justice."

—Desma Simon, Executive Producer and Director, *Very Scary People*, Investigation Discovery/HBO Max

"The story of serial killer Scott Kimball is one of the most haunting and captivating stories I have ever covered. And there is no one better to tell this intense, riveting saga than former FBI Special Agent Jonny Grusing. This relentless lawman spent more than a decade studying, interviewing, and investigating Kimball—all in the pursuit of justice for the many people whose lives Scott Kimball destroyed. Get ready for a roller coaster ride deep into the mind of pure evil."

—John Quinones, *20/20*, ABC

"A former Division 1 basketball star, Jonny Grusing brought that same competitive spirit and team mindset into the FBI. As a Colorado-based Special Agent, he doggedly pursued notorious serial killer Scott Kimball. *The Devil I Knew: Unmasking a Serial Killer* takes you inside the twist-filled hunt for a devious con man and maniacal murderer. A must-read for true crime devotees."

—Joel Waldman, Host of the true crime podcast "Surviving the Survivor" and the book *Surviving the Survivor*, and Former Fox News National Correspondent

"Jonny Grusing's life is focused on faith, family, friendships, and the willingness to attack evil whenever it appears. His unique skill as an investigator for the FBI and his inspiring faith proved to be the perfect combination to uncover the truth revealed in this book."

—Bo Mitchell, NBA and MLB Chaplain

"Controlling con man Scott Kimball used his role as an informant to manipulate his prior encounters with law enforcement. But when FBI Agent Jonny Grusing took over the case, Kimball had finally met his match. Listening to the pleas of the family members of Kimball's victims led Grusing to the shocking conclusion of this unbelievable murder investigation."

—Jerri Williams, Retired agent and host of the "FBI Retired Case File Review" Podcast

"Scott Kimball is one of the most cunning, ruthless, and elusive serial killers in history, but he met his match with FBI Special Agent Jonny Grusing. For over fifteen years, Grusing relentlessly pursued Kimball across the country like no other investigator, finally bringing him to justice. *The Devil I Knew: Unmasking a Serial Killer* is a riveting inside account of Grusing's exhaustive investigation and face-to-face dealings with the man who simply called himself . . . Hannibal."

—Robert Dean, Producer/Director, Vantage Point Productions, and Former Producer, *Dateline*, NBC

"It's been well over a decade since I covered this story, and I still think about it weekly. Scott Kimball is one of the most dangerous and duplicitous killers I have ever met. It took someone with Jonny Grusing's intelligence and investigative skills to outwit him and help bring him to justice, but it was his empathy for Kimball's victims and their families that really sticks with me."

—Lourdes Aguiar, Senior Producer, *48 Hours*

"Jonny Grusing spent years untangling Scott Kimball's decades-long trail of cons, deceit, and murder, a history so complex and devious it almost defies belief. It's likely the truth would never have surfaced if not for Grusing—his tenacity, his deep empathy for Kimball's victims and their loved ones, and his unrivaled investigative talents."

—Sara Burnett, Former journalist, *Rocky Mountain News* and *The Denver Post*

For the families of Jennifer, Kaysi, and LeAnn.

And Justin and Cody.

And April, Bethany, and Ben.

Special thanks to Larissa, Lori, Bob, and Rob for being my sounding boards and guides throughout the writing of this story. Thanks to Kay Agnew, Lindle Humble, and Kelli Andrews for review. And thanks to my editorial and design team: Nancy Albright, Editor; Ella Kirshbaum, Proofreader; Teddi Black, Cover Designer; and Megan McCullough, Interior Designer.

"Life is pain, Highness.
Anyone who says differently is selling something."
—Westley, *The Princess Bride*

"The world is not full of evil because of those who do wrong.
It is full of evil because of those who do nothing."
—Albert Einstein.

"The purpose in a man's heart is like deep water,
but a man of understanding will draw it out."
—Proverbs 20:5

# CONTENTS

Preface .................................................................................. 1

**1** That's Not Her .................................................................. 7

**2** We've Got a Problem ..................................................... 11

**3** The Detective Dad ......................................................... 27

**4** Montana & Alaska Roots .............................................. 41

**5** The Minion, the Girlfriend & the Brother .................. 67

**6** CB & X-Man .................................................................. 83

**7** Two Bags of Trash ......................................................... 93

**8** The Dangerous Vacuum ............................................. 105

**9** Laptop, Lottery & Left Hook ...................................... 109

**10** Scott Wins ................................................................... 117

| 11 | Seconds Away | 123 |
| 12 | Scott As Hannibal | 131 |
| 13 | A Friggin' Miracle | 149 |
| 14 | Circling Around | 159 |
| 15 | Deeper Deceit | 171 |
| 16 | Deal with the Devil | 183 |
| 17 | Body Hunts | 193 |
| 18 | The Last, Last Trip | 211 |
| 19 | Three Billy Goats Gruff | 223 |
| 20 | A Surprise Trial | 229 |
| 21 | Trashed Terry | 233 |
| 22 | Sentencing | 241 |
| 23 | I Framed Scott Kimball | 249 |
| 24 | Larissa Revisited | 257 |
| 25 | Cat | 263 |
| 26 | Other Murders | 269 |
| 27 | Profiling Scott | 275 |

**28** 21 Homicides ............................................................. 283

**29** The Opportunity Killer ............................................. 289

**30** An Unexpected Death .............................................. 293

**31** The Helicopter Escape Plan ..................................... 297

**32** Making Scott Cry ..................................................... 305

**33** Mod Pizza ................................................................. 311

**34** Lori & Kaysi Revisited .............................................. 317

**35** Kay Revisited ............................................................ 323

**36** Perspectives .............................................................. 327

Epilogue .................................................................... 337

Appendix A: Timeline ............................................. 339

Appendix B: Persons Involved ................................ 341

References ................................................................ 343

# PREFACE

THE KILLER's birth name wasn't Hannibal, though that's how LeAnn knew him. After about eight years into my investigation and correspondingly unfortunate close relationship with him, he told me that he needed a "name." I was driving back to the jail with the killer cuffed in the back seat beside Detective Gary when the killer asked me, "Jon, why didn't you ever name me?" It's been over ten years since that drive, yet I could still point to the portion of the road on eastbound I-70 where we were when he asked that question.

I asked the killer, "What do you mean, name you?"

"You know, like Green River or BTK? Why didn't you name me?"

Famous murderers who got named—of course that's what he was talking about. That, after all, was why we were transporting him from our Violent Crimes Task Force FBI office—where he had been telling his attorneys about all the people he'd killed over the past twenty years—back to the jail, where he would have the privacy needed to name names.

Instead of telling him that the thought of naming him hadn't entered my mind or that we had plenty of names for him, none of which he would appreciate, I asked, "Okay, what name should I give you?"

"The Opportunity Killer. Because I killed people whenever there was an opportunity."

Detective Gary and I just sat there, speechless. Although Gary was gifted at quick, dry, funny retorts, we both knew that this man detested sarcasm and we knew when *not* to poke him. I don't think either of us responded as we continued to transport the killer back to jail.

"The Opportunity Killer" *did* fit all of my investigation to date. He killed a lot more people than I will ever know about because the opportunity cost for me to find those things out was way too high. It will become tiresome for you, the reader, if I only refer to him as "the killer" in telling this story. The killer is Scott Kimball. His crimes are a matter of public record. More importantly, he is the prototype of a predatory hunter of human beings. Scott is an expert at appearing to be the Average Joe. He is your next-door neighbor. Handyman. Outdoorsman. And the classic, attentive gentleman, charming and seducing every woman in the room.

He used the name "Joseph Scott" as one of his aliases while he was killing people in 2003 and 2004. The nondescript name fit perfectly because those who knew him never suspected him of being the most violent and dangerous person they would ever meet. And that is why he labeled himself the Opportunity Killer.

I'm using quotes from my conversations with Scott, the victims, and the witnesses who are part of his story. While the exact words are close, I did not audio record every conversation. I have tried to convey the context and the emotion of the interactions instead of the precise details. This story is how I remember these experiences. I have changed the names of some of the people for a variety of reasons, and I'm not using last names as a general rule for two reasons: (1) there are a lot of critical people in this story to keep straight and last names simply add another layer of detail; and (2) Scott was able to make a lot of people look stupid and feel foolish. Even guilty. Myself included. My intent is to give humanity back to these victims instead of more notoriety to Scott. Those of us closest to him learned valuable lessons in recognizing dangerous behavior in others and ourselves. These lessons are worth passing along.

Through nearly fifteen years of studying, interacting with, and battling against Scott, I learned what a murderer looks like on the inside. After witnessing and experiencing his uncanny intelligence and manipulation, combined with his sadistic and improper expression of emotion, I developed a template of how to deal with subsequent predatory suspects like him who may have killed someone.

Because Scott Kimball, a serial killer, is at the top of the scale for deception, intelligence, manipulation, cold-bloodedness, and charm, I developed one extremely valuable tool: I learned to listen to a new voice in my head during other murder investigations. I could almost hear Scott saying to me, "Jon, if you ever smell even a hint of these things that you've seen in me inside the person you are investigating, that's probably your guy."

And guess what? His unintended instruction was pretty damn effective.

Scott seized money, dignity, reputations, security, and sometimes life itself from doctors, church leaders, prosecutors, his family, my family, his neighbors, the FBI, inmates, judicial systems, law enforcement agencies throughout the western United States, and almost anyone who came across him. Scott's murders have been reported in several documentaries and numerous articles, but none of these accounts can accurately report the important but embarrassing details when everyone is named outright.

This serial killer had three wives. During the investigation I spent enough time with two of them to move from investigator-to-witness status to friend status. Together we walked through the horrors of uncovering the extent of Scott's truly evil self. Scott was married to his first wife for a few brief years in the early 1990s. She has spoken to me when necessary but wants no part of the investigation and would not want to be named at all. His second wife, Larissa, married him in 1993 and gave birth to his two sons. But when she eventually divorced him she became the brunt of his laser-focused manipulation, anger, and sadism. Larissa is very lucky to be alive today and she knows it. His third wife, Lori, married Scott on August 31, 2003, eight days after he was last seen with her only daughter, a beautiful nineteen-year-old named Kaysi.

Hopefully, the story of this investigation of Scott will help you recognize a predator when you see one and prevent you from being conned, or worse. I have often admonished audiences with these words: "Have your antennae up! Pay attention to your spider sense!" You cannot cruise through life assuming your nephew, next-door neighbor, or fellow churchgoer does not possess the ability to be a threat just because he's nice to you. This story should not lead you to become the cynic and the recluse who refuses to leave your house. That is an unhealthy response. Instead, I want to encourage a balanced and healthy awareness that will allow you to live with both eyes open and to accurately assess risks, if and when dangerous people enter your life.

After years of being with Scott in jail cells, deserts, prison transports, court hearings, and car rides, I came to know this man better than his mom, dad, and brother knew him—I knew the adult, criminally exposed Scott. When you're the family member of someone like this serial killer, you never suspect that he's capable of doing the very things he is hiding from you. Killers like this man do not broadcast that they are violent. Scott led everyone around him to believe that he did not have claws or fangs. He continuously and very effectively broadcast a persona that asserted, "I'm just a check fraud guy—I've never been violent." Scott was only violent to people who would never be able to talk about it. Because once he targeted and isolated his victim, they ceased to exist. His assertion that he was not dangerous continued to appear true to everyone around him because he knew how to manipulate the legal premise that everyone is innocent until proven guilty.

This serial killer's mother, Barb, gave me more insight into his true nature than anyone else. But it took a long time for her to become convinced that he *could* do the things we were accusing him of doing. It is almost impossible to convince a mom that her son is a monster—no evidence, no news report, no law enforcement report, no judge, no jury with a guilty verdict is guaranteed to change her mind. That mother must wait until the light finally clicks on, in that deep place inside herself that she has guarded from everyone. And that click is unique to each person. We in law enforcement cannot force that light to click on. It is just too hard for a parent to accept such a horrible truth, because a parent's identity is deeply and intimately tied to what kind of child she raised.

The same goes with dads. I know because I am one. I've seen it in my own dad, and now with other dads, when sons do awful things. We dads give our kids the benefit of the doubt until proof, far beyond a reasonable doubt, finally crushes our last defenses. Reality tries to step through the door, but the parent pushes it back out and slams the door closed again until more evidence begins to seep in through the vents and windows. Sadly, law enforcement tries to shine that light too quickly and too brightly many times, forcing it into the eyes of a family member who loves their child, and the result is alienation. But once that light finally clicks on, the parent can become the investigator's greatest asset. This acceptance won't happen until the mom or dad, or both, trusts you not to judge them, and their soul chooses to allow the possibility of the "awful" to venture inside. It took me a long time, over a year, but I eventually earned Barb's trust, and that opened multiple doorways that led her to know her son for what he truly is.

The serial killer also knew that Barb knew *what* he was. He tried twice to kill her grandson, Justin, his own ten-year-old son, for insurance money in 2004. Scott rarely failed at killing people. Justin is the only survivor who lived to talk about Scott's well-concealed murderous side, and what it looked like just before his life almost ended. However, Scott managed to make both attempts look like accidents, and he skated away with no charges.

I applied what I learned from Scott's two murder attempts on Justin to a handful of future child homicides I was later assigned to investigate. The phrase "there's nothing new under the sun" is appropriate to address the hellish motives behind the drive for any parent to harm their kids. This killer absorbed my time, my energy, and a lot of my career, as his manipulation and intelligence humbled me daily. However, at the same time, he provided me with insight and a new definition and application of patience and persistence. From the families he had victimized, I made friends for life. I developed a template that helped me see into Machiavellian and psychopathic offenders. It is my sincere hope that by reading this you can gain some of the experience and insight that we gained, while only having to travel vicariously with me into the depths of Scott's incredibly twisted mind.

I was unable to take my FBI reports with me when I retired. However, my supervisor, Phil, told me early on in this investigation, "Jon, you better write some of this stuff down 'cause this is a once-in-a-lifetime case. It'll make a good book someday." So, I kept a journal at home. I wrote a few notes each night during my fifteen years with Scott. With the FBI's permission in 2010, I handed over 151 pages of my journal to two investigative reporters who covered this story so they could write the book. It was a very messy affair because of the tangled and complicated timelines of Scott's victims. The journalists took a stab at writing it, but they got busy with life and work and did not complete it. That's why I'm writing my own version. I will reference a handful of documentaries, news articles, and court documents, as well as FBI documents authored by me that Scott had squirreled away in his prison cell. Scott's cousin Ed cut-and-pasted these FBI documents to create a 503-page book that challenged Scott's twisted stories using the assertions in my reports, and Ed attempted to merge the two accounts. Our two stories don't mesh well because, to no one's surprise, Scott remembers and interprets things quite differently than I do.

This is not an exhaustive account of my investigation into the murders and other crimes committed by Scott Kimball. I attempted to write such an account a few years ago, and even after paring it down it was twice as long as this story and still omitted large chunks of the investigation. It read like my affidavits—factual, dry, and packing in copious amounts of probable cause to support investigative conclusions that Scott said what he said and did what he did. Upon review, the FBI did not like it and neither did I. I scrapped everything, used only what was publicly available, and wrote from memory, as I've relived this story for fifteen years through formal and informal presentations about the investigation. I went through what I call a "narrowing." When I retired from the FBI it required a separation of identifying myself as "I'm an FBI agent" to "I worked for the FBI." This account of Scott's horrific taking of lives, money, reputations, and dignity went through the same narrowing.

I placed Appendix A at the end of the book to serve as a simplistic timeline of major events, and Appendix B to illustrate the relationships between Scott's families and his victims.

In accordance with my obligations as a former FBI employee pursuant to my FBI employment agreement, this book has undergone a prepublication review for the purpose of identifying prohibited disclosures but has not been reviewed (by the FBI) for editorial content or accuracy. The FBI does not endorse or validate any information that I have described in this book. The opinions expressed in this book are mine and not those of the FBI or any other government agency.

# 1

# THAT'S NOT HER

"There's a truth to everything I said, Jon. This is a puzzle. You have to figure it out." The killer told me that five years into our relationship, and yet, it defined my entire fifteen years with him.

Two years earlier he told us, "There's a bone." It wasn't significant to any of us at the time. We'd seen lots of sheep bones over the past two months in these canyons as we looked for two of his victims. One of the deputies who had grown up in the area agreed that it looked like another sheep bone. I wasn't good at determining which type of bone came from what. Minutes earlier the killer had told us, "LeAnn might be by a waterfall." And now we were standing by a vertical wall of rocks at the end of a dry creek bed that could have passed for a waterfall, but it was only about eight feet high. He had also said that she could be "in a lot of different places" by this day, March 11, 2009.

As I've replayed the scene in my head over a hundred times, I think it was more his comment, "Okay, let's head the other way," and the nonchalant way he said it that triggered something inside of me. I could never tell when he was lying because he was always lying—even he'd tell you that. It was probably less about my own sense of when he was lying or not, and more about my mom and her church group in West Texas praying that we'd someday find something that made a real difference in this awful case. Maybe it was a combination of all those things and just plain serendipity. The best definition I've heard for the word serendipity is "looking for something and finding something even better."

The killer started heading back down the dried creek bed away from the waterfall with our search party that included his defense attorneys, several FBI SWAT agents, Grand County Sheriff's Office deputies, and Gary, a solid detective who'd become my close friend over the past three years. It was my job to be with the killer at all times. I'd written the memo to get him out of jail, which included shipping him from the middle of Colorado to the Utah border and supervising his supposed "guaranteed plan" to find both of these female victims in one day. When the first attempt failed, I wrote a second memo to the Attorney General's Office to check him out of jail again, assuring their office and the Department of Justice that we would find someone or something on this trip, which had led us to where we now stood by the waterfall. As the search party walked back down the dry creek bed, I just let them go as I looked at the supposed sheep bone lying there in the dry sand and white rocks. I hadn't parted from the killer on any previous trip because he'd already tricked one of my FBI squad mates into thinking that he wasn't the guilty party in any of this, even though I'd warned them all not to listen to him or be alone with him because of his uncanny persuasive and manipulative abilities. However, I let the others leave with him on this day. I started walking up the side of the horseshoe canyon wall, grabbing onto little shrub trees and finding rock footholds as I tried to trace a vertical path up the slope to see if the bone that had tumbled down the riverbed was from something other than a sheep.

After five minutes of climbing, I saw a large, red rock slab that was resting downward and at an angle in the reddish-gray sand. The slab partially covered some vertical rocks on the canyon wall and resembled a natural shelter or lean-to that had slipped downward from the erosion and torrential rains that came in the spring. Just to the left of the slab I saw something small that didn't belong out here. It was gray, plastic, and shaped differently than anything else on the cliff face. I leaned in for a full view of a girl's hair clip, with long strands of brown and blond hair still clasped in it. Immediately, the last photo of LeAnn that had been taken before her death, found on the killer's computer, flashed into my mind. LeAnn's hair was tinted dark brown in that photo, but when she had left her parent's house weeks before her disappearance it had been blond. This hair clip had both colors of hair from those last sightings still clutched in its teeth. LeAnn was here.

I'd spoken with Howard, LeAnn's heartbroken father, at least a few times each week for the past eighteen months. The killer was an FBI informant, and since he was responsible for LeAnn's disappearance, it was my duty to keep Howard and his family informed of our progress. I spoke to Howard much more than investigators normally do, because he'd become a hell-bent investigator in his own right—he *was* going to find out what had happened to his beautiful girl.

I think it was the summation of my hundreds of interactions with LeAnn's dad that caused my voice to crack as I yelled, "I FOUND HER!" It came out as more of a raspy squeak than a yell, so I had to say it again, this time louder. I had to get the search party back here.

The second-clearest memory I have after finding the hair clip was seeing the killer return to where I was, as I kept vectoring them in with my voice. He was standing with my boss, Phil, and a few of the sheriff's deputies. The killer looked at me through his glasses, soaking up the scene. His affect was completely flat. He wasn't happy, but he wasn't overly upset either. He looked like a professor who was disappointed with his prize student after the student had given an answer that both undermined the lesson and confused the entire class.

After an uncomfortable moment or two he said, "That's not her. Let's keep moving."

Those two sentences cost him twenty-two more years in prison.

Phil said, "He's acting weird, let's get him outta here." The sheriff's deputy and one of our SWAT guys, Daryl, walked him down to where all of our SUVs were parked. I later heard that Daryl dared the killer, "Hey Scott, why don't you try to run and see how far you can make it?" Daryl, armed with an assault rifle, was an excellent shot and no one doubted what the result would've been. The killer's attorney complained to us that Daryl simply wanted to shoot his client. The attorney wasn't wrong. We all wanted to do the same thing that day.

We began to see a few more bones under the large red slab as we gently probed around. And these didn't look at all like sheep bones.

The slab had covered over 99 percent of LeAnn, with her hair clip, hair strands, and one partial bone being the only items easily visible. We were *supposed* to find her that day. The sheriff called the coroner and a few sheriff's deputies waited for him as the rest of us walked down to the killer to find Girl #2.

## 2

# WE'VE GOT A PROBLEM

On November 10, 2006, I was assigned my first serial killer investigation—it would change my entire career and, candidly, my life. I was sitting in our squad area working on one of many armed robbery cases when my boss Phil said, "Hey Jon, come into my office. We've got a problem."

I knew he'd been meeting with someone because all visitors had to walk by the wavy glass windows in the hall outside of our workspace on the way to his office. They couldn't see us clearly through the glass and we couldn't see them. About ten of us, mostly from different agencies, were part of an FBI Violent Crime Task Force. Our focus was chasing down the city's more violent fugitives, kidnappers, armed robbers, and murderers. Following the attacks on September 11, 2001, most of the larger cities banded local and federal agencies into task forces to effectively combat serious crime as unified teams. The horrific events of September 11th might have been prevented if we had all been talking to each other, to put together the puzzle pieces of the pilots from other countries training in our states to take down buildings. These specialized task forces tied the resources of the federal government to the local cops who knew their cities, and we were hopping as we responded to significant criminal acts in the Denver metro area that local agencies didn't have the bandwidth to work. Our team sat together on the fourth floor of a hundred-year-old building, one that was not up to modern-day fire codes. The windows were sealed shut and no fire sprinklers worked. However, it was incredibly cool to work in an old building that oozed personality: brick, thick wood trim, wooden floors, ornate ceilings, complete with a massive hundred-year-old bank vault.

We were often in and out of the office, each taking another investigator with us as we went back to crime scenes to collect more video, went to the jails to get our arrestees before judges, or tracked down witnesses who could help further our cases. On this particular day I was the only investigator in our bullpen, so Phil summoned me to his office with a tone of gravity. I knew something had not gone well during that meeting.

Not many people call me by my name, Jonny, likely because it seems like a child's name, and it makes them uncomfortable to call an adult that. Yet, it still fits me because I never outgrew being childish in many ways—I still try to play competitive sports in my fifties, I love cartoons, and I still tell dad jokes almost daily around the house. Phil was a huge, manly man from Montana and I don't think "Jonny" could ever exit his mouth.

Once I sat down, Phil started with, "Jon, you need to clear your cases because I'm assigning you one case that needs all of your attention."

He explained that the two men who had come into his office were fathers of young women who had gone missing. These beautiful adult children, Jennifer and Kaysi, had disappeared from planet Earth over three years ago. Jennifer's dad, Bob, told Phil that he'd been looking for his daughter all over Denver, putting up billboards, putting ads in the paper, talking to the cops, and talking to Carle, an FBI agent on our squad who was Scott's "informant handler." Bob, after quite a thorough investigation, had figured out that Jennifer had last been seen with Scott Kimball. *And* Bob had confirmed that Scott was indeed an informant for our FBI task force. Bob brought to Phil's office his new friend Rob, the father of Kaysi, another girl who had last been seen in Scott's company. Kaysi had vanished six months after Jennifer. No wonder Phil was so somber.

Both dads had been searching for their girls for over three years.

Bob had met Scott, with the consent of FBI Agent Carle, an easy-going senior agent whom I knew fairly well. Carle had operated Scott as an informant because Scott knew the identity of the person inside the federal prison system who was working to get witnesses outside the prison killed. For those who have not seen *The Shawshank Redemption*, it's a must-see fictional account of how prisoners know they should not be in jail and how they blame anyone but themselves for being there. When inmates allow the blame to grow it sometimes turns into a plan to kill the witnesses and then becomes an action—paying a third party to do the crime. It's called a "murder-for-hire." I had been assigned to work crimes in the federal prison for several years and had spoken with a handful of inmates who had threatened to kill the people who had put them there. These targets included judges, U.S. Attorneys, their own co-conspirators who testified against them, and even their families who had turned their backs on them. Scott reported to Agent Carle what was almost universally true in prison—that his fellow cellmates wanted revenge, and one cellmate even tried to persuade him (Scott) to be the instrument of such violence and death. Scott quickly gained not only the attention of agencies like our FBI, but also our favor and our money.

Investigators like Carle thought that Scott was a criminal who was on "our side," and together they were working to save these people outside of prison from being killed. Yes, Scott was slippery, deceptive, and a thief, but he was money-hungry to the point that he would give up his own family to get paid. So, why shouldn't he cooperate with the cops to solve these impending murders? It would benefit him tremendously, unless his fellow inmates found out about it. The terms "rat" and "snitch" aren't as polite as "informant," nor are they safe labels to have in prison.

## THE INFORMANT FILE

Phil brought me a cardboard banker's box that held payment receipts, printed emails, typed reports, and court documents from Scott's informant file. He said, "I've just assigned this case to you. It's gonna be a really messy one, but I need you to get to the bottom of it."

I placed the box on my desk and thumbed through the handwritten file labels and the many copies of documents. I had been with the FBI for ten years at this point, considered experienced when compared to our new investigators, but still a youngster to the thirty-year veterans. I had learned firsthand that most agents don't take the time to thumb through old, disorganized files like this one. It'd take hours just to organize it. It was easier to talk to the prior investigator and get a brief summary from him on what went on, to figure out where to focus one's time and effort. Except, that's only effective if the previous case agent gives you an exhaustive debrief of everything you need to know. And that just doesn't happen very often. By now, I had been handed a handful of cases that had been briefly summarized and closed without resolution.

In the very first criminal investigation assigned to me eight years earlier, two bank robbers had been unknowingly identified by one of our agents who was investigating a tip or a lead during a neighborhood canvass. However, the agent who was covering the leads of the vehicle descriptions that had ferried away the robbers just typed up his report and sent it to the file. He then forgot to speak directly with the agent assigned to the bank robbery case. The case agent either had no inkling that he should read back through his own file, or decided it was a waste of time. He missed the "serial" (the term used for sequential reports in FBI files) that described the getaway vehicle seen by witnesses—a description that led me to identify the two robbers and arrest them. The case was closed as unsolved because, well, the case agent knew what was in his own case file, didn't he?

I came to the FBI with no police experience, no real investigative experience, and my only exposure to the criminal element had been the times my younger brother had been arrested. However, when this first closed-and-unsolved bank robbery case had been assigned to me, I walked down to the Closed Files room, pulled the hard copies, and started taking notes. I found that the robbers drove away from the bank in a U-Haul with a stork scene on the side. The agent covering the lead had driven to the local U-Haul facility and obtained a list of who had rented U-hauls with stork scenes on that day, learning that four people had rented such trucks. I don't think he ever told the case agent about his findings though—he just sent his report with the four names to the case file for the bank robbery investigation. I searched through the rest of the file and was confident those names had never been explored as suspects. After a few months of database checks, phone calls, knocking on doors, handwriting samples, and an upset girlfriend who learned it was her boyfriend who had rented the U-Haul, I made my first two arrests as a criminal agent.

But it begs the question: How many other names of robbers, child molesters, and murderers are sitting in the closed case files of unsolved cases across the country today?

I tell this side story because that first case taught me something, and I made a promise that I would keep as long as I was an FBI agent: Do your damn homework! These matters were too important for half-efforts.

The files in the banker box containing information about Scott Kimball revealed a lot of disjointed and jaw-dropping stories. The case started with Agent Carle opening Scott as an informant. Carle had received a call from the federal prison informing him that Scott knew of a murder-for-hire plot. Carle went to the federal prison on a July afternoon in 2002 and met with this persuasive inmate, who told him that he had already saved the lives of some very important people—one in Seattle and two in Alaska. Scott told Carle that if he didn't believe him, he should call the FBI agents in those two states and see for himself. As a matter of fact, he gave Carle the names and numbers of the agents up there.

Scott said, "People are about to die if you don't get me out of this prison and on the streets. Yes, I'm a check fraud guy. I've made mistakes. But we're talking murder, here!"

Agent Carle assessed this man, a middle-aged, slightly overweight, stocky, balding average-Joe-type inmate who possessed some intangible talents that Carle had never seen before and never would again. Scott showered attention on Carle. He wanted Carle to succeed at his job and he was intelligent enough to help Carle get there. He was a lot like Carle: they both liked to hunt, they loved the outdoors, they knew the mountain towns well, and they were about the same age. This inmate was . . . likable. Maybe even magnetic. Scott quickly knew what was important to Carle—success in a fascinating and newsworthy investigation—and it was obvious to both of them that Scott could deliver the prospects of bringing down some dangerous drug dealers and killers, while saving innocent people's lives. After all, what investigator signs on to law enforcement and puts his own life at risk without hoping to succeed in at least one major, significant investigation that warrants a significant reward?

Scott told Carle, "Look, right now I'm in a cell with Steve, a bodybuilder who's all up into using steroids and selling Ecstasy. He's a scary guy. Steve's pissed that two people testified against him in a DEA case and he knows he's looking at the rest of his life in prison if they take the stand. Just today, like maybe an hour ago, he's telling me he's gonna use his girlfriend, Jennifer, to hunt down these witnesses and kill them."

Scott gave Agent Carle the names of two targets and later said that Steve had also asked if he (Scott) could help Jennifer get rid of these guys. Scott again told Carle to call the Alaska and Seattle FBI agents, because the same stories had played out there and Scott was already the hero. Scott hammered the point that he saved lives and could make Carle the hero in the process.

Agent Carle returned to the office, called the two agents in Seattle and Alaska, and learned that Scott's claims had checked out completely. Scott's timely information had saved the lives of a U.S. District Court Judge and a prosecutor in Alaska. Carle also called the local Drug Enforcement Agency (DEA) to ask about their case against Steve, Scott's cellmate, and found that the two names of the targets were indeed witnesses in the trial against him. Scott was scheduled to be released from prison in less than five months because his prison term for check fraud and forgeries, stemming from Alaska, would be completed in December 2002.

Carle returned to the prison numerous times that fall to meet with Scott and learn more about this murder plot. He triangulated with the investigators in the other states, who were also looking at similar cases. The murder plot in Alaska happened in late 2001, about one year prior to the emerging murder-for-hire in Denver, and involved Scott's cellmate, "Wes," who wanted two witnesses, along with the federal judge and the prosecutor in his case, killed. Wes attempted to hire Scott and an associate, who was actually an undercover agent working with the Alaska FBI, to kill these four targets. If not for Scott's timely information, both judicial figures would have been dead. I saw a copy of the transfer letter from Washington D.C. that authorized the Alaska prison system to transfer Scott out of there to "save his life" because he was now a "valued informant" for the government. They quietly shipped him down to Spokane, Washington, where he informed on yet another murder-for-hire plot—except this killing had already happened. A different cellmate in Alaska confessed to Scott about killing a well-known federal prosecutor in Seattle and the murder had been all over the local news. The Seattle Assistant U.S. Attorney (AUSA), named Tom Wales, was shot in October 2001 while sitting in his own house, the bullets striking him through the plate-glass window of a sliding door. No one had been arrested. Yet, "Jeremiah," Scott's second Alaska cellmate, had bragged to Scott about the job and provided details that only the killer would know.

After talking to the Seattle and Alaska agents and spending time with Scott, Agent Carle was convinced that Scott was telling the truth about a third murder-for-hire that was spinning up in Denver. Jennifer was part of this new murder plot that was hatched by her boyfriend, Steve. Agent Carle started talking with the U.S. Attorney's Office in Denver about using Scott as an informant to prevent this third set of killings from happening. The next steps involved signing Scott up as an FBI informant in Denver (even though he was already an informant in Alaska) and giving him a protected name in our files, paying him cash for good information, recording conversations between him and the co-conspirators, and possibly giving him a break on his current check fraud charges. The Denver U.S. Attorneys and the federal judge, however, were hesitant to give someone like Scott any breaks. His criminal record showed that he'd been convicted almost fifteen times for different forms of theft and fraud and had talked his way out of jail time on most of the sentences, serving only parole. Scott did not appear to be violent from his arrest history, just a habitual thief. The Colorado U.S. District Court Judge presiding over this case, Marcia, had a lot of experience—I recognized her name in the case file because I'd done her background check years ago. She knew that if she gave *anyone* a break on a legal sentence, *she* would be on the hook for anything wrongful he did during the interim period that she had let him out of jail. So, Judge Marcia stood fast and Scott had to stay in jail until December 2002. But the pressure kept mounting, and Scott and Agent Carle were insistent that lives would be lost if Scott could not work outside of prison as an FBI informant.

On December 18, 2002, Scott was released from federal prison and was supposed to be supervised by the U.S. Probation Office (USPO).[1] Their office wouldn't supervise him, however, if any agency, including the FBI, was using him as an informant. Inevitably, any law enforcement agency's usage of a former inmate as an informant would create situations (buying drugs, watching robberies happen) that would eventually clash with that informant's probation requirements. So, in a few heated hearings that I could read about in the written court logs, the USPO eventually said they wouldn't supervise Scott because it would be a losing ordeal, with the transcripts reading something like this:

The Court: "This defendant (Scott) has a long history of violating the terms of his probation. How can we be assured that he will report to Agent Carle, who's not even a probation officer?"

Agent Carle: "Your honor, I have thoroughly checked out this defendant with other law enforcement agencies in Alaska and Washington. I will supervise him if the U.S. Probation Office can't or won't. We're talking about some check fraud violations versus the risk that witnesses might be killed."

Other conversations went on behind the scenes between the U.S. Attorney's Office (USAO) and Agent Carle. Bill, a Denver Assistant United States Attorney (AUSA) who met with Scott Kimball and Agent Carle prior to one of these hearings in front of Judge Marcia said, "I won't forget this guy (Scott Kimball). I met him once. I was present when Agent Carle asked him some questions . . . I had some significant concerns. I deferred to the FBI. They knew him. They knew the case. Agent Carle was convinced that (Scott) would be key to drawing admissions out from other suspects on this homicide . . . I was concerned that Agent Carle wasn't seriously considering the possibility that the reason Kimball knew things about this was that he might've been involved."[2]

---

1 John Aguilar, "Chapter 3: The Informant," *Daily Camera*, March 7, 2010 (Archived from the original on January 11, 2020. Retrieved June 29, 2024.)
2 David Payne, *Somebody Somewhere*. (February 7, 2018) S1 Episode 3. "A Man Named Kimball." Rainstream Media

When AUSA Bill was asked how Agent Carle reacted when he told him his concerns, Bill replied, "He laughed. He laughed and pooh-poohed me."

I also saw the flip side when Bill's co-workers at the USAO were advocating for Scott's release to keep society safe. A different USAO prosecutor assigned to the matter stated: "I would move the Court to allow the defendant, Scott Kimball, to cooperate with law enforcement authorities based on what the Court has heard so far, in that there is an ongoing investigation concerning the death of an Assistant United States Attorney in Seattle, Washington. It happened about a year and a half ago or so, as I recall. And Mr. Kimball has indicated to authorities that he knows something about that, and they're trying to confirm that with him . . . it's a matter important to the Department of Justice.

"He has previously given information which has led to the conviction, I believe, on a plea of guilty of two people for putting a contract out on a federal judge and an AUSA in Alaska. And he's come about these matters to my understanding because he was in jail pending charges while these other people were in there with him."[3]

So, what happened? Inmates who are released must be supervised to make sure they don't start off doing the same things that put them in prison in the first place. I couldn't believe the words I was reading—Agent Carle had agreed to supervise Scott. We in the FBI did not have the tools, training, or legal authority to do those things! This veteran U.S. District Court Judge essentially pulled a Pontius Pilate, washing her hands of this sizable risk without completely approving or disapproving of it. She was irritated by the continued appearances of Scott and Carle in front of her, and the federal prosecutors didn't oppose it.

Scott was now a free man, reporting to a violent crime FBI agent about a murder, maybe two, that might happen in the near future. He had no ankle monitor. No probation rules. No wonder what happened, happened.[4]

We in the FBI have no training or tools on how to supervise parolees. We are investigators. Probation officers accept a form of liability

---

[3] Damon Antal, "Kimball Files." Alternative Reality Television. Received by Jonny Grusing, August 5, 2024. (Attachment p. 800)

[4] I learned later that even when Scott was under USPO supervision in 2005 and early 2006, very bad things continued to happen.

with each person they supervise, even as they are checking to see if their clients are truly working, not getting into trouble, have a place to live, not using or selling drugs, and so on. It's not as though probation officers can see their clients twenty-four hours a day. However, it's much more comprehensive than any attempted supervision by an FBI agent having an informant on the books. Informants give us information on crimes happening. We don't supervise them or keep track of them during the day. Otherwise, they could not get involved in the things they do to hang around the people who commit such crimes. Informants give law enforcement information for money, a sense of justice, revenge, and a variety of other reasons.

"There are no swans in the sewer," Phil often told us. All FBI agents assigned to criminal matters are *required* to have informants, and only people involved in criminal activities can report on such things. As long as their criminal history wasn't violent—no murder, rape, serious assault, or robberies, we would sign them up to possibly tell us about bad things that were happening out there.

Scott's not being under U.S. Probation supervision was a one-in-a-million situation with the justice system. Scott knew how to pull the right strings like no one you or I will ever know. He centered on what he knew the justice system was all about—saving lives—and exploited its weaknesses to the furthest extent possible.

As I thumbed through the payment receipts, I saw *my name* as a witness to pay him. Wait! I met Scott? While he was killing people? Looks like I did. When I saw the details of the expense receipt, I remembered meeting him. Agent Carle took me to meet his informant at a Starbucks in the Denver Tech Center. Per agency rules, we couldn't pay informants by ourselves; we had to have a law enforcement witness. Seeing the receipt helped me remember the day I drove down with Agent Carle to meet Scott in late 2003. Carle had told me that his informant was working on a case involving the missing girlfriend of a drug dealer. I shook hands with the informant and watched Carle count the cash and hand it to him. I signed the witness receipt and let them talk while I went to get coffee and make some calls. Scott was just as Carle saw him in prison—a plain, middle-aged, stocky, average looking, balding white guy. He seemed friendly and confident, and nothing about him screamed, "Beware!"

I flipped forward to the end of the file, reviewing the most recent communication. I saw that Gary, a local detective from Lafayette, a small town near Boulder, Colorado, had spoken with Carle a few months ago. From Carle's writeup and my future conversations with Gary, their conversation went something like this: "Hi, Agent Carle, I'm Detective Gary Thatcher. I'm investigating Scott for check fraud and forgery on multiple counts. I've heard from multiple people that Scott is either an FBI agent or an informant. I'm *hoping* he's not an agent because he's been arrested multiple times. I just spoke with Scott's wife, Lori, and I learned about the case he's working on involving Jennifer Marcum."

Carle responded, "Thanks for letting me know, Gary. I can confirm that Scott is definitely NOT an FBI agent. He's been helping the FBI on a missing person case involving a young woman named Jennifer."

"Missing person?" Gary asked. "You probably need to know that *two more* people besides Jennifer have disappeared after hanging around Scott."

"Who are these other people?"

"Well, Carle, Lori is the mother of one of the missing people. This girl was nineteen years old when she went missing almost three years ago. Her name is Kaysi."

"Yes, Gary, I know about that one—from what I've heard, Kaysi was a drug user who ran away. Who's the other?"

"Scott's uncle, Terry. He disappeared from their living room a year later in 2004. Supposed to have gone to Mexico or something."

"Heard about him, too, Gary. Won the lottery, I think. Interesting. Who knows? You might have a serial killer on your hands. Thanks for the information, detective. Please let me know if anything else comes up."

I reread Carle's write-up of their short dialogue at least five times. The "serial killer" comment was not in the FBI file, but that offhand comment was made that day. The second dad who came in to speak with Phil on November 10, 2006, was Rob, Kaysi's dad.

Carle's communication record had a phone number for Detective Gary and I called him right away, introducing myself and telling him that I had just been assigned to this investigation into our own informant. Gary was instantly disarming, joking that he had been waiting for the FBI to "snatch him off the street, put a bag over his head, and make him disappear" because he had called Agent Carle about one of our informants. I gave him the good news that my brand-new assignment was to investigate that informant *with* him, if he was up for that. I told him about my boss clearing my plate of other cases and the visit of the two dads. Though I'd never met this detective, I had a good sense that we were about to become not only investigative partners, but friends. I told him that my boss learned from Jennifer's dad, Bob, that Denver Police Homicide was going to speak with him again the following day about his missing daughter.

I told Gary, "I'll sit in on the interview with the dad, take good notes, and let you know everything I learn. You're also welcome to come sit down and let me explain this informant file to you."

He responded, "I've spoken with Kaysi's mom, Lori, a few times and confirmed that she's still married to Scott even though he's spending time in a Montana prison. She's caught in the middle and doesn't know what to believe. They're holding Scott on a long-deferred probation violation escape attempt from Montana. I don't know when they're releasing him, but it could be any day now."

## SCOTT THE CON ARTIST

I met Gary in person the next day. We reviewed the basics of his investigation into the check fraud and trailer theft that Scott had committed before taking off to California in December 2005 to start his new life. I learned that Scott's mom, Barb, ran a life insurance agency, sharing office space with Dr. Cleve, an affable older man who ran a small clinic specializing in optometry. Dr. Cleve had watched Scott and his brother grow up and noted that Scott started telling fibs at an early age and valuable items kept disappearing from Dr. Cleve's office. As a teenager, Scott started having run-ins with the law but always seemed to get away with a slap on the wrist because he could effectively shift the blame to someone else.

Unbeknownst to the FBI, from 2003 to 2005 Scott had been forging money orders and cashier's checks, and stealing from local businessmen, former convicts, friends, and neighbors while he was running Agent Carle and other FBI agents in circles with the Who-Killed-Jennifer goose chase. Detective Gary was assigned to a few of these scams, including one with a trailer that Scott had reported stolen, filed an insurance claim on, and fraudulently collected the insurance money while the trailer sat on one of the properties he was using for a different scam. Another more personal theft included Scott writing $77,000 worth of bad checks from Dr. Cleve, who had been their longtime family friend.[5] The doctor's personal checkbook disappeared when he left town in late 2005 and Scott's fake business account grew exponentially overnight. However, Scott was able to talk a ranch hand, Gamblin, into signing the checks so he could (truthfully) deny he had "forged Cleve's signature on anything." Gamblin would later explain to both Detective Gary and me not only how he got pulled in on this scam, but the unnerving details of Scott's planned, fantasized, and actual homicides. Gamblin thought that Scott had gotten him freed from a Montana jail because Scott was acting as if he was Gamblin's parole officer in Colorado.[6] The Montana parole department had also been fooled into thinking the same for a while.

As Detective Gary investigated Scott's fraud, he spoke with Lori, Kaysi's mother, about Scott's activities, including the cashing of Dr. Cleve's checks. Lori was still married to Scott through 2005, during the check fraud activities, even though he was living in California with his new girlfriend, Denise. Lori told Gary about Scott helping the FBI with murder cases, and about her interactions with Scott's "boss" named Carle. Gary quickly caught on to Lori's confusion about Scott being the last person with Kaysi when she disappeared, and Scott supposedly using the FBI to find her. Gary also learned from Scott's mom, Barb, that Scott was an FBI informant, or possibly an employee—she didn't really know—who was helping solve murders. According to Barb, Scott's role involved rescuing prostitutes from the streets of Denver who were being transported to a trailer in Colorado

---

5   Jordan Michael Smith, (2021). "The Snitch." *The Atavist*. No. 115. Retrieved June 29, 2024. P. 28 (Though the article listed the total as $83,000, when Gary consistently told me it was $77,000).
6   Detective Gary recovered Scott's printed fake documents with official-looking gold seals and probation headers that he used to pose as Gamlin's "P.O."

Springs. As the story went, a group was shooting a snuff film inside the trailer and selling the film on the black market. The prostitutes were being murdered during the filmmaking, thus the term "snuff." Scott said that his job was to "rush in and rescue them at the last second." There was a reason Scott posed such a fantastical scenario to his mom while he was living at home with her. I would not understand that reason until three years later.

Lori and Barb were consistent in their interviews with Gary: Scott was helping the FBI find Jennifer, whom he described as a drug dealer's girlfriend. I told Gary that I could share some of what I learned about Scott from the FBI file. Agent Carle had authored an affidavit to search Jennifer's car after it was abandoned at the Denver airport in 2003.[7] We read through the five pages together and learned the following:

Scott was listed as "CW-1," who pointed the FBI to Steve (Scott's former cellmate and Jennifer's boyfriend) and Jennifer, as having plans, locations, and photos to facilitate killing the witnesses in the drug case against Steve. After being released from prison, Scott met with Jennifer twelve times between December 2002 and February 16, 2003, in attempts to get her to talk about the murders on a recording. However, none of the recordings indicated Jennifer was involved in a plot to kill these witnesses or anyone else.

On April 19, 2003, Scott reported to Agent Carle that Steve's dad told him, "Jennifer's dead. Nobody will have to worry about her cooperating."[8]

The affidavit noted, "On June 17, 2003, CW-1 (Scott's protected informant designation) was arrested for violation of his probation in a 1999 case in Spokane, Washington. This unauthorized criminal activity caused him to be deactivated as an informant."

On June 19, 2003, while sitting in jail on the Spokane charges, Scott asked Agent Carle and DEA agents to give him a polygraph. He asserted that Steve's friend, Jason, "strangled Jennifer and that her body had been buried in a creek bed north of Rifle, Colorado. Jason told CW-1 her clothes were stripped before burial, but he felt law

---

7  John Aguilar, "Chapter 4: Catch and Release," *Daily Camera*, March 10, 2010. (Archived from the original on January 12, 2020. Retrieved June 29, 2024.) (Copy of Affidavit)

8  This was the first "breadcrumb" in the case file that Scott knew about homicides. I think today that Scott wanted to test and taunt the FBI because killing Jennifer and getting away was too easy.

enforcement could identify her from breast implants and a copper IUD." The polygraph examiner at the Denver Police Department found Scott's answers truthful.[9]

Agent Carle further wrote that he contacted Jennifer's ex-boyfriend on June 19, 2003, and that man had said, "She hasn't visited our four-year-old son since February 16, 2003." Carle learned that Jennifer's green Saturn had been initially parked at Denver International Airport in the early morning hours of February 18, 2003, abandoned until it was towed. Within days of talking to the ex-boyfriend, Carle identified a wealthy Denver businessman who had seen Jennifer dance at a strip club, and had paid for her breast implants, as well as a client in New York whom she was supposedly flying out to visit. The New York client, however, was adamant that she had not arrived in February 2003, nor were there plans for her to travel there in the future. The source of Jennifer's travel plans eventually trickled back solely to Scott.

Finally, from the affidavit, "Jennifer's last telephone conversation with Steve was on February 17, 2003, at 9:30 p.m. Agent Carle listened to the recorded call. Jennifer and Steve exchanged loving words, indicating a long-term relationship was intact. Jennifer said she'd call him the next day. Steve attempted to call on her numerous occasions . . . but not had any telephonic conversation with her since February 17, 2003."

Gary's agency, the Lafayette Police Department, recognized alongside the FBI that this investigation into Scott Kimball was going to be a full-time job. Gary and I became ad hoc partners to see what we could find out about these missing people while investigating Scott's other crimes.

---

9  John Aguilar, "Chapter 4: Catch and Release," *Daily Camera*, March 10, 2010 (Archived from the original on January 12, 2020. Retrieved June 29, 2024.) (Copy of Affidavit)

# 3

# THE DETECTIVE DAD

PARTNERING WITH Denver Police to chase fugitives and bank robbers had afforded me an access badge that allowed me to enter their investigations building through the basement. I asked one of the Denver detectives on my squad where the meeting with Jennifer's dad was being held. He ushered me to the interview that had started early. I snuck into the room and sat as invisibly as I could, knowing that Bob, Jennifer's dad, was not a fan of the Denver FBI. Bob and Jennifer's older sister, Tammy, sat across the table from two veteran detectives. Unfortunately, both investigators displayed an obvious lack of interest in what Bob had to say. Looking at Tammy and hearing her voice was eerily like seeing Jennifer. Bob looked to be about ten years older than I was. He was thin, wore glasses, and possessed the intelligence and doggedness of a seasoned investigator.

Bob said, "Look. I've been talking to your department for over three years now, and each time I deliver the same basic message: Scott, whom we all know by now was an informant for the FBI, took my daughter Jennifer and, from all accounts, killed her. I'm getting no help from Agent Carle at the FBI or his replacement, or any other law enforcement. She was last seen in Denver, which falls to you two guys. Can you please help us find out what happened to her?"

Tammy spoke more directly. "Will you guys please get off your asses and do something? What are you two waiting for!?"[10]

I listened as this father talked about the first call he had received from Agent Carle in May 2004 and learned that Jennifer had been missing since February 2003. Carle told Bob that her car had been recovered from the parking lot of the Denver International Airport. The FBI did not know where she was. Bob had confirmed to Carle that Jennifer was in a high-risk line of work, dancing at a local strip club called Shotgun Willie's. The family did not talk to her very often, choosing to let her live her own life. Her boyfriend, Steve, had been arrested on an Ecstasy case by the DEA and had been serving time in the same federal prison, in the same cell with Scott, months before Jennifer disappeared. Steve was still in prison at the time of this interview of Bob and Tammy at the Denver Police Department.

When Bob learned of Jennifer's disappearance, he called Steve, who referred Bob to his dad, who had been in contact with Scott during the time Jennifer disappeared. Steve's dad told him, "Scott was released from prison two months before Jennifer disappeared. My son trusted him because he promised that he would get Jennifer out of stripping and would give her a job in one of the coffee shops he owned in Washington. Scott looks and acts like a 'business genius' with lots of money, claiming he has connections throughout the western states, and was only in prison for some screwy financial misunderstandings."

Bob explained to the detectives, "From inside the prison, Steve told Jennifer that she should trust Scott and try a career change. She moved all of her furniture from Colorado Springs, where her ex-boyfriend lived, to Scott's condo in Lakewood (Colorado) on February 16th, two days before she left for Washington."[11]

As I sat in the room listening to Bob's story, I remembered something Bob did not know. After Jennifer started spending time with Scott, in one of their recorded prison phone calls she told Steve, "Scott doesn't give me a good vibe, honey. There's something about him that's off. But, you know him better than me. If you trust him, I'll go along

---

10 Personal journal, (provided to authors Kevin Vaughan and Sara Burnett with consent of OPA and PIO K. Wright from Denver FBI on 09/14/2010)

11 John Aguilar, "Chapter 3: The Informant," *Daily Camera,* March 7, 2010 (Archived from the original on January 11, 2020. Retrieved June 29, 2024.)

with the plan because this (working in a strip club) wasn't my life's dream either." The next thing Steve knew, Jennifer wasn't returning calls. Her friends did not see her at work. His best friend, Jason, did some asking around, but nobody knew what had happened to her.

Bob continued to press his argument to the salty Denver detectives. "Scott conned Steve's dad and mom into believing he was flying Jennifer to Washington on the day she vanished. Scott told them she booked a flight around February 17, 2003, and he asked Steve's parents to meet her at the airport. Jennifer was *not* on the plane when it landed. Scott convincingly provided a long list of possible excuses to Steve's dad as to why she didn't arrive as planned. Then, Scott took advantage of Steve's dad thinking that he was a successful businessman. He started meeting with Steve's dad in Montana and persuaded him to purchase some forest land for a land acquisition venture he was putting together. But neither the land nor the business existed. It was all a con."[12]

Bob continued, "Steve's dad told me that Scott was very convincing. He believed that the business deals were legit. Scott managed to trick Steve's dad into cashing checks in several neighboring states for a business that did not exist. Within months, Steve's dad began getting calls from multiple collection agencies and law enforcement entities that he was cashing fraudulent checks and was going to be arrested. In order to resolve his own jeopardy, he was forced to pay back all of the money from the banks that had been defrauded. He was left with nothing but Scott's finger-pointing and excuses that none of this was his fault."

Bob had told Agent Carle in 2004 that he thought Scott might be involved in Jennifer's disappearance because she didn't show up at the airport to meet Steve's dad in February 2003. When Bob learned from Jennifer's ex-boyfriend that Jennifer, with Scott's help, had moved her furniture into Scott's apartment one day before she disappeared, he became even more convinced that Scott knew what had happened to her.

I had learned from the FBI file that Scott had in fact moved Jennifer's furniture into his apartment on February 16, 2003, because he convinced her to sign a receipt with that date on it. Over the next several years, Jennifer's dad, Bob, continued to periodically reach out to Agent Carle,

---

12 State of Colorado, County of Boulder v. Scott Lee Kimball. Warrant for Arrest Upon Affidavit. 2009-CR-0001626. Signed October 5, 2009. Received July 26, 2024, p.3.

hoping to learn more about Scott. Bob's persistence put the agent in a tough spot. Carle could not ethically disclose Scott's relationship with the FBI. It is an FBI mandate that the identities of confidential informants (CIs) must be protected. Releasing information about a source who is providing help to the FBI on cases can result in serious injury to that person, or even death. I've seen it in more than one of my own cases. Friends and family members of a CI tend to become upset over the secret reporting and deception required for such work. They understand that the FBI has a job to do to uphold justice and solve crime; they just do not want their own friends or family members involved in such justice. We have to keep the identity of CIs confidential. Our duty to protect the lives of people who are providing critical information to the FBI is a sacrosanct rule because, as I learned firsthand, *people* are our best source of information about what is happening in the criminal world. All of the wiretaps, crime mapping, profiling, and other methods do not come close to providing the quality of inside information that only another human close to the suspect(s) can provide. In 2005, Agent Carle eventually gave in to the pressure from Jennifer's dad, knowing that Bob was going to meet with Scott with or without help from Carle.

As this ever-worsening situation was unfolding in front of my eyes in that police interview room, I made myself a promise: If I ever found myself in Carle's position, confronted with a dad saying, "Your informant took my daughter," I committed that I would do whatever I could to help him get to the bottom of what happened to his daughter. I would ask my co-workers, my boss, and the informant coordinator, "What the heck do I do with this?" I appreciated Bob's dilemma because I have a daughter. And I was grateful I was not in Agent Carle's position in 2003 as this was unraveling, because I would not have had good answers either.

The detectives listened to the story about the interactions between Bob, Steve's dad, and Scott with the same attitude you and I would listen to elevator music—eyelids half closed and a little slumped in their chairs. It was clear they wished the time would pass more quickly so they could end the meeting. I could not really blame them. They were a local agency. Tracking down check fraud in Montana or the FBI's informant problems was not part of their job description.

The bigger issue for Bob was that his daughter was twenty-five years old when she went missing and was working in a high-risk occupation. Nobody in her family knew that she had been missing for four months. Now, her father was blaming an informant, who had supposedly been helping law enforcement, for taking her and what? Killing her? There was no evidence that she was dead. Anyone over eighteen years of age has the personal prerogative to leave their old life behind and start fresh somewhere else. It is not up to the cops to be involved in personal life choices, especially when the person is in a high-risk lifestyle. Bob had heard that exact rebuttal often and pointed out the sleepless nights and his tireless efforts trying to find even the slightest clue that Jennifer was alive. None of her co-workers, family, friends, her lover Steve or his family, or anyone else Bob could find to speak with had any evidence of her existence after February 17, 2003. Even Agent Carle did not learn until June 2003 that she was missing.

After a series of five or six meetings, including phone calls, Agent Carle dismissed the multiple theories Bob had continued to develop. Agent Carle simply could not believe his informant was capable of killing people.[13] Then, in 2004 and 2005, Bob became focused on the "mystery guy" named Scott who had moved Jennifer's furniture into his apartment. The longer Agent Carle refused to reveal the informant's name, the more curious Bob became that Scott and the informant might be the same person. In a 2004 meeting with Agent Carle, Bob demanded, "I want to talk to the guy who has her furniture!" Agent Carle discussed a murder plot involving Jennifer, Steve, and Steve's friend Jason, but did not introduce Bob to the informant.

Another year went by. In May 2005, because of Bob's continued persistence, Agent Carle finally agreed to let him meet the informant. However, Agent Carle held fast that he could not reveal the informant's true name. In arranging the meeting, Carle told Bob to use the name "Joe Snitch" when he addressed the informant. Bob called the number that Carle gave him to set up the meeting and the informant answered, "This is Scott." Bob, his second wife, Noelle, and his ex-wife ("Jennifer's mom"), met this Joe Snitch man at a restaurant in Lafayette, Colorado. The noise level was so high that no one could hear each other, so they

---

13 Phone call between me and Bob on 07/14/2024

agreed to move to a different restaurant. When the informant, Joe Snitch (Scott), drove out of the parking lot in his maroon pickup, Bob wrote down the license plate number. It only took a couple of calls to find the true registered owner of the truck—Scott Kimball. They had a margarita with Scott (though they kept calling him "Joe") at the next restaurant but did not learn anything significant about Jennifer. Scott kept telling them, "Agent Carle is calling," and he would leave the table to take the calls.[14]

Unbeknownst to Bob, Scott had led the FBI around Denver to strip clubs, trash runs, and dead-ends as they pursued Steve's friend, Jason, who supposedly had killed Jennifer. Scott had passed a polygraph in June 2003, in which he asserted that, "Jason killed Jennifer and put her in a creek bed near Rifle." This kept the FBI focused on Jason being Jennifer's killer for two years. During 2004 and 2005, Agent Carle was working on other cases that required him to travel back and forth to Washington, D.C. Because of his caseload and relocation, his attention to Jennifer's disappearance was sporadic.

Bob continued to describe the events of May 2005: "We were putting out flyers and working on the billboard beside Jennifer's strip club when my wife, Noelle, along with Jennifer's mom and I, decided to call Scott and see if he would meet with us again. Scott requested Jennifer's mom and I to come to a park in Broomfield that evening. Scott told Jennifer's mom, 'I'm not gonna talk to you with him (Bob) present about what happened to your daughter.' She followed him to an outdoor restroom a few hundred yards away out of my sight. Jennifer's mom later told me that Scott said he had to 'make sure she wasn't wearing a wire' and had to search her. He thoroughly groped her up and down, spending a significant amount of time searching around her breasts. Finally satisfied there was no wire, Scott told her, 'Your daughter, Jennifer, was strangled and killed by a guy named Jason. He left her in a creek bed in Rifle, Colorado. I can tell you what happened but I do not trust your ex.' Scott said that when Jennifer was dying, she told Jason that I had abused her. Jennifer's mom was drawn in by his story and told Scott she wanted to know what had happened to her daughter, regardless of the consequences. He asked

---

14  Phone call between me and Bob on 07/14/2024

her where she was staying and she told him. Then Scott said, 'I'll meet you at your hotel room at midnight. If you tell Bob about this, the deal's off.' She swore to Scott that she would not.

"When Scott and Jennifer's mom returned, Scott confirmed to me that he posed as a hit man to cellmates, and that a guy named Jason killed our daughter and said she was buried in the mountains and that Scott could probably take us to the location. He left and we headed back to the hotel. My ex (Jennifer's mom) wouldn't talk to me about anything they had discussed. She wouldn't even look at me. At about 11 p.m. she called me from her hotel room and said, 'I'm meeting Scott at midnight and he's going to reenact for me, in my room, what happened to Jenny.' I warned her, 'This man killed our daughter! He will kill you too if you open that door for him!' At midnight there was a knock on her door. Scott was standing in the hallway ordering her to open the door. When she refused he started banging on the door, telling her she needed to find out what happened to her girl. The cops were called and Scott fled the parking lot, screeching the tires and his truck fishtailing.

"Jennifer's mom called Scott several days later and managed to record the call. He repeated the same thing he had told her behind the park bathrooms—except this time he wanted to have sex with her before he would tell her what happened to Jennifer. I brought the tape for you guys if you want to hear it."

There was not even a nod from the detectives. Bob was not making any progress with them. He then referenced his meeting two days earlier with my boss, Phil. Bob asserted, "The FBI was finally going to look into whether Scott killed my daughter." The detectives used that opportunity to steer this determined man back to the FBI for answers. I took a ton of notes during the interview and spoke briefly with the detectives when the interview was finally over. There really was not much they could do. But one thing was clear: the heavy lifting was going to be all mine.

I went back to the informant file and sure enough, there was a CD from Jennifer's mom that recorded the phone conversation between her and Scott after the May 2005 meeting. I obviously do not have that recording now that I'm retired from law enforcement. But luckily, Jennifer's mom sent it to the media.[15] Even though she knew "Joe Snitch" was not Scott's real name, she called him "Joe" during the conversation, according to Agent Carle's instructions. Here are some lines of that conversation:

Jennifer's mom: "Hello? Joe?"

Scott: "Hello? This is Joe."

Jennifer's mom: "Yeah, it's (Jennifer's mom). I've been trying to get ahold of you."

Scott: "Hey (Jennifer's mom), what's up?"

Jennifer's mom: "I've been trying to get ahold of you. Do you really, really, really know how my daughter died? Actually?"

Scott: "I already told you what I knew. I told you what I can and can't say and I told you what I was willin' to show ya. Now listen, we're not going down this road. I'm not doing it."

Jennifer's mom: "Okay, okay. Just talk to me, damn it."

Scott: "You had your chance and now you regret it."

Jennifer's mom: "I couldn't let you perform those things on me."

Scott: "All . . . all I asked you to do is let me look in your room and you wouldn't do that. You know, you're really lucky I'm talkin' to you now."

After some discussion, Scott continued.

Scott: "Well, you know what? Then hire an escort and you can watch an escort and I'll show you what happens with an escort. There you go. Then you don't have to worry about it."

Jennifer's mom: "Joe!! Do you hear yourself?"

Scott: "Yeah, why? You didn't want to go through with the acts, but you wanted to see what happened? Guess what? All you

---

15 CBS News: "Scott Kimball's Chilling Offer." https://www.youtube.com/watch?v=0AfsIVcmans. Downloaded June 30, 2024

have to do is you come back to Colorado, you hire an escort and I'll show you exactly what happened. You can be a bystander."

Jennifer's mom: "The only thing that means a damn thing to me is my daughter. And I don't know where in the hell she ended up."

Scott: "Why don't you have your other daughter talk to me?"

Jennifer's mom: "My *other* daughter? You . . . you want my other daughter to talk to you?"

Scott: "Maybe she'll be reasonable."

Jennifer's mom: (Gasping, sounds of disgust) "What are you going to do? Ask her to strip?"

Scott: "You have to understand I'm protecting myself here."

Jennifer's mom: "That's not what it sounds like to me. It sounds like you're doing it for gratification, or . . . or it just doesn't make sense to me."

Scott: "It doesn't make sense to you, but that's how it is."

Jennifer's mom: "Are you working for Jenny or against her?"

Scott: "I'm working for her . . . some things that you think are important, that you know are classified and I'll be in huge trouble if I tell you. I'll have to show you."

Jennifer's mom: "I don't get it! What can you show me, Joe?"

Scott: "I gotta go. I'll see you later, bye-bye."

Jennifer's mom: "Joe! Joe!" (call ends)

I waited a few days, thinking about the police interview with Jennifer's dad, Bob. Typing it up I first felt, and then knew, that we, the FBI and law enforcement in general, had failed this man on multiple fronts. I resisted the initial urge to call him, understanding that he did not trust us after his interactions with Carle. However, I wanted to know more about what he knew. I thought that Bob's investigation had been better than ours in some ways up to this point. After several days I finally called him and introduced myself. I told Bob that I was looking into the disappearance of his daughter, Jennifer, and reminded him that I had been there in his interview with Denver Police. I told him that I was working with Detective Gary on the other people who had disappeared, namely Uncle Terry and Kaysi. For what it was worth, I told him that I would give him and his family all of my effort to find out what had happened to Jennifer, and that I sincerely wanted to know what he knew. If he called my phone I would answer. I explained why I could not share much of what I already knew with him, because he would one day be a witness in court if this case went the way I hoped it might. All he could know was *his* part in this investigation. This was true, and so was the fact that I would be fired if I shared the results of an ongoing investigation with Bob.

Bob said he knew at the time of the meeting in Broomfield Park with Scott that Scott was an informant for the FBI. Scott had told them he knew *exactly* where Jennifer's body was buried and that he could take them to that spot in the mountains.

I explained to Bob that despite Scott's statements to his family about the whereabouts of Jennifer's body, Scott had never reported to the FBI, or any other law enforcement agency, that he knew the precise spot where she was located. We both agreed that Scott had said "in a creek bed near Rifle, Colorado" and nothing more specific. Scott had promised Jennifer's mom that he'd take her to the exact spot if she would open her hotel room door and go with him that night.

During their 2005 meeting in the park, Scott told Bob, "This isn't the first time I've been in a jail cell with someone like Steve. I told Steve, 'I'm a hit man' in order to see if he wanted someone killed."[16]

Bob did not appear to be opposed to me right off the bat, though he was brutally honest about not having any reason to trust my agency. I told him that was completely understandable and rational. While I loved working in my department, sometimes I did not understand why we did things the way we did, either.

---

16 State of Colorado, County of Boulder v. Scott Lee Kimball. Warrant for Arrest Upon Affidavit. 2009-CR-0001626. Signed October 5, 2009. Received July 26, 2024.

## THE JAIL & THE POLY

After talking to Bob in November 2006, I turned back to the FBI case file for more answers. The significance of what had happened in June 2003 matched up with one of the communications I had seen in the murder-for-hire file using Scott as the informant. An arrest warrant out of Spokane, Washington, had been issued for Scott on May 28, 2003, and Agent Carle was notified about it. However, Scott was up in Alaska testifying in the trial against Wes (Scott's previous cellmate), so Carle had to wait for Scott's return. On June 17, 2003, when Scott showed up at the FBI building to pick up his Jeep, Agent Carle assisted the Denver police in arresting Scott for that Spokane warrant. By this time, Agent Carle was mentally exhausted from the drama and deception surrounding Scott and deactivated him as an informant. Carle later told the media, "He (Scott) was being squirrely with me, so I decided to be squirrely with him."[17] After Scott was arrested and booked into jail, he called Carle and told him, "I've got something you're gonna want to hear right now. I haven't been completely honest with you, and I'm sorry. But you're really going to like what I need to tell you."

Agent Carle said, "Look, unless you've got something big to trade, I can't help you."

Scott replied, "It's Jennifer. She's been murdered. I know where she's at."

Carle immediately grabbed a DEA Agent, a couple of Denver PD detectives, and a polygraph examiner and met Scott at the jail. Scott's interview went something like this:

"So, when I was in the cell with Steve, he was using his best friend, Jason, to keep eyes on Jennifer while they were trying to figure out how to kill the two witnesses who were gonna testify against Steve. Things went sideways and for some reason, Jason killed Jennifer.

"I know this because Jason showed me a photo on his laptop of her body. In the photo, I saw Jennifer—she was nude, tied up and gagged, and lying on the floor of Jason's bedroom.[18] Unconscious. Maybe dead.

---

17 Jordan Michael Smith, "The Snitch," *The Atavist*. No. 115. (2021): 19 (Retrieved June 29, 2024)
18 https://web.archive.org/web/20151009192738/http://scottleekimball.com/wp-content/uploads/2003/07/affy2.pdf (Search Warrant for 1996 Saturn, Signed July 10, 2003, Downloaded on 06/29/2024)

I asked Jason what he was going to do and he said he was going to take her out west and bury her in a creek bed near Rifle, Colorado."

A detective interrupted, "Where?"

"Rifle," Scott continued. "Three hours west of Denver. I'm confident that I can get him to tell me where he put her if you can get me alone with him. Please give me a polygraph test, as I know this sounds crazy and you won't believe me otherwise."

I scanned through the next few pages of the file and saw "Denver Police Polygraph Test Results" with the questions being along the lines of:

1. What's your name?
2. How old are you?
3. Are you going to tell us the truth today?
4. Did Jason kill Jennifer?
5. Did Jason say that he buried her in a creek bed near Rifle?

At the bottom of the report, the polygrapher had written that he concluded Scott's answers were "truthful/no signs of deception."[19]

I was required to take six polygraphs during my tenure with the FBI. Every five years, a new background check is required for us to have Top Secret security clearance. All FBI agents have to fill out financial affidavits, sign multiple forms and waivers, and agree to take a lie detector test to determine if we had become a spy, or worse. I sweated through each and every polygraph. In answer to the question, "Have you ever cheated?" I would quickly volunteer a confession of an instance in the fourth grade when I had cheated on a math test. Then, I would think about other times when I had lied or forgotten to log off of my computer properly. Once I had passed the polygraph and was relieved that the agency would keep me on for another five years, I would walk out of those cramped, white rooms grateful for the five years that separated me from the next test. I suppose the polygraph proved that I still have a conscience and my body still responded to any untrue statements.

---

19 https://web.archive.org/web/20151009192738/http://scottleekimball.com/wp-content/uploads/2003/07/affy2.pdf (Search Warrant for 1996 Saturn, Signed July 10, 2003, Downloaded on 06/29/2024)

For Scott to pass the polygraph, he was either telling the truth or he somehow had convinced himself that his lies *were* the truth.

After Scott passed the polygraph, Agent Carle contacted the prosecutor who had issued the arrest warrant in Spokane, Washington. Carle asked him to drop their warrant so Scott could help the FBI find Jennifer. A Washington Department of Corrections supervisor memorialized this in a memo to a Spokane County Superior Court Judge.[20]

I called the Spokane prosecutor and confirmed the conversations he had with Agent Carle about Scott. He explained that he had weighed the outstanding check fraud charges against the claim that Scott could help the FBI solve a murder and send the killer to jail. The Washington warrant was dismissed and Scott was released from jail. The FBI reactivated his status as an informant ten days later.[21]

## JENNIFER'S TIMELINE

My head was spinning with all of the investigation findings that were trapped in the head of Jennifer's dad, Bob. I needed to sort out and establish a very simple timeline of what had happened to his daughter. So, I went back to the July 10, 2003, search warrant issued for Jennifer's Saturn to break things down for myself and create a timeline. (See Appendix A)

This timeline grew to twenty-five pages over the next three years as our team attempted to determine how many people had disappeared when they were around Scott. What floored me later was learning what Scott had been doing to other victims during these same busy months that Jennifer went missing, while he adeptly misdirected the FBI and other law enforcement agencies in the western United States.

---

20 John Aguilar, "Chapter 4: Catch and Release," *Daily Camera*, March 10, 2010 (Archived from the original on January 12, 2020. Retrieved June 29, 2024.)
21 John Aguilar, "Chapter 4: Catch and Release," *Daily Camera*, March 10, 2010 (Archived from the original on January 12, 2020. Retrieved June 29, 2024.)

# 4

# MONTANA & ALASKA ROOTS

AGAIN, I went back to the informant file, writing notes to myself. It was the only way I could keep the many details straight in my mind. There, I found references to a large payment to Scott from the FBI in the amount of $18,000, made on August 31, 2003. It set off all sorts of alarm bells for me as it was out of the range of what normal informant payments were back then, regardless of the magnitude of the case or relevance of the information provided.[22] This one was huge, and it could not be ignored. I flipped back to the most recent communication, in which Detective Gary called Agent Carle and found that Lori, Kaysi's mom, reported that Kaysi disappeared on August 23, 2003. So, if Scott was responsible for killing Kaysi, why did the FBI pay him eight days afterwards? It appeared that payment was for Scott having saved the life of a federal judge in the Alaska murder-for-hire, initiated by Scott's Alaskan cellmate, Wes. It was not until years later that I learned from the Alaska investigation that FBI and federal prosecutors up there had remained convinced that Scott was a lifesaver and Wes was the one with murderous intent. This murder plot was hatched back in November 2001 when Scott was in an Alaskan prison for check fraud and forgery.[23] Though I learned this information gradually over a few years, it only makes sense to

---
22  John Aguilar, "Chapter 5: Misplaced Trust," *Daily Camera*, March 11, 2010 (Archived from the original on January 11, 2020. Retrieved June 29, 2024.)
23  Ed Coet, *SLK Serial Killer* (Publishamerica, Inc., 2010), 179

provide most of this critical information to the reader up front, because it provides context for understanding Scott and his relationship with law enforcement prior to the awful things that would take place later. It was a painstaking process of collecting the pieces of a puzzle that had been scattered throughout multiple investigative files, from multiple states. I finally put together the series of events that led to Scott being considered a "reliable informant" who was saving people's lives. I had to go back even further to learn about Scott's beginnings as an informant and con man.

In 1993, Scott married his second wife, Larissa. Together they had two sons, Justin and Cody. After a rocky marriage that included multiple affairs by Scott, process servers on their front porch every month, and Scott being in and out of jail for various fraud charges, Larissa divorced him in July 1997. From 1997 to 2001, there were police reports from Spokane, Washington, of Scott allegedly abducting Larissa from her house at gunpoint or knifepoint, handcuffing her, assaulting her, and leaving her across the state line in Idaho or Montana. These allegations made by Larissa were investigated by local police through polygraphs of both her and Scott, often with Scott calmly telling police that she was just trying to get custody of the boys and there was no evidence to support her claims. Scott's interviews and lie detector tests contrasted significantly with Larissa's, who seemed desperate to be believed. Her mind was frantic and her nerves frayed to the point that her polygraph tests were considered inconclusive. These disconcerting reports documented Larissa's failed attempts to have Scott arrested, and thus he was never convicted of any crimes of violence.

Larissa called the police again in August 2001, reporting that when she arrived home, she found Scott hiding in her attic. He then forced her at knifepoint into his Jeep and handcuffed her to the sliding bar underneath.[24] He drove her across the state line, assaulted her, and left her near a pay phone so she could call her dad to come get her. This time, the police searched the attic and found a half-empty Coke can with Scott's fingerprints on it, along with the knife he had left behind. When they tried to call him to come to the station he was nowhere

---

24 Personal journal (provided to authors Kevin Vaughan and Sara Burnett with consent of OPA and PIO K. Wright from Denver FBI on 09/14/2010)

to be found. Added to that, Leo, a prosecutor for Lewis and Clark County in Montana, had called the Spokane Police Department and informed them that Scott had violated his probation on a check fraud case. Leo explained that Scott stole money out of the cash register from the small business owner in Montana who was helping supervise Scott under the terms of his probation for the fraud charges. After grabbing the money, Scott stole a truck and fled the state of Montana on the day before the kidnapping and assault on Larissa.

The Spokane police finally filed charges on Scott for kidnapping and assault. However, I could not find the charges listed in his criminal history, nor had Agent Carle found them in 2003 when he had signed up Scott as an informant. Where did those charges go? Leo, the Montana prosecutor, definitely wanted to know the answer to that question as well, since he wanted Scott arrested for the parole violation, theft, and escape charges. I had to combine the Washington reports and the Alaska reports to find the answers.

Following the August 2001 escape from Montana and kidnapping in Washington, Scott assumed his brother's name, Brett, and used his brother's social security number to flee Washington. He secured a job on a deep-sea fishing boat that left Seattle bound to Dutch Harbor, Alaska. While enjoying an extended stay at the Unisea Inn in Dutch Harbor, Scott became engaged to the bar owner, a salty woman named Catherine. I never met Catherine in person, but I picture her as about 5'7", sturdy build with strong arms, long hair, and a weathered but attractive face.

I interviewed Catherine by telephone midway through the investigation, but what she told me fits here into the story chronologically. I called her once I had determined her story would give me critical information about Scott. Catherine was one of the few people in this investigation who was not hesitant to talk, and she told me the following:

"Scott was the most romantic, attentive person I had ever met, and I fell for him, hard, until I learned that everything about that man was a lie. I knew him as 'Brett' but found out later that was his brother's name. He *proposed* to me under his brother's name. Scott lived a cloak-and-dagger life, disappearing for weeks at a time and making whispered calls to me from pay phones in Seattle during the middle of the night. He flew back and forth from Dutch Harbor to Seattle while we were dating. Scott somehow caught a fishing treble hook in his leg that got infected and almost killed him.[25] There's no way a treble hook should ever catch in your leg 'cause the prongs turn inward. Anyway, that infection is what landed him at my inn and got him off the fishing boat. Scott was the most energetic and persuasive man I've known. And the most frustrating. We once got into a fight in my hotel room, smashing glass, and punching and kicking each other while yelling and screaming. I won that one because he was drunk."

Catherine had filed a report with the police department in Unalaska, Alaska that was vintage Scott. I got a copy of it, with her written statement, and it went something like this:

"In October 2001, I was tending the bar when Scott came up and said he thought someone was in our room. I'd been missing cash from my Crown Royal bag containing the bar proceeds that I hid in my room over the past few weeks and Scott kept telling me someone must be sneaking in and grabbing it. We headed to the room late one night and the door was closed. Scott asked, 'Did you hear that?' I didn't hear anything, but he said, 'Someone's in there right now! I'm going in. Stay here!' He opened and closed the door quickly, then yelled at the thief. I heard some commotion and opened the door after it became quiet. The window was raised and I could hear Scott yelling at someone as he ran through the snow. I called the cops.

"The officer came and I told him what happened as Scott confirmed what I was saying. The officer looked out the window and turned around to us. He asked Scott if he could see the bottom of his boots. Scott showed him and the officer said, 'I only see one set of footprints headed out of that window into the snow, and they match your boots.' Scott and the officer spoke separately out of my earshot."

No one was arrested for the supposed theft from Catherine's room by the invisible and unfooted man.

Eventually, Scott was arrested months later for manufacturing checks issued by Fisherman's Finest, made payable to himself in his brother's name. Even with the evidence of fraudulent checks and forgery right in front of two police officers and a detective in Cordova,

---

25 Personal journal

Alaska, Catherine watched Scott almost talk them out of arresting him. This was the first time she learned his true name. When she later visited Scott in the Alaska jail to find out who, in reality, she was engaged to, he confessed to three things:

1. He was Scott not Brett.

2. He *did* steal money from her Crown Royal bag; there was no one in the room.

3. There was never a "sex trio" going on the night he rushed her to their room and asked her to throw away the bed sheets. He said, "I threw up on the sheets and was embarrassed, so I made up the story."

With regard to number three, Catherine explained to me that a red-haired prostitute had been hanging around the hotel for several weeks, having arrived on one of the fishing boats. One night when Catherine was tending bar she passed Scott sitting in a chair in the lobby. He was looking straight ahead with a thousand-yard stare—she walked right in front of him and he did not even know she was there. Hours later, Scott came tearing into the bar exclaiming, "Come quick! There's two men in our room having sex with that red-headed woman!"

Catherine, momentarily confused by the statement, hustled down to their room with him. No one was there, but the bed sheets were crumpled and tossed around. Scott told her, "They must have left. Do you want to keep the sheets?" When she said, "Um, no," he threw them away.[26]

I asked Catherine at the end of our interview if anything stood out to her during her time with Scott. She returned to the thousand-yard stare scene, saying, "He looked like someone else, not himself. I think he gave himself over to someone or something evil." She added, "Scott will do anything for money."

Scott and I would revisit Catherine's statements many times over the next ten years.

Scott's incarceration for the check fraud case in Alaska jump-started his process to become an informant for the FBI—Wes was assigned as his cellmate a few months down the road, and the murder-for-hire plot

---

26 Personal journal

that began this chapter materialized. I called Detective Gary and told him about the beginnings of Scott's informant shenanigans with the FBI. The news did not surprise him. Gary said that when he interviewed Scott about the check fraud and theft cases in Colorado in 2005, he was doubtful that Scott was truly guilty, seeing him as a decent guy who had probably been in the wrong place at the wrong time. It wasn't until Gary got back to his desk and thought about exactly what was said that he figured out Scott was manipulating him. The best term that Gary and I could come up with to describe Scott's uncanny influence over people was "pixie dust." If you were in direct contact with him, his ability to influence your thinking was completely inhuman.

None of the information in the Alaska case file answered my question as to why the kidnapping and assault charges filed by Washington prosecutors against Scott on Larissa's behalf had disappeared. I did, however, see a phone number for Leo, the Montana prosecutor who wanted to get Scott back to his state for all the crimes he had committed in August 2001. Maybe he knew the answer. Here's how my call with Leo went:

Leo: "Hello?"

Me: "Hi Leo, I'm Special Agent Jonny Grusing with the FBI in Denver. I'm working on missing person cases involving Scott Kimball and I was wondering if you could help me fill in some blanks."

Leo: "Yeah, I've been keeping an eye on him for the past twenty years or so. There's nothing that man's not capable of doing. FBI in Denver? Are you working with Agent Carle? You folks are the ones who let Scott out of jail to circumvent my warrant."

Me: "Yes, that's my squad, but Carle's in Washington D.C. now and I'm trying to clean up the mess that Scott made of us and about everyone else in Denver."

Leo: "Good deal! Carle kept running interference between me and Scott for years. I don't know how many calls I made trying to get Scott back in jail and he kept slipping away."

Me: "Yes, I saw your Montana warrants for theft and escape, and the Washington warrants for kidnapping. How did Scott slip out of those?"

Leo: "I don't have answers for the Washington piece, but I sent a signed governor's warrant to Alaska when Scott was in jail up there. Those warrants are ironclad and somehow the feds helped him slip around it. I got the runaround for months before I found out he was loose on the streets of Denver in early 2003."

Me: "What happened next?"

Leo: "I called FBI Agent Carle and asked how in the hell that happened. Carle said that Scott was 'saving the lives of people who were about to be murdered.' I said that I didn't really care about that— and I warned Carle that Scott was a con man with a silver tongue who could talk his way out of anything. Carle didn't listen and Scott was able to avoid me for years. Eventually, Scott was arrested by the U.S. Marshals in California for some probation violation in March 2006. That's when I *finally* got to serve my warrant on him. Scott's currently in a prison up here in Montana for my warrant I issued way back in 2001, but knowing him, he might get released soon."

Leo gave me the name of the warden at the Montana prison, whom I called immediately. The warden told me that Scott was there, but "could be out and on the street any day now." Apparently, Scott was helping them prove they had a dirty guard who was smuggling drugs into the prison. The warden believed that Scott needed to be out of jail to help them track down where the drugs were coming from.[27] I told the warden that Scott was a suspect in the disappearance of multiple people and that I was working with other detectives, hoping to file more charges against him.

"Please don't let him go," I requested, trying not to sound desperate but wanting to communicate my sincerity. The warden agreed to hold Scott. I asked if he could send me the recordings of Scott's jail calls and

---

27 Personal journal

copies of his letters. He said, "Be happy to," and the following week, I got my first CD of Scott's unreal, soap opera-like life.

Within two weeks, the warden was forced to fire one of his senior female officers at the prison for violating policy by acting as Scott's attorney as she put a watch on his incoming and outgoing mail. This prison guard compromised her ethics and lost her job by pretending to be a defense attorney, an offense that would get any prison employee fired, maybe even prosecuted criminally. It was more Scott manipulation. If I had not called the warden, I imagine Scott would have had another girlfriend—an ally—to help him achieve his goal of slithering around the justice system.[28]

## PRISON CALLS & PROFILERS

As I kept pouring through the case file, I saw the three phases of Scott's reporting to the FBI about how Steve (Scott's former Colorado cellmate) had supposedly wanted witnesses killed: (1) Steve was attempting to hire someone to kill witnesses that were going to testify against him, (2) Steve wanted Jennifer to kill the witnesses and Scott volunteered to stop that from happening, and (3) Steve hired Jason to kill Jennifer, and Scott was getting close to finding her body. Yes, I thought, people's circumstances can change, especially when they involve plans to murder someone. However, these shifts were significant and apparent to me now that the dust had settled. It's like I had the stadium seats to see what had happened on the field of play. At the time, Scott's variances in reporting to Agent Carle were subtle enough that Carle couldn't discern how Scott had shaped the versions to fit the narrative needed to get him out of jail.

Word spread around our office that I was now working a possible serial killer case. The informant file box had sat on the desk of another FBI investigator, Nick, for a year before making its way to my desk. Nick and I had been investigators for about eight years at that point, and we enjoyed an amicable relationship. Nick was one of the most intelligent agents I knew, destined for an executive management career

---

28 Personal journal

if he wanted to pursue it. Nick strolled over and asked me how the case was going. I told him a little about Jennifer's dad, choosing to keep the Alaska story to myself for the time being. Nick said, "This case is a tangled mess that's going nowhere; it's filled with a bunch of contradictory statements which will lead you in a circle and you will wind up back where you started. Don't waste your time on it."[29] I thanked him for his advice and promptly went back to work after he walked away.

Carle also stopped by my desk on occasion, whenever he had reason to visit from Washington D.C. He remained adamant that Scott was telling the truth, pointing to the polygraph tests and the fact that Scott was the only person who could find Jennifer. Carle told me this:

"Jon, I've got the complete trust of Scott. He'll tell me things that he won't tell anyone else. If you could get me alone with Scott in an interview room at the jail, even for a short time, he'll tell me where Jennifer is."

I nodded and told Carle I'd consider that. Several months later when Gary and I were standing outside the FBI building with Carle, he proposed the following:

"You guys should get a court order to check Scott out of jail, let me meet him in the mountains and *not* Mirandize him so he'll be comfortable talking. Scott would then actually take me to Jennifer's burial site because he trusts me. We could arrest him once he confesses to the homicide. This might even overturn Miranda because although he won't be in custody when he confesses to me, he should've been."[30]

Carle's plan was so far-fetched that Gary and I looked around, checking to see if someone was playing a joke on us. There were no cameras rolling or iPhones recording. Carle was serious. Pixie dust. We politely thanked him for the idea and reported his suggestion to my boss, Phil. He shook his head and said, "There's no way that Carle's getting anywhere near this case, Jon."

I listened to the first CD recording of prison calls the warden from Montana had sent me. Scott had convinced three women to put money on his books—his mom, Barb, his third wife Lori, and his girlfriend

---

29 Personal journal
30 "Miranda" refers to the right for defendants to refuse to answer questions or provide information to law enforcement or other officials, named for the U.S. Supreme Court's 1966 decision Miranda v. Arizona.

from California, Denise. Nothing had provided me with deeper insight into Scott's uncanny, manipulative abilities than listening to these calls. I could tell that his mom loved him. She desperately wanted him to stop his life of thievery and lying, and she dangled her wealth, that *he* desperately craved, in exchange for his promises to turn his life around. Scott consistently blamed Neighbor Ted for "Bad Scott," and could not stop grabbing money or any other asset of value to demolish the dignity of his friends and family. In blaming Neighbor Ted, he was indirectly blaming his mom because she had allowed him to spend time with this man, her friend. In one call, Barb asked her son if Bad Scott was still around. He said that while in jail he could keep Bad Scott away, and he hoped he would only be Good Scott once he was released.[31]

When Scott was about ten years old, Scott's dad, Virge, came to their Colorado home and found his wife, Barb, in bed with another woman. The story goes that Virge, being a hard, conservative, outdoor type from Montana, did not say a word as he packed up his things to move back to Montana. Divorce papers arrived in Barb's mailbox. He remarried another lady named Barb (True!), who will hereafter be referred to as "Barb 2." Barb 2 had children of her own from a prior marriage who were the same ages as Scott and his brother Brett. Barb's new partner, Kay, moved in to help parent Scott and Brett, and became as married as two women could be in Colorado in 1976.

And Scott hated Barb for that.

The prison calls between Scott and Barb primarily focused on the subtle guilt he laid on her shoulders for having allowed Neighbor Ted to molest him well into his late teenage years. When the discussion inevitably came around to Scott being incarcerated, Barb would try to get him to accept responsibility, but he would point to being molested. With each telling the molestations became more horrific in detail. As the calls continued, it seemed Scott was going for shock value. One time he told Barb, "You know, Mom, Neighbor Ted once buried me in the dirt with only my head sticking above ground, then he poured a jar of ants on my face and laughed as they crawled around and bit me. After that, he put a glass jar over my penis and I screamed as the ants bit me there over and over."

---

31 Personal journal

I heard stories of Scott being "strapped to the four corners of the bed" while Ted sexually assaulted him; he spoke of awful things that Ted did to him in the bathroom. Neighbor Ted even "tied Scott up, put knives around him like his head was cut off, and poured fake blood all over him." The conversations with Barb started with pleasantries and updates on Scott's brother, who was a pilot, and that "both families are doing well." Before Scott would request that Barb put more money on the books, he would slap down the Neighbor Ted guilt card like the high card in a poker game. Sometimes Barb would push Scott about his potential involvement in Uncle Terry's disappearance, then ask why Jennifer and Kaysi were missing. Scott was always quick to assert that he had passed the polygraph tests and would then propose alternate suspects. He would feign grief and pain that his mom would bring up such accusations about "things that were already settled." The calls always ended with her returning Scott's professions of love for her. Barb would promise to call the next day, though she often chose to wait several days between calls. When the next call would finally come, Scott would begin with "I haven't heard from you"—a move designed to establish his power to manipulate her.

Barb rarely fought back on Scott's unspoken assertions that it was *her* fault for who he had become. Both mother and son agreed that he was better off in jail, and that he could not help himself from stealing from those who trusted him.

Scott's calls with his current wife, Lori, were also almost daily, and consisted of his professions of undying love for her, assurances that her daughter, Kaysi, would come home any day, and sporadic arguments about his fling with Denise. Lori was still living in Colorado and Scott, on each call, asked her to come see him in Montana. She reminded him that she knew he was still talking to Denise after he admitted to having an affair with her. Scott swore that the affair was a mistake, that he truly loved Lori, but Denise had control of some of his finances. Unsurprisingly, Lori argued that it was demeaning for her to have to ask this fling of his for rent and utility payments, when she, Lori, was Scott's wife. Scott promised Lori, "I'll be out soon—this whole ordeal with Denise is completely done. I promise. Please just be patient and know I love you. Come see me. I need to see you."

And, finally, Scott's calls to Denise were centered around their six months of secret love in California before his arrest in March 2006. Scott asked her to keep the payments going to his "pitiful" wife and into his prison account, to keep the money flowing while he was in custody. I could not tell if Denise thought they were still a thing, because she remained guarded in her own professions of affection. I learned from Detective Gary that Denise's dad was a California Highway Patrol (CHP) sergeant and was none too happy when Scott was arrested by U.S. Marshals in a high-speed chase through his territory. Scott and Denise spoke once or twice about that arrest and, although no details were given because Denise knew the prison calls were being recorded, I had a strong sense that she shared responsibility in covering up something that would prove damning for Scott. So, I added her to my "To Be Interviewed" list.

Scott spoke often about his former cellmate, Gamblin, who seemed to be one of Scott's soldiers. Gamblin was conceivably a minion who would have done whatever Scott asked him to do. Gamblin had been an inmate buddy from the Montana prison system, who had come down to Colorado in 2004 and 2005 to work with Scott in a beef-selling venture. Scott's requests for Lori and Denise to find out what Gamblin was up to made me want to talk to him because, like Denise, he was complicit in something. As mentioned previously, Gamblin was the same guy involved in the check fraud when Scott stole from Dr. Cleve. If I could approach Gamblin in just the right way, I was hopeful he would feel he had the freedom to speak candidly, because Scott was in custody and could not exert control over him.

The Montana warden continued to send me these prison calls each week, sometimes ten to fifteen hours of listening homework. I sped through them but began entrusting an FBI intern named George to share the workload of this love triangle beatdown. My list of people to speak with kept growing, and I began to think about how I needed to prepare for an interview with Scott. I kept Detective Gary and Phil in the loop, and they agreed that a big interview was on the horizon. I just needed a solid strategy. I had never dealt with anyone like Scott before. He was more than likely a serial killer, and a very good one because we had no crime scenes, witnesses, or deceased victims (recovered remains). Phil advised that I call the FBI's profiling unit since they specialize in this sort of thing. I had used them once or twice in past years for media strategies on our more serious serial bank robbery cases. Their advice had been right on the money back then, helping us identify a very dangerous, armed takeover crew through a media strategy to develop an informant. Thanks to their careful wording, one of the robber's relatives put two and two together after seeing the news and told us enough to get his brother and partner arrested. I called the main number of the Behavioral Analysis Unit (BAU), asked for the help I needed, and was transferred to a profiler named Art.

Art's voice was deep and intelligent and seemed to be accompanied by a perpetual smile. He asked me what office I was in, what case I was working on, and how BAU could help. I brought him up to date on the three missing people, the two detective dads, the prison phone calls, and the previous informant stories. After asking several clarifying questions, Art said, "Jonny, the key is turning this from a missing person case to a homicide case. If you have to trade everything with this guy to get just one homicide, it'll change everything."

I didn't think his advice was very profound at first. Of course I wanted a homicide charge against Scott. Duh! However, those two sentences resonated in my brain for years down the road, as we continually battled with Scott to get him to tell us what had happened to the vanishing young women and his Uncle Terry. And we definitely needed something to trade to get there.

Art talked with me about how to deal with someone like Scott, who demonstrates both psychopathic and narcissistic tendencies. He said that Scott needed to control any interview or interaction with an investigator like me, and that I would have to be very judicious on when and how to either exert my will or walk away from him. I would need to let him win most of our battles. Art used terms like "victim selection," and talked about the attributes each victim had possessed, like desirability, availability, and vulnerability. He said that a predator like Scott assesses each of these traits and learning how he did so could help me determine how each of these people disappeared. He spoke of victimology and told me that a heavy workload was in my near future if I wanted to determine *why* each victim had been targeted by Scott. Art talked about predatory violence and the planning and premeditation that would need to be unearthed if I wanted to investigate this matter thoroughly.

Talking directly to a profiler, especially someone as experienced, accessible, and likable as Art, was an absolute privilege for me. I took notes furiously as he spoke and told him how grateful I was that he took my call and how helpful his advice was in giving me some direction moving forward.

Art said, "Jonny, I'll be your point of contact for this investigation and I'll run the case summary of what we talked about past my team. With your experience in criminal investigations, you should apply to be a local BAU coordinator for Denver. You could be our liaison to give consults to law enforcement and other FBI agents for cases like this."

For me, it was like being invited to suit up and play in the NBA or at least warm up with them. People like Art—a profiler with such intelligence, talent, and experience with serial killers— were asking *me* to join them, in a sense. Who wouldn't jump at the chance? I put in that day to be Colorado's BAU liaison to the profiling unit.

I told Detective Gary about my interaction with Art and the directions I had received. He agreed that the advice on approaching Scott was sound, especially after Gary's initial dealings with the man.

Gary asked if the FBI had a child forensic interviewer who could interview Justin, Scott's oldest son. As noted in the prison phone calls, Scott supposedly tried to kill Justin twice in one day for insurance money, however, Scott was never charged for the attempts. Gary said that Larissa was willing to talk about her awful marriage to Scott and that if she talked maybe her sons, especially Justin, might speak about the homicide attempts that happened in July 2004.

I told Gary that we had one of the best child interviewers in the country, my co-worker Stephanie, and I knew she'd be up for the challenge even before I asked her. I called Larissa and introduced myself as the lead investigator for the FBI on her ex-husband's role in the disappearance of a handful of people. Since Gary had laid the groundwork, she was happy to talk to me and was sitting in my office within a few days with her two boys and her father, Larry, beside her.

I introduced Stephanie, the FBI's Forensic Child Interview Specialist, to the Kimball family members, and we expressed our hopes that

Justin would be willing to talk to her. Justin instantly liked Stephanie and they went off to an interview room. I stayed behind and spoke to Larissa and her dad, who had driven down from Idaho to support her during the interview. I'd heard some pretty wild stories by then about missing kids, prison homicides, bank robbers, and fugitives, but nothing compared to what Larissa told me that day. Listening firsthand to what Justin told Stephanie unmasked the depravity and evil lies lurking beneath Scott's disarming smile and personality.

This flurry of events took place between November and December 2006—it's amazing how much work can be accomplished when your boss clears your plate of other cases. I was still responding to bank robberies and going to court for plea deals and small trials, but Phil was fine with 90 percent of my time being devoted to this investigation. Kaysi had now been missing for over three years, Jennifer almost four, and Uncle Terry just over two. The two near fatal injuries to Justin happened just weeks before Uncle Terry disappeared in 2004. I'd next learn that these two attacks by Scott on his own family members weren't coincidences.

## THIS CAN'T BE REALITY

Gary and I sat with Larissa and Larry in our back-office space at the FBI near the holding cells. Prior to the interview, Gary told me that Larissa had completely blocked out some of her memories of the abductions and assaults by Scott. Although I had no responsibility in operating Scott as an informant, I briefly told them about how he had fooled not only us, but our other FBI offices in Alaska and Washington. Larissa didn't flinch, saying, "That doesn't surprise me at all. He worked for a different federal agency in Spokane prior to working for your FBI. That's the main reason why the local police let him get away with kidnapping and assaulting me."

Larissa continued, "There were a series of gun thefts in Spokane in 1999, and Scott supposedly hid in a gun store to help the feds catch a group of thieves. I don't know much more about his role as an informant for them." I asked if she knew anything about him being an informant for other law enforcement agencies. She and her dad exchanged glances. Larry told us about a time when he had argued with Scott and how Scott managed to have him and his wife arrested.

"My wife and I drove from Idaho to visit Larissa and the boys around 1996 while she and Scott were still married. I got into an argument with Scott shortly before getting into the car to come back home; it was about something so insignificant I don't even remember what it was about today. Just before we got to the state line, we were pulled over by three highway patrol cars with their lights and sirens on, and they ordered us out of the car at gunpoint. With our hands in the air, they put us face down on the side of the highway."

The cops searched Larissa's parents thoroughly and methodically searched their vehicle. While this was unfolding, Larry *knew* that Scott was behind the stop because of their argument just hours ago. Once the patrolmen had confirmed there were no drugs or weapons in the car, Larry insisted on driving with them back to the Spokane police station. Larry told the sergeant that he knew who had made the anonymous call stating that Larry and his wife were dangerous drug runners. The sergeant allowed them to listen to the audio recording of the 911 call and, though Scott disguised his voice, they could tell it was him. With disgust in his voice, Larry told me, "Guess what? I don't think Scott was ever charged with false reporting, even though they had the evidence right in front of them!"

Larry continued speaking with Gary and me, agreeing that Larissa had memory gaps resulting from being kidnapped and assaulted by Scott from 1997 through 2001. He confirmed that such abductions *had* happened and were horrific. Larry received phone calls in the middle of the night from Larissa saying she was at such and such gas station and that, "Scott has done it again." Larry would take her to the hospital to be evaluated and help her file a police report, but Scott kept getting away with it over and over. When Larry was watching the grandkids on the weekends, he would sit with them on the front porch while holding his shotgun, waiting for Scott to try to take them. Larry told us, "Scott's the most dangerous person I know. Mostly because he can trick and manipulate people to think he's the good guy and make the rest of us look like we're the crazy ones." He turned to Larissa and asked her to tell us about the concert, one of the few assaults she could recall.

Larissa took a deep breath and said, "Let's back up a little to why Scott hated me so much and would've killed me if he could. He was furious that I had the . . . what would you call it? Maybe gall? Or nerve, to divorce him. I knew that he'd been cheating on me for years, but I couldn't prove it. About a year before the divorce, Scott and his brother, Brett, spent a few weeks in eastern Montana—they told me they were working on Scott's tree business venture, and I finally caught him cheating on me." She explained that Scott had pretended to accept her beliefs in the Mormon faith. Once they got married, he used the pretense of faith to con her church leaders into investing in a tree business that did not exist. A few bishops in her church lost tens of thousands of dollars to him.

(Years later, Scott told me how he did the bishop scams. He had hired a homeless man for $100 cash, put him in the back seat, and told him to act like an investor in the tree-cutting industry. When one of the bishops got into the truck, all the homeless "investor" had to do was talk like he'd made big money from Scott in the business and that, "if anyone had any business sense, they would invest in this quick moneymaker before it's gone." Scott used the religious talk of being part of the church and convinced the churchgoers that he was only letting them in on such a deal because they shared the same faith.)

Shortly after their marriage, Scott began to sneak out of the house from late night through the early morning hours. He told Larissa that the after-hours work was because he was "out late burning slash piles." Larissa suspected he was sleeping with someone but never would have guessed that he was having sex with prostitutes. One night, one of her male friends was with Scott when he went trolling down Sprague Avenue in Spokane. The friend observed that Scott appeared to know way too much about which street women would be located near which hotel, and the friend told Larissa what he observed. This information triggered Larissa's memory. While she was dating Scott, he would drive her down Sprague Avenue and play the game "Find the Prostitute." She thought it was entertaining at the time, never dreaming that her future husband was scoping out the same women he would be seeing later that night, while bringing his future wife in on the "game." Since Larissa was skeptical of the slash piles, she smelled his clothes several nights in a row before she washed them. She even challenged Scott by asserting, "Your clothes don't smell like smoke." That accusation led to the first of their big fights over his sexual prowling and things went downhill from there.

Larissa's memory of the abductions was sketchy at best. She recalled taking a shower and, suddenly, when the shower curtain flew open, Scott was standing there pointing a large handgun at her face. Her next memory was calling her dad from a pay phone at a gas station in a remote area. Larissa also remembered when Scott gave her a mickey at a concert, rescued her, assaulted her, then rescued her again. She explained it somewhat like this:

"We had times of peace, even in the middle of him kidnapping me, because he still had visitation rights to the boys. At an outdoor concert in southern Washington, Scott brought us both mixed drinks from the bar and after a few sips I could *not* keep my eyes open. I have a vague memory of Scott carrying me over his shoulder like a sack of potatoes out of the arena. The next thing I knew, a man was on top of me in the parking lot having sex with me. There was some type of short break, then I saw and heard Scott sprinting out of the bushes and yelling at the man who supposedly assaulted me, though he was chasing no one. For years, I accused Scott of slipping something in my drink but he would never admit to it. About ten years later, Brett told me that Scott gave him permission to tell me it *was* Scott who slipped the mickey in my drink, and that the statute of limitations had passed."[32]

As the interview continued, Larissa moved to the topic of Justin's two almost fatal "accidents" on the same night in July 2004. Larissa had received a call from the emergency room in Louisville, Colorado. Justin had been admitted in critical condition. The trip north usually took an hour, but she drove it in forty minutes that night. She got there in time to see Justin briefly before they put him into a helicopter and flew him to Children's Hospital in Denver. Justin was in the hospital for several weeks, and Larissa and her father stayed in the hospital room with him continually. They feared Scott would come after Justin

---

32  Ed Coet, *SLK Serial Killer* (Publishamerica, Inc., 2010), 143

and try to kill him again. The child remained in a medically induced coma and on a ventilator for two weeks. One day, after the ventilator had been removed, he woke up while Larissa was the only one there. He asked, "Why did Dad do this to me?" Larissa reported his question to the Louisville detective and to the neurosurgeon. The neurosurgeon did not believe they could "take the statement as factual" because of the amount of trauma to Justin's brain.

Detective Gary interjected that those words, uttered by the surgeon, created a massive hurdle to being able to file the "accidents" as attempted homicide charges against Scott. However, the detective from Louisville made it her mission to find a way to file such charges against Scott. But she got little cooperation from the neighboring county where a cattle grate had "fallen" on Justin's head. The cattle grate had disappeared by the time there was a serious investigation into what charges could be filed, and Scott was able to convince the locals that "the wind must've blown it over." Scott agreed to take a voice stress analysis test, which was less intrusive than a polygraph, at the insistence of the persistent Louisville cop. The investigation centered around the question that was in everyone's mind: Did Scott try to kill Justin?

Scott, of course, passed the test and once again another investigation died on the vine. A few weeks later, Justin abruptly stopped asking questions about why his dad had tried to kill him. He did not want to talk about what happened that night and did not bring it up again.[33]

Months later, Scott's mom, Barb, told Larissa in confidence why she had not come to the hospital that night to check on Justin. When she learned of the horrible injuries to Justin, she immediately went to her office to remove Scott as the beneficiary from the life insurance policy in the event Justin died.[34] Her exact words to Larissa were, "I wanted to remove temptation from him." The unspoken insinuation from Barb was that she did not want Scott to be tempted to finish the job in order to make a claim on the insurance policy on Justin's life. Considering what happened to Justin on that day in July 2004,

---

33 Larissa updated me on July 17, 2024, with this fact and the ones following regarding Justin gaining consciousness.
34 Barb ran her own insurance agency and took policies out on both of Scott's children shortly after they were born. The beneficiaries were listed as Scott and Larissa, with the intent to cover medical bills and funeral expenses.

Larissa told us that she was convinced Scott had also tried to kill their younger son, Cody, six years earlier. Barb had life insurance policies on both boys for $50,000 that were in force at the time of both attempts.

I perceived Larissa as being extremely traumatized, but also authentic and believable. She was another victim in the ever-growing wake of Scott's broken toys who had managed to make it into the group of survivors who had been in close contact with him. Larissa told me that in 1998, when Cody, Justin's younger brother, was three years old, he was playing on a playground in Spokane. Larissa was working at Costco when she got a call from the emergency room. The doctor explained, "Cody had (supposedly) eaten some fertilizer off the grass." She immediately rushed to the ER and found Cody was going to completely recover—but she never accepted Scott's explanation that Cody was eating fertilizer. Weeks later, she found an odd vial of an unknown substance hidden in the basement of her sister's home. She knew Scott had recently been there, but she never had the liquid tested because she had no way to prove it was Scott's.

Both Larissa and her father were understandably relieved that Scott was in prison, for now, and that law enforcement was finally seeing the violent side of him for what it was. They had other stories of Scott's scams and fraud schemes that I don't have time to record here. Suffice it to say, Larissa convinced Gary and me that we were likely outmatched in a battle of wits. Her stories did not help me find any of my three missing people, but they gave me a valuable ally who knew Scott well and was willing to talk. And, just as importantly, I was confident that she would never tell Scott about me. Since this investigation was in its infancy at this point, I did not want Scott to get wind of what was coming. I needed to catch him unprepared for our first encounter.

I asked Larissa when her divorce from Scott had been finalized.

"July 14, 1997. I had filed back in November of '96, but it wasn't final until July. And things just got worse after that as you can see from the police reports."

That month, July 1997, would become very significant three years down the road. Scott would not kill Larissa for divorcing him, but that did not mean someone else would not die.

Larissa filed a report with the Spokane Police Department on December 8, 1999. She alleged that Scott kidnapped her at gunpoint, raped her, and forced her to drive to Montana with her two sons. No charges were filed due to lack of evidence. On December 18, 1999, ten days later, she filed another report that a locksmith friend of Scott's had helped him pick the locks and break into her house. Scott put a gun to her head, sexually assaulted her, then made her take a bath to dispose of evidence. He also took over $200 in cash from her purse. The Spokane police again cited lack of evidence to file charges.[35]

As we were finishing the interview, Larissa told me about a police report from the Spokane Police Department dated January 10, 2000, which documented that she and her then-boyfriend, Trey, reported Scott breaking into her house, using zip ties to restrain them, and threatening them with a handgun.

In the report, I found an unforgettable set of quotes as Scott was tying them up. Trey said, "Oh, my God! Please don't kill us! Take what you want!" And to Larissa he asked, "How'd he know we were here? Is he with the mafia or something?"

She replied, "Worse. He's my ex-husband."

Scott tied up Trey and pistol-whipped him across the face with the gun. Larissa reported that she was sexually assaulted by Scott during the invasion. She was hopeful that this time something would happen because she finally had someone to corroborate her story. However, again there was no arrest from this home invasion and assault, even with Trey's corroborating statement.[36] Larissa mentioned yet another Spokane police report that noted Scott was arrested on January 26, 2000, for violation of a restraining order.[37]

Gary and I thanked Larissa and her dad for their time and the two of us went to watch the interview of Justin that was underway. Stephanie, the FBI Forensic Child Interview Specialist, had taken a break from the interview and was eager to show us the disturbing doodles of twelve-year-old Justin as they were getting to know each

---

35  Ed Coet, *SLK Serial Killer* (Publishamerica, Inc., 2010), 138
36  Scott bragged to an inmate later (2009) about pulling this off without getting charged.
37  U.S. District Court, State and District of Colorado. Application and Affidavit for Search Warrant, Search of Toshiba laptop and Dell computer tower, Case 07SW-05116. Signed June 1, 2007. Received July 3, 2024.

other. He was quite an expressive artist, using black and red and yellow crayons to show stick figures using flame throwers against one another. A more significant drawing showed one stick figure cutting off the top of another stick figure's head with spurts of red coming out of the top, while the decapitated crescent-shaped head piece, hair included, lay bleeding on the ground.

Stephanie told us that Justin was warming up to her and they had covered a lot of the groundwork necessary for them to talk about the "accident." Our timing was perfect. Or dreadful.

Gary and I watched through the one-way glass in the fourth floor north room of the FBI Safe Streets building as Stephanie and Justin sat back down. He'd had a chance to talk to his mom and grandpa briefly during the break and appeared to be very comfortable with Stephanie. She jumped into July of 2004, around nine or ten o'clock in the evening, when Scott had led Justin and Cody into the yard and told them to dig for worms because they were going fishing the following day. They were a couple of hundred feet from the house and the truck was parked nearby. Scott told Justin to start digging. He then said, "Wait just a second, Justin, I've got to get Cody back in the house." Justin figured it was late and Cody needed to go to bed. Scott returned from taking Cody inside and moved Justin over a little bit, telling him, "That's the spot, start digging."

The next thing Justin remembered was "seeing a star." He had been knocked unconscious. Justin drew a picture of the star in the middle of a blank sheet of paper and showed it to Stephanie.

Justin resumed his story. "Next thing I remember is I woke up in the passenger seat of the Jeep. My dad's driving and I feel like I'm going to throw up. I see blood running down my left arm and hand and it's filling up the cup holder between the seats. With my right hand, I try to roll down the window (motions in the air) to get some air but I accidentally pop the door open."

Justin motioned with his left hand, holding it up to the left side of his face, and pressed his palm against his cheek as he said, "I can *still smell the sweat* on my dad's hand as he pushed me in the face and out of the car."

This interview took place two years after the horrific event. We listened as a twelve-year-old boy described that life event with incredible detail. He was able to describe the sensory experience of blood running down his arm, of how the sweat from his father's hand smelled, and how he had seen the star when he was hit. No one listening doubted for a second that Scott had pushed Justin out of the Jeep. I still get a sinking feeling in my lower gut when I recall hearing Justin tell that story; that this boy had been forced to live through such a nightmare.

Justin rolled right on through what he could recall of that night and of the next few weeks. He said, "I tried to grab on to something inside of the Jeep, but the blood on my hands was so slippery I couldn't hold onto anything." He did not remember anything else of the Jeep ride. His next pertinent memory happened weeks later, after he had been transferred to Children's Hospital.

As Stephanie was wrapping up her interview with Justin, she asked him what had happened after he got out of the hospital and spent time with his dad again. Justin said he initially told his mom and family that he couldn't understand why his own dad would push him out of the Jeep. After asking these questions several times, Scott pulled him outside of a restaurant, possibly a Red Lobster, and asked Justin something like, "Do you *really* think I tried to kill you that day? Back in July? If that's the case, what do you think I will do if you keep trying to make me look like a murderer and send me, your dad, to prison for life? It was an *accident*, Justin!" Justin did not mention the incident again to anyone until this December 2006 day when he felt relatively safe in a law enforcement building with Ms. Stephanie.

I gave this highly traumatized family the nickel tour of our unique office space with the heavy wood paneling and trim, the ornate doors and molding, and the glass display cases featuring some of our surveillance photos of masked bank robbers and newspaper clippings of the more notable cases we had worked. Justin paused in front of one of the blown-up bank surveillance photos of a man in a coat wearing a ski mask and holding a shotgun. He turned and asked me, "Is that my dad?" I said I didn't know for sure but didn't think so—not an answer I would give to any other child on the planet. He accepted my answer with a shrug and we said our goodbyes.[38]

---

38 Personal journal

## FILLING IN THE GAPS

Lori, Kaysi's mom, who had been married to Scott for over a year by July 2004, previously told Gary her version of the Justin "accidents" story because she was there when it happened. After Larissa and Justin left the office, Gary provided me with a copy of Lori's statement. She later confirmed to me her firsthand account of that night:

"Scott scooped up Justin and ran to the house, yelling at me, 'Call 911! Justin's been hurt!' I saw blood everywhere, coming from a wound on Justin's head and smeared all over Scott's arms, as I ran to grab the phone. But before I could dial, Scott said, 'Wait, remember how long it took them to get here for the fire? Forget calling 911, I'll just take him straight to the hospital.' Scott threw Justin into the Jeep and sped off to the Louisville, Colorado hospital."

Lori called Scott's mom, Barb, and told her about the horrible event.

Gary said that Scott was going over fifty miles per hour when Justin fell (was pushed) out of the Jeep. There were no brake marks on the pavement. Justin's head hit the pavement and his blood and brain matter splattered up onto the passenger-side door of the Jeep. Scott made a U-turn, picked Justin up, threw him back into the passenger seat, and sped off to the hospital. Scott came in through the ER doors pleading for the staff to save his son, tears streaming, and screaming, "Save my son!!" and vomiting in the trash can—appearing to all as a dad desperate to save his little boy. No one doubted his grief.[39] However, the Louisville Police Department detective who was in the ER felt the whole thing smelled bad. She's the one who later advocated for Scott to take the voice stress analysis test, which he passed. When the neurosurgeon from Children's Hospital made his statement that Justin's assertion could not be considered valid, the case died on the vine.

However, years later Scott's mom, Barb, confirmed that she did not even go to the hospital that night. Instead, she went to her insurance

---

39  As I would speak to many forensics and psych classes in the years to come, I have stressed that people like Scott, with narcissistic tendencies, can "act" better than you and me; their expressed grief can be more believable than our actual grief. Law enforcement and eyewitnesses cannot afford to be swayed by these performances, or they will end up switching off their BS meters.

office in the middle of the night and removed Scott's name as the beneficiary on the life insurance policy she had taken out on Justin. Scott's request that she remove Larissa from the policy just days before these two "accidents" was not a coincidence to Barb.

Detective Gary and I had a lot to digest after learning the horrific details about Scott's violence toward his family members. He *had* to stay in prison and we needed to figure out criminal charges necessary to keep him there.

# 5

# THE MINION, THE GIRLFRIEND & THE BROTHER

I CONTINUED listening to the audio CDs of Scott's phone calls from prison, talked to Profiler Art almost daily, reviewed Scott's informant file from Colorado and the criminal history files of his arrests over the past twenty years for check fraud and forgery, all while speaking daily with Detective Gary about how we might gather enough evidence that would hold up in court to convict this man. I also reached out to my favorite prosecutor, Dave, and told him about this uncanny investigation. Dave was an Assistant United States Attorney (AUSA) who had prosecuted approximately twenty of my bank robbery cases. He was a master in the courtroom. Dave had seemingly memorized the criminal codes, Colorado statutes, and predicate cases. I had watched him in awe many times during trials as he educated judges on legal points he believed the Court needed to take into consideration before making a ruling. To my great chagrin, Dave asked me the same question that Art had: "You find any bodies yet? No? Then this guy's not guilty of anything besides check fraud." And my disappointment nearly turned to despair when he added, "They've put you on a fool's errand, Jon-Jon."

Dave, with his bald head, thin, rectangular glasses perched on his nose so he could look over them and down at me, wearing his expensive silver cufflinks and a light-colored suit with his signature matching dress shirt and impressive but loud tie, asserted that the only federal charge he could think of filing against Scott, if we found one of the victims alive or dead, was "F*cking kidnapping." Dave dropped the F-Bomb inside of any phrase or word when he had the chance. No one ever challenged him on it because he was dying of cancer and we all knew he would just dish out a second helping of F-Bombs for good measure. He advised that I look up the kidnapping statute and start tailoring my investigation to meet the criminal elements. It was sage advice, and I did exactly as he suggested. Dave was more than my prosecutor; he was my mentor and my friend. We shared with each other what our wives and kids were doing; we talked about what we did for fun when away from work; we complained about our bosses and our dysfunctional co-workers; and of course, we shared many unforgettable courtroom experiences, sitting across the table from the violent and dangerous people we had worked hard to incarcerate. We were both committed to protecting society. Here is what the kidnapping statute required:

"Whoever unlawfully seizes, confines, decoys, kidnaps, abducts, or carries away and holds for ransom or reward any person, or when the person is willfully transported in interstate or foreign commerce across a state boundary is guilty of kidnapping and shall be punished by imprisonment for any term of years or life and, if the death results, by death or life imprisonment."[40]

So, in layman's terms, Scott had to take a victim for some kind of reward and move the victim out of state in order for Dave to prosecute him. We had no clue where any of these victims might be, but we did know that Jennifer's phone had pinged off a Utah tower three days after she went missing in February 2003. A very small start, but it was a start. With the kidnapping statute and Dave's counsel, I had a specific direction to head in, instead of just continuing to uncover how many times Scott had managed to trick our agency. We had to find either a missing person . . . or a body.

---

40  https://uscode.house.gov/view.xhtml?req=(title:18%20section:1201%20edition:prelim) %20OR%20(granuleid:USC-prelim-title18-section1201)&f=treesort&edition=prelim &num=0&jumpTo=true. Downloaded July 1, 2024.

# THE MINION

By January 2007, I was ready to take a run at my first witness from Scott's circle of friends. Gamblin was a co-worker and former cellmate, and he was still serving time in Missoula, Montana. By now, FBI Headquarters (FBIHQ) had caught wind of this case. Specifically, they were briefed on the part about how an informant in Denver had likely murdered at least three people while law enforcement and the courts had allowed him to be free without formal supervision. Add to that, he was being paid out of informant funds, supposedly to keep other people from being killed in murder-for-hire plots that in reality probably never existed. Every organization I have ever worked for has sought to protect its reputation and the FBI was no different. So far, the facts in this case were *not* improving the reputation of the FBI. The FBIHQ unit had given me the green light to get this quickly, and quietly, taken care of before it could hit local or national news. So, when I asked Phil if Detective Gary and I could interview Gamblin, he did not hesitate: "Go, Jon, I'll book your flight if you need me to."

Within a few days, Gary and I found ourselves in a cafeteria in Missoula waiting for Gamblin—a cafeteria inside a prison that is. After an hour, a guard appeared and said, "We're bringing him down. It always takes a while with him and he's very nervous to talk to you guys." Gamblin then walked into the large room, wide-eyed, with lots of dark, bushy facial hair. Gary and I introduced ourselves, told Gamblin we were there to find out more about Scott and acknowledged that Scott had gotten him into a lot of trouble.

After eyeing us with distrust for a few seconds, Gamblin spoke. "I've got a lot of things going on right now. Sorry you detectives had to wait on me, but you see, I got voices in my head that won't be quiet. The only way I can get them under control is to hold my head under the shower for, well, a long time. That kinda drowns them out. So, I got that. Also, Scott was a good friend of mine. I trusted him. He was with the FBI, just like you (nodding toward me), so you should know all about him, anyway. Regardless, Scott tricked me really good. Not once or twice but lots of times. I don't think I'm ever getting out of here."

I explained to him that Scott was not with the FBI, but an informant of the FBI who had taken us for a ride. I added that the ride was much like the one Gamblin had taken with Scott. He interjected, "If I talk about Scott and he finds out, I'm a dead man. I don't know of anyone more dangerous than that man."

We started the interview with a ground ball. Gary asked Gamblin about the checks that Scott forged from Dr. Cleve. Gamblin told us how he watched Scott manufacture official documents, complete with court headers and seals. Scott assumed the role of Gamblin's parole officer and proceeded to move his parole from Montana to Colorado. Gamblin confirmed the parole "reporting" and the check fraud stories we had heard from Lori and Barb—Scott had talked Gamblin into signing the checks as if he were Dr. Cleve. Scott managed to steal about ten checks from the doctor and made them payable to himself, in an amount totaling over $70,000. Scott filled out the top part of the checks and talked Gamblin into imitating the doctor's signature on each one.

I asked, "Why or how did Scott talk you into doing that? Did you get any money from it?"

Gamblin stared at me for a moment with a puzzled expression before saying, "That's just Scott. He has that effect on people. I think he gave me some money, but it wasn't much."

We assured Gamblin that Scott was currently in jail and we were planning to file as many charges against him as possible, but we needed his help to do that. I said, "We heard Scott carried around guns—guns he wasn't supposed to have, and he may have asked you to do something about them."

Gamblin responded, "Scott needed a handgun because he was a probation officer and an FBI agent. I think it was around 2004, just after his Uncle Terry disappeared and Scott's oldest boy was hurt really bad, when I was paroled from here (Montana). I knew Scott from spending time with him in jail years before. He convinced me to come down to Colorado and work for him in the Rocky Mountain All Natural Beef business. I said that'd violate my parole, but Scott said that he'd work it out with his bosses and Montana corrections. He convinced me that it wouldn't be an issue. I went ahead and made my way to Colorado and asked him for some documentation to send to my P.O. (parole officer)."

Scott provided Gamblin with a document, supposedly signed by an Adams County Court Judge, complete with the gold seal and notary stamp, which transferred Gamblin's parole supervision from Montana to Colorado, and listed Scott as the acting officer. (Note: Agent Carle was supervising Scott as his FBI informant at this time, while Scott was pretending to supervise parolee Gamblin.)

Gamblin continued, "Scott began taking me on beef runs from Colorado to his brother's restaurant in Palm Springs, California. He kept cattle on a few different plots of land and every few months he took the cows to a slaughterhouse and sold them to local farmer's markets or to his brother. Scott's wife (Lori) and some kids out of high school helped us set up for the farmer's markets."

The cattle business operation Gamblin described was intriguing. Gary told me that Scott was selling these "All Natural Beef" cows at a premium price, when he had actually bought some of the sickest cows around and paid 25 cents on the dollar for them before taking them to slaughter. However, we were not here for that, or other rabbit trails. We had to remain focused. We were trying to find missing people. I asked Gamblin to share any stories of people going missing or dead around Scott.

"When we drove to and from California, sometimes we'd see a woman hitchhiking. Scott would tell me, 'We should take her, throw her in a hole and torture her for a few days and use her as a sex slave before killing her.' Once, we came upon a broken-down travel trailer and he asked me, 'What if we pulled over, I rushed inside and shot everyone? Would you be my getaway driver?'[41] Also, he showed me a brand-new rifle with a scope and told me, 'I'll pay you two thousand dollars if you shoot a woman who deserves to die.' I later found out that the woman Scott wanted to kill was his own mother, Barb. I told him, 'No thanks.'"

Gamblin was holding up remarkably well for someone with multiple voices in his head. The next story he told was the one I had been

---

41 U.S. District Court, State and District of Colorado. Application and Affidavit for Search Warrant, Search of Toshiba laptop and Dell computer tower, Case 07SW-05116. Affiant Jonathan Grusing. Signed June 1, 2007. Received July 3, 2024.

waiting for. He said that one morning in 2005 he and Scott went to a Sonic near one of their cattle pens in Broomfield, Colorado, for breakfast. Scott asked him, "Do you think that fake tits can be traced?"[42]

Gamblin replied, "I think so, Scott, because I'm guessing the serial number and manufacturer's name are stamped inside the implants for lawsuit filings, in case things go poorly."

Scott responded, "I know a guy that will pay you to cut implants out of a dead body."[43] Confused, Gamblin asked why anyone would be concerned about breast implants when the body would have fingerprints and footprints.

"Because Gamblin, this drug dealer's piece-of-shit girlfriend is hidden away. There'll be no skin left when some hiker comes across her someday. I promise you the drug dealer will pay you $10,000 to cut out her implants and her IUD."

Gamblin waited and Scott continued, "She was killed and left up in the mountains..."

"C'mon Scott. You and I are both hunters. You know better than anyone that a body left up in the mountains will be scavenged. But, if they find her bones scattered around one day, there would still be her teeth and skull to worry about."

Scott answered, "Not on this one. This girl was downsized. You know. Cut off the feet, head, and hands and there's no trace of it."[44]

Scott assured Gamblin that the drug dealer's girlfriend was under large rocks and that animals had not disturbed her.

Gamblin asked him, "How can someone do something like that??"

"The girlfriend was a piece of shit and a drug addict. It's just like field dressing."

"Scott, how do you know people who would do this sort of a thing?"

"Through my federal parole officer. This girl had to disappear."

Gamblin couldn't tell Gary and me *where* in the mountains this victim might be, but he was proud to say that he declined the offer.

---

42 State of Colorado, County of Boulder v. Scott Lee Kimball. Warrant for Arrest Upon Affidavit. 2009-CR-0001626. Signed October 5, 2009. Received July 26, 2024, p.4

43 U.S. District Court, State and District of Colorado. Application and Affidavit for Search Warrant, Search of Toshiba laptop and Dell computer tower, Case 07SW-05116. Signed June 1, 2007. Received July 3, 2024.; also, Personal Journal.

44 State of Colorado, County of Boulder v. Scott Lee Kimball. Warrant for Arrest Upon Affidavit. 2009-CR-0001626. Signed October 5, 2009. Received July 26, 2024, p.3

Scott never brought up the drug dealer or the dead girlfriend to Gamblin again.

I brought Gamblin back around to the handgun and the rifle. "Do you know where those guns are today?"

"I was in California when Scott was arrested after the big U.S. Marshals helicopter chase that made the news," he replied. "When I was watching TV, I got a call from Denise, Scott's girlfriend, and she said, 'I need you to come to my house right now.' When I got there, she gave me two guns—a rifle with a mounted scope and a silver handgun that was still in a Velcro holster. She told me to take 'em directly to Brett (Scott's brother) and not to get pulled over on the way. I drove them straight to Brett and handed them to him. I haven't seen Denise, Brett, or the guns since."[45]

Gary then followed up on a statement that Gamblin had made earlier, "You said Scott wanted to hire you to kill his mom? What was that about?"

Gamblin explained that Barb was gay and that Scott "has a real problem with that." Gamblin said his own brother, Michael, was gay, and Scott didn't like Michael for that either. Gamblin said during a conversation at a farm, described as the old Waneka Farm off of Highways 7 and 119 in Lafayette, Scott asked him, "How much would you charge to get rid of someone?" Gamblin asked, "You mean like shoot someone with a rifle from a hilltop?" Scott said that this person needed to be taken care of because her "companion was going to be put into the will and get all the money." Gamblin said he asked Scott, "This person you're talking about is your mother, isn't it?" Scott told him that it was, and that he was upset because his mother had cut him off financially and she was giving all her money to her girlfriend. Scott said that he would provide the gun. Gamblin said he told Scott, "No," and Scott didn't bring it up again.[46]

We thanked Gamblin profusely for his time. As he was being escorted away by the guard, Gary and I agreed that the "drug dealer's girlfriend" was Jennifer. Also, Scott's guns, if we could find them, would give the

---

45 https://www.ca10.uscourts.gov/sites/ca10/files/opinions/01018349505.pdf Appellate Case: 09-1245 Document: 01018349505 Date Filed: 01/15/2010. Downloaded 07/18/2024.

46 Damon Antal, "Kimball Files." Alternative Reality Television. Received by Jonny Grusing, August 5, 2024. (Attachment p.1104–1105)

federal felony charges some teeth to use against him. Since Scott had been convicted many times of theft and fraud counts, I might finally have a federal investigation against Scott for my mentor, AUSA Dave, to formally charge him. First, though, we had to find the guns and tie them to Scott.

## THE GIRLFRIEND

I used two FBI intel analysts to identify and research Scott's secret girlfriend Denise and his brother Brett. Neither one had a criminal history. Both were gainfully employed and lived in Palm Springs, California. I briefed Phil and Dave about what we had learned from Gamblin and Larissa. They agreed it would be worthwhile for me to travel to California and take a run at Brett to see if we could get our hands on those guns. If we could successfully file weapons charges, we would be able to keep Scott in jail. So, in February of 2007, I was on a plane with Detective Gary, headed to Palm Springs. We were soon sitting in front of a very intelligent and professional Denise in her pristine real estate office. I had mistakenly pictured her as an airhead blonde with some beauty, but little self-confidence. I could not have imagined that such a confident, attractive woman would have fallen so quickly for Scott and then stuck with him even after learning he was married and had an extensive criminal record for theft and fraud. Denise was engaging, intelligent, confident, and well-spoken. She held our gazes as she spoke unapologetically about being conned and taken in by the FBI informant.

Denise had fallen in love with Scott while he was renting her casita (travel trailer). He stayed in Palm Springs hoping to avoid an arrest warrant from the U.S. Federal Probation Office out of Colorado for violating his probation. Scott was hauling beef to his brother's restaurant during 2004 and 2005 until he learned of the warrants that Gary and federal probation officers issued for him in December 2005. He did not tell Denise about being a fugitive until March 2006. To avoid arrest, Scott drove his F-350 for over a hundred miles at high speeds, off-road and through cornfields while being chased by law enforcement. The chase was aired on local news from the helicopters filming it. He called Denise as he screamed, "Go! Get in your car!" When she asked, "What's going on??" she could hear the sirens and a helicopter through the phone.

Scott said, "I'm being chased by the cops. I have a lot to tell you, but I can't right now. Go to your bedroom closet and get the guns I left in there." Denise told him, "Turn yourself in!" He said, "I can't! They'll kill me if I stop!"[47]

During Scott's desperate call, he asked Denise to wipe the laptop and remove his prints from the handgun and rifle. He told her to give the guns to Gamblin who would give them to his brother, Brett. Denise, the law-abiding daughter of a California Highway Patrol sergeant, uncharacteristically did exactly what he asked, thus tampering with the future evidence of multiple homicides.

She told Gary and me, "During our three-month romance, the only warning sign I can point to today, besides knowing he was married of course, was Scott faking a call with his boys when we were on a trip to Utah. We were alone in Bryce Canyon when he answered his cell and was talking to his boys for quite some time as I stood beside him. He told Cody, 'You can't talk to your mom that way,' and gave him some hints on how to get along with his new stepfather. I got a glimpse of the screen on Scott's phone and clearly saw there was no call connected.[48] For some reason I didn't challenge him on it, though I'm a pretty plainspoken person. From everything I saw, he was a successful businessman with a lot of money who showered me with expensive gifts, praise, and attention."

During the Utah trip, Scott let Denise shoot his silver semi-automatic handgun in a remote, hilly area where he had been previously. Denise didn't have much more to add except that she was presently "done talking to Scott and handling his money and doling it out to his wife (Lori)."

Denise would later summarize for the media what she had told us that day, "I would never in my whole life have guessed (that he was a serial killer). The Scott I knew wouldn't have hurt those people," she said. "He portrayed himself as someone else."[49]

---

47  John Aguilar, "Chapter 11: Rockstar," *Daily Camera*, March 16, 2010 (Archived from the original on November 3, 2018. Retrieved June 29, 2024.)
48  Personal journal
49  John Aguilar, "Chapter 1: On the Loose," *Daily Camera*, March 7, 2010 (Archived from the original on January 12, 2020. Retrieved June 29, 2024.)

As we walked to our rental car, Gary agreed that he also had been floored by how savvy Denise appeared. It made both of us pause to guess how many seemingly smart people Scott had been able to compromise—to make them risk going to jail for him, lie for him, and continue to support him while under his spell, even while he was in jail. As we drove to meet Scott's brother, Brett, we added Denise to our "Got Conned" list, which now included multiple law enforcement agencies, Lori, Larissa, Gamblin, Catherine, Wes, Steve, and the Spokane bishops. We knew we would be adding many more names to this unenviable club.

## BRETT & THE GUNS

Gary hopped out of the passenger seat when we arrived at the storage shed. He shook hands with Scott's brother, Brett, who asked to meet us in this desolate spot. Although the television series *Breaking Bad* had not come out yet, this looked like a scene from that show—metal sheds on isolated desert sand surrounded by yucca plants. Our plan was that Gary would talk first because we knew Brett did not trust my agency as law enforcement. He believed that Scott worked for the FBI, and Scott had screwed him over again and again since childhood. Brett figured that the FBI would protect his brother, lie for him if needed, and maybe even throw anyone in jail who was a threat to Scott or the FBI. So, Gary talked to Brett and his wife about the check fraud investigation, the U.S. Marshals chase, a little about what we were currently looking into, and eventually, about the guns that Brett had supposedly received.

Brett's physical characteristics were eerily identical to those of Scott—the same stocky build and round head, and even voice patterns and mannerisms that caused both Gary and me to feel like we were talking to our main subject. Brett immediately took an offensive stance.

"You know I have a hard time trusting anyone in law enforcement because Scott used all of you guys to take everything from me and my family. He really screwed me over with this Rocky Mountain All Natural Beef business—just another scam in a long line of his. I lost tens of thousands of dollars in that one. I'm sure you know by now that Scott was using my name and social security number up in Alaska in 2001. I lost thousands of dollars in that one, too, and even got told there was an arrest warrant out for me! And this woman in Alaska thought she was engaged to me!"

Brett continued, "I swear to you, though, Scott never gave me any guns. I knew about all his crimes and I'd be a fool to hide guns for him. You think I'd go to jail for him after what he's done to me and my family? No way. I want no part of his life of crime. I've got a wife, two kids, and a good job that I'm *not* throwing away for him."

Gary tried several avenues to get Brett to budge on the guns but he was not budging. I sat back and watched the nonverbal responses and glances between Brett and his wife during Gary's questioning. Her eyes widened briefly at some of Brett's denials, and I almost expected her to jerk involuntarily at his continued assertions of not knowing anything about the guns.

After nearly an hour of just listening, I jumped in. I identified myself as an agent for the FBI, the same agency that operated Scott as an informant. I said that I was not supervising Scott in any capacity when these people had disappeared, but Scott was a lot smarter than me and I probably would have been fooled by him too. I explained that our mission was to find out what happened to these girls and his Uncle Terry, who had last visited Scott. Brett was not overly concerned about his uncle, explaining to me that Uncle Terry was a drifter (the same word Scott used) and was known to disappear for periods of time.

Before I pressed Brett on the guns I told him some of my family story: "My younger brother was arrested routinely during high school and into his thirties. More than once, I had to point the cops to where my brother was hiding, and he was not happy with me. When I applied for the FBI, the last two questions I was asked before being hired were, 'When is the last time you talked to your brother?' and 'When did he last visit your house?' Like you, Brett, I steered clear of getting pulled into the tar pit of crime my brother lived in, but I also had to maintain a relationship with him because he's my brother."

I wanted Brett to know that I understood the situation he found himself in more than most people would. However, I told Brett plainly that if Scott had somehow used him to hide guns, a case of this magnitude was just going to keep growing and Brett would not be able to avoid criminal exposure. Gary and I were hell-bent on finding these girls because of how badly Scott had used, manipulated, and tricked all of us. We *were* going to recover the guns, one way or another, because it might be a means to find the girls. This wasn't about Brett. This was about Scott.

Brett didn't answer, but his wife asked, "Can we have a minute?"

After their brief conversation, Brett asked us to step aside with him. He whispered to me and Gary, "I can take you to the guns, but you have to promise me that you'll keep my name out of this. Scott's blackmailing me with a photo he took of a stripper wearing my shirt in his hotel room. He said he'll send it to my wife and wreck my marriage if I ever give up the guns. He's right. It probably would wreck my marriage! How are you going to protect me?"

I do not remember what I said to Brett—it wasn't like his name would never appear in any document that Scott could someday read. I would have been able to say that none of this investigation would ever be disclosed to Scott if criminal charges *weren't* filed. However, the gun charges could put Scott in prison for a while, years that he would not be out stealing from Brett and blackmailing him. Whatever I said or didn't say, Brett agreed to take us to the guns. He took us across town to the trailer home of his friend Bender.

As of this writing, it has been more than seventeen years since Gary and I climbed the metal stairs and walked through the paper-thin door of the old, white trailer. However, I remember Bender's trailer like I had been there yesterday, because of the significance of what had happened there. After meeting the middle-aged, scraggly, friendly-but-unclean Bender, Brett told him, "Please take us to the guns." Without hesitation, he led us to a small, messy bedroom with a huge fish tank filled with orange and red fish—it was blocking the closet door. In the back of the closet, on the left side, I pulled out a rifle with a scope and a silver handgun in a Velcro holster. Gary, Brett, and I thanked Bender, and left his humble residence.

On the way back to the storage shed Brett finally let down the rest of his defenses. He said, "I think you two will be interested in a box with some of Scott's things that the U.S. Marshals pulled out of his truck when they arrested him. Do you want to see it?"

Yes, please!

After some deep digging in the back of the storage shed, Brett came out with a small box that held forgettable trinkets and clothing—except for one piece of paper. The first line read:

"I _____ do give Joseph Scott permission to enter my hotel room." (Joseph Scott was one of Scott's aliases that will be explained in Chapter 6.)

I glanced down at the last line which indicated that the permission expired at 6 a.m. on August 24, 2005. This was Scott's own typed "consent form," by which Jennifer's mom would allow him to reenact Jennifer's death in the hotel room. It mimicked one of our FBI consent forms, except it contained terminology like "agree to be bound, gagged, and consent to sexual acts," and that Scott would not be held liable in case Jennfer's mom had second thoughts or something went wrong during the reenactment and all that entailed. I thanked Brett and grabbed the document and secured it as evidence, along with the guns. Gary and I took our newly found, very valuable items directly to the FBI office in Palm Springs and asked them to please ship the evidence to Denver. Gary and I had plenty to talk about on our way home. Our primary challenge would be how we could definitively put those guns in Scott's hands. We concluded that although other fingerprints would include Gamblin's, Brett's, and Bender's, Denise had wiped them down so by now there were other fingerprints and DNA all over them. We would have to rely on witness statements, which would come down to Brett, Denise, Bender, and Gamblin—a motley crew, except for Denise.

The next morning, I called my friend from Alcohol, Tobacco and Firearms (ATF) and asked him to run traces on the two guns. Gary and I were very curious about how Scott had gotten his hands on the weapons since he was a convicted felon and prohibited from purchasing them legally. My ATF buddy asked if this was a rush job and I said, "Please." In the time it took to fly back to Denver we had the traces on the gun purchases. The Winchester rifle had been purchased from a Walmart near Broomfield, Colorado, by someone named Melissa in December 2005, just days before Scott fled Colorado to avoid arrest for stealing from Dr. Cleve and beginning his affair with Denise in California.

The silver Firestar handgun had last been owned by a firearms dealer in Hermiston, Oregon, who sold it to an unknown party for cash in January 2003 while Scott was running around Denver strip clubs and meeting with Jennifer before she disappeared.[50]

Detective Gary already knew about Melissa because Lori had told him that Scott was having *another* affair, with a waitress also named Melissa, who worked at a local Perkins restaurant. Lori even had to spend a few days in jail and was issued a restraining order after she confronted Scott about the affair.[51]

In my efforts to track down Melissa I learned that she lived out of state. I also researched the Oregon firearms dealer and called the owner and learned that "his business had burned up in a fire along with all of his receipts." So, for now, our only viable option was to pursue the history of the rifle; Gary and I settled for a phone interview with Melissa because we weren't ready to hop on another plane just yet.

## THE STRAW PURCHASE & MELISSA

In February 2007, Melissa told Gary and me that she had dated Scott for the last six months of 2005. She had weathered a tough last three months once she found out that Scott was married. Scott's wife, Lori, found out about their affair and Scott informed Melissa he had to file a restraining order on his "nutty wife." Scott and Melissa first met at the Perkins restaurant where she worked. He showered her with attention and always seemed to have a lot of cash on hand. He often disappeared on trips to the mountains or to California. Scott loved to hunt, and in December 2005 he told Melissa that he would enjoy teaching her how to hunt and painted a romantic picture of going on some hunting excursions with her. She thought it sounded fun and Scott told her they needed to get a rifle. He drove to a Walmart north of Denver and gave her cash to buy the gun, saying that they "wouldn't sell to him because of a BS check that bounced." She agreed to help him out and bought a rifle with a mounted scope, as Scott had

---

50  State of Colorado, County of Boulder v. Scott Lee Kimball. Warrant for Arrest Upon Affidavit. 2009-CR-0001626. Signed October 5, 2009. Received July 26, 2024, p.16
51  Explained in the next chapter.

instructed, while he waited in his truck. As we would later introduce in federal court in 2009, Melissa said, "Scott talked me into (buying) it. He put the rifle in the back seat and I never saw it again."[52]

For those unfamiliar with federal laws, such a gun acquisition is termed a "straw purchase" because the convicted felon cannot pass the criminal history instant check and thus cannot buy the weapon. Someone like Scott is forced to get someone like Melissa to buy it for him. Melissa could have technically been charged criminally for such an offense, but she, like all the other characters in this account, had been conned by Scott and therefore was not necessarily an accomplice to his criminal acts.

This was the same rifle that Scott wanted Gamblin to use to shoot Scott's own mother, Barb, despite the fact that his mother was the only person who consistently cared for him. Thanks to Melissa, we now had bookend events that connected Scott with the rifle. Scott gave Melissa the money to purchase the rifle, and then she gave it to him. Four months after the purchase, Denise, Gamblin, Brett, and Bender also pointed to Scott as the owner.

I would not be able to piece together who bought the silver handgun for Scott until much later, after we learned of a third young female victim of Scott's. In that instance, we would find a bullet fired from that silver gun in the place where the victim's head should have been.

---

52 UNITED STATES OF AMERICA, Plaintiff-Appellee, No. 09-1245 (D. Colorado) (D.C. No. 1:07-CR-00249-MSK-1) v. SCOTT KIMBALL, Defendant-Appellate Case: 09-1245 Document: 01018349505 Date Filed: 01/15/2010, Downloaded July 17, 2024.

## 6

# CB & X-MAN

My second interview after Jennifer's dad in November 2006 was with Kaysi's boyfriend, CB. He was a slim, dark-haired, handsome young man who looked like the actor James Franco—at least that's what I tell my forensic classes so they can picture him. Detective Gary and I met twenty-six-year-old CB in the parking lot of the same Motel 6 in Thornton, Colorado, where he last saw Kaysi. His mother, Charlene, was there to support him, to assist him with explanations, and to protect him. She and CB knew Scott worked for the FBI and therefore did not trust me. CB told his story to Gary and me, not once looking at us, and he often struggled to find the right words. Occasionally, he would start laughing and nodding, as if an invisible person was telling him an inside joke. CB's mom said that he had experienced some kind of psychotic break after Kaysi's disappearance and that he was getting help. He told us that he met Scott in February 2003, when Scott began dating Kaysi's mom, Lori. Scott represented himself as an FBI agent to CB, and as being employed by the National Security Agency (NSA) to a select few of CB's friends. Scott carried a holstered gun on his hip and had the FBI seal on his laptop.[53]

CB described a date that will never leave him—August 23, 2003. Scott came to this Motel 6 where CB had been staying for almost two days with

---

53 State of Colorado, County of Boulder v. Scott Lee Kimball. Warrant for Arrest Upon Affidavit. 2009-CR-0001626. Signed October 5, 2009. Received July 26, 2024, p.9

Kaysi. Scott said, "I'm here to take Kaysi to work." Kaysi and CB were employed at the Subway shop on 144th Street and Lowell Boulevard, close to where Scott and Lori lived. CB told us, "I was going to marry Kaysi and I'd bought her an engagement necklace. Before she left with Scott, I put the necklace around her neck, kissed her, and watched her get in Scott's truck and drive away. A few hours later, I got a call from Subway that she had never showed up for work. I tried her phone over and over but it went straight to voicemail. I called her mom (Lori) and she said that Scott was in the mountains hunting for elk. I said, 'No he's not. I just saw him a few hours ago. He picked up Kaysi and said he was taking her to work. They drove away in his truck with a travel trailer attached.'"

CB and Lori then blew up the phones of Kaysi and Scott, but no one answered either phone.

CB continued, "We heard nothing for over a day and I was freaking out along with Lori. When Scott finally returned in his truck, as it was coming up the driveway I ran out to him and asked, 'Where's Kaysi?? What did you do with her!?' He said that he'd been in the mountains hunting and didn't know what I was talking about. I opened the trailer door and started yelling for her. I came back out and told Scott, 'You did something to her!'"

After CB paused in a moment of silence, I asked what had happened next.

CB had no more to tell us that day. His memory and cooperation were finished. His mom, Charlene, picked up where he left off.

"CB didn't win that argument. He was convinced then and is convinced today that Scott is an FBI agent. He came running through my door later that day sobbing and told me the story of what happened. It was just like he told you today. That same night, within hours of CB coming home, Scott called me and threatened, 'I'm gonna have the FBI come over there right now and search your house for Kaysi. I *know* CB did something to her!'"

Charlene continued, "I told Scott, 'Please do! Bring the FBI, the police, anyone you want! You can turn this house upside down. Kaysi is not here! Stop saying that my son took her!'"

It was obvious to both Gary and me that this woman was not afraid of Scott. Neither Charlene nor CB had any proof that Kaysi was alive after Scott picked her up from the motel, though they had heard stories that she had been seen in Arizona and back at her mom's house.

After the interview with CB and Charlene I waited five months before I felt it was safe to speak with Lori. She was still married to Scott and I did not want him to know that I was investigating him. I had an idea that I wanted to run by Phil and Gary: What if we used Jason against Scott to see if Lori would be willing to talk to us? (The reader will recall that Jason was Steve's friend, whom Scott had blamed for Jennifer's death.)

I knew from listening to Scott's phone calls to Lori that she had a lot of questions about Kaysi. Hitting Lori directly with "Guess what? You're married to a serial killer," would likely not be successful. She might not have been ready to face that reality yet because it would force her to take the next logical steps:

1. You let this monster in your life.
2. This monster took and killed your daughter.
3. You are somewhat responsible.

Considering the awful reality looming for Lori, I knew she wouldn't listen to *me*—especially because of Scott's association with the FBI and her prior dealings with Agent Carle. I didn't know how I would make it past introductions before she slammed the door on me, possibly forever. I told Phil that I was thinking of using an intermediary to talk to Lori on my behalf. He asked who I wanted to use against Scott and I answered, "Jason. I'm confident he's not responsible for killing Jennifer. I'd like to interview him to see if he'd like to work for us." Phil cautiously agreed, not wanting to blow up the case if Jason seemed untrustworthy. So, I called Jason, the primary suspect in the FBI's murder-for-hire case, the guy who supposedly killed Jennifer, and asked if he wanted to chat.

## X-MAN TATS

I needed to see what Jason had to say about his interactions with Scott while Scott was steering the FBI to investigate him. We were growing confident that neither Steve nor Jason had been responsible for kidnapping and killing Jennifer, but we needed to know what Scott had told them and how far their knowledge extended into her disappearance.

On February 6, 2007, Jason and his attorney showed up at our office, just a few days after my phone call to him.[54] Based on the communications in our informant file and a few emails between Scott and Agent Carle, I pictured Jason as a hulking, mindless thug. The FBI file contained printouts of emails to Scott from Jason that alleged Jason and Steve needed Scott to "stay around at the club" and "reach the place where the old car wad (sic) dumped."[55] Jason's email address was supposedly XMAN_TATS@yahoo.com, and his emails to Scott contained numerous and egregious spelling errors. After introductions were made, I went straight to the heart of the issue: Agent Carle had relied upon this email—"the old car wad (sic) dumped"—as proof that Jason was involved in Jennifer's murder. I asked Jason what was meant by the "old car," but Jason had no clue. It was impossible for him to fake the look of cluelessness and anticipation, so I explained my odd question. I knew from the case file and search warrant that Scott had told Agent Carle the code Jason used for Jennifer's burial site was the "old car," but I did not share that with Jason quite yet. The Jason in front of me was the complete opposite of the murderous mobster Scott had portrayed to Agent Carle. Shocker, I know.

Dressed in a casual suit with a white shirt and no tie, Jason proceeded to tell Gary and me the following:

"I found out about Jennifer going missing from my wife, who worked with some of Jennifer's friends at the strip club. I had talked to Steve earlier about it during some visits to the prison and he was all excited about Jennifer getting out of stripping thanks to Scott. Scott sold Steve on the plan to put Jennifer and some other strippers in some drive-up coffee shops in Washington modeled after Hooters. Supposedly, people would park while waiting on the order and pay double the price for pretty women on roller skates in bikinis to serve hot drinks.

"Shortly after Jennifer started hanging around Scott, she disappeared. No one heard from her for a few months. Steve's dad told him that she never showed up to meet them at the Washington airport.

---

54 Personal journal
55 Convenient that Scott gave Agent Carle the "suspect's request" for Scott to hang out more at the strip clubs. Tough assignment for an informant.

"Within a few months, Scott was calling me and asking to meet him, then asking me questions like, 'What drugs do you want to move?' and 'Do you want an alias? Cause I can get it for you. See, I got this one saying that I'm Joe Scott,' or something like that. I never liked or trusted the man and I told my wife that. He felt slimy and was always trying to talk me into doing something."

Scott pretended to be Jason's friend but Jason knew something was off, and so did his wife. They stopped returning his calls. For a few months in late 2003 and into 2004, Scott kept showing up at strip clubs asking where Jason was. When Jason saw the article in the news about Jennifer going missing, he and his wife called the FBI office and reported it. No one got back to them.

With knowing glances, Gary and I agreed that Jason played no role in this and we showed him the copy of the supposed email he sent to Scott in late 2003. When I share evidence like this email to the potentially guilty person who wrote it and the person refuses to take responsibility, they most often manufacture indignation and anger. They blame the person who told on them for being a snitch and a liar, claim ignorance and innocence in the victim's disappearance, or turn to their lawyer for advice before answering. Jason did none of those.

Jason just laughed.

He pointed us to the spelling mistakes, commenting that Scott obviously did not know that he (Jason) had a college degree and could write. Jason was truly curious about references in the email that did not make sense to him, trying to figure it out along with us. He was happy to help us however he could. I asked him and his attorney if he would be willing to call Scott while Scott was sitting in jail and ask why he had pinned this murder on him. He said, "Sure."

This would accomplish two things for us. I had been monitoring Scott's calls and mail and knew he had not been talking to Jason. If those two were complicit in Jennifer's death, it would be tough for them to talk about such things without rehearsing it while I was recording them. Secondly, we had a slim chance Scott might say something incriminatory and we would have the audio. Jason made the call. Scott was very guarded and gave lots of excuses about why the cops might think Jason did this, but he never gave up that *he* was the one who had told us about Jason. Scott was clearly off-balance for the first two minutes of the call but quickly gained control and started talking in analogies of Jennifer being a "stone in the pyramid" and that the "pyramid could fall."[56] Scott often launched into similar off-topic and odd segues during my next fifteen years with him. Scott finally told Jason, "I know where you live," which we all took as a veiled threat. Our recorded call to Scott gave us nothing new, other than confirming that Jason had never been involved in Jennifer's murder.

Jason told us that we should interview his wife since she had firsthand knowledge of Jennifer's disappearance. I confirmed through a name search that Jason's wife contacted the Denver FBI office on August 27, 2005,[57] and reported that she had pertinent information regarding the disappearance of Jennifer. After Jason and his attorney left, I called Jason's wife, who confirmed that she was friends with the owner of Shotgun Willie's, the nightclub where Jennifer danced. She was also friends with some of the dancers at Shotgun Willie's during the time period following Jennifer's disappearance. The club owner told Jason's wife in 2005 that Jennifer's mom had come to the club and was talking about the disappearance of her daughter. Jason's wife went home and looked up Jennifer's name on the internet and found her listed as a missing person. That's when she and Jason called the Denver FBI. Her statements lined up nicely with my own research.

I now felt comfortable asking Jason to speak with Lori on our behalf. We met with him again about a week later, this time without his attorney. I told him that we weren't only looking for Jennifer; other people had disappeared when they were around Scott. Other parents were looking for their daughters, but they did not trust the FBI because Scott had worn us like a security blanket to shield himself from the families' questions. Jason didn't hesitate. He was in.

I explained to Jason that Lori and Rob, Kaysi's mom and dad, had appeared in several local news stories about their daughter going missing. It would not be too far-fetched if Jason called and asked them if they would talk, especially since he was being framed for Jennifer's murder. I did not give him any details on Kaysi when he

---

56 Personal journal
57 State of Colorado, County of Boulder v. Scott Lee Kimball. Warrant for Arrest Upon Affidavit. 2009-CR-0001626. Signed October 5, 2009. Received July 26, 2024, p.4

asked, explaining that if the parents wanted to share, he would learn about it then. I was hopeful that Jason's likable personality and his indignation at being thought of as a murderer would make the plan succeed. Jason made the call.

## EYE-OPENING

Lori agreed to meet with Jason in a church parking lot in southwest Littleton. She asked to bring her ex-husband, Rob, and explained the parking lot "would be a very public, visible place." As I listened to the call, I understood why she wanted to meet in the open—Scott had been telling her for three years that Jason was a killer. Of course she was nervous to meet Jason, but her curiosity overrode her fear.

I heard during a lecture once, "We're all on a yardstick in coming to know a significant truth—whether it's about God, ourselves, or someone close to us. Sometimes we move an inch or two at a time; rarely do we move an entire foot. Our job, most often, is to move ourselves or those we love a few inches at a time toward truth."

That day, Jason moved Lori a few inches toward what was true about Scott. Here is some of the conversation, midway through:

> Lori: "Yes, I'm still married to Scott, but part of me still wonders if he was involved in Kaysi's disappearance."
>
> Jason: "He pretended to be a friend to me, like he was looking out for me. I found out later that he was just setting me up to the FBI as a murderer."
>
> Lori: "I still can't get over what Kaysi's boyfriend said: that Scott picked her up from the hotel. Scott convinced us, though, that—"
>
> Jason: "Sorry, but someone else said that Scott was last with your daughter?"
>
> Rob: "Yes, her boyfriend, CB, who really had no reason to lie. Scott bullied him and his mom by using his FBI connections."

Jason: "That's almost exactly what happened with Jennifer! Scott was the last person with her. I know that firsthand from her boyfriend, Steve, who's also my close friend. Steve set her up with Scott for a new job and he was supposed to fly her to Washington. Steve's parents waited up there at the airport and she never showed up. Guess who he blamed that one on? Me! And I had absolutely no idea!"

Lori (shaking her head from side to side): "This is almost exactly what happened to my Kaysi. It can't be a coincidence."

Their meeting lasted for almost two hours and proved to be a therapy session for Jason, Lori, and Rob as they commiserated about their many losses to Scott. I think they even hugged each other at the end, but I wouldn't swear to that on the stand. Jason came away happy and confident that he had helped Lori move closer to the possibility that her current husband had murdered her daughter. I could hardly wait to hear the next few phone calls between Lori and Scott as he sat in the Montana jail.

## IT'S YOUR SOUL, NOT MINE

A few weeks went by and nothing significant came to light during the prison calls. Then, I listened to one of the calls during the first week of April 2007. Lori finally found her footing and challenged Scott's story about what had happened to Kaysi. Here are some of the statements made during that call:

Lori: "Kaysi's been missing for almost four years now, Scott. My life is a wreck!"

Scott: "You know it's been hard for me too! My mom choosing Kay over me. Then Ted molesting me! Lori, despite all of that, I'm trying to be a better husband and dad. I need to feel loved by you."

Lori: "What about Kaysi? What about Justin?"

Scott: "I have nothing to hide about Kaysi or Justin. Ask me anything."

Lori: "Scott, it's your soul, not mine."

Scott: "I understand that. I haven't done anything to Kaysi."

Lori: "Yes, you have."

Scott: "I'll take truth serum, I'll take hypnosis, I'll take twenty-five polygraphs, I'll take whatever it is." (Scott asserted that he was talking to her openly on a recorded phone, claiming that he had nothing to hide.) "Guilty people aren't willing to take polygraphs."

Lori: (in a much calmer tone) "Several months ago, I had a very disturbing dream. It came back last night for a second time. The exact same dream. In it, I'm talking to Kaysi. She's leaning against a wall, just kind of smiling. I ask her, 'What's going on? Are you here or aren't you here?' Kaysi looks right at me and says, 'Mom, I'm dead.'[58] Those were Kaysi's exact words, Scott."

Scott seemed to be on the ropes. However, he took control of the conversation by asserting that Kaysi was alive. He reaffirmed his love for Lori, regardless of the awful things she was saying. He again veered into the horrific details of his victimization at the hands of Neighbor Ted. Lori finally stopped pressing him on Kaysi's whereabouts.

As I took off my headphones, I was as happy as I had been about anything in the case. Lori had found her footing and was finally challenging Scott! I told Gary about the call and he agreed—we should take a run at her now that she was seeking answers.

---

58  She would later tell me this paragraph line-for-line outside the elevator at the Safe Streets Task Force after she had this dream a third time.

# 7

# TWO BAGS OF TRASH

ON APRIL 10, 2007, Detective Gary and I spoke with Lori at her apartment in Westminster, Colorado. She was not hesitant to talk with me, thanks to Jason laying the groundwork that the FBI might be "trying to make things right." I assured her that I was not there to "cover the FBI's ass," though I was careful not to use the exact words I had heard her say on the recording. I told her up front that I knew the FBI's 2003 version had made a lot of mistakes in handling Scott; I was simply pursuing *what happened*, wherever that led us. She confirmed to Gary and me the same story we had heard from CB, that she and CB blew up Scott's cell phone on the night of August 23, 2003, after her nineteen-year-old daughter, Kaysi, disappeared. Like the other parents in this story, she would relay this account numerous times over the next few years, adding minor details each time as she recalled them. Basically, Lori's story went like this:

Scott and Lori's relationship began on Valentine's Day 2003, when Barb, Scott's mother, made room for Lori to sit down at a casino table in Blackhawk, Colorado. Scott was by all appearances a loving and caring son toward his mom, who was in a wheelchair. He seemed almost too good to be true. After an hour or so of observing him, Lori asked jokingly, "You're not a felon or anything, are you?"

He said, "Just the opposite. I work for the FBI."

Lori told us, "Scott gave me just the right amount of flattery and attention, showing intense interest in me like few men ever had. We were dating immediately after Blackhawk. I had no idea that at this exact same time, Scott was moving Jennifer's items into his apartment and spending three days with her just before she disappeared. I learned about that from Agent Carle when Scott was arrested in June 2003 when he (Agent Carle) asked to see my day planner for that week in February 2003.

"Scott proved that he worked for the FBI by introducing me to Agent Carle within the first week or so after we met. A few months later, Scott told me that some drug dealers killed Jennifer and that he was going to help the FBI find out who killed her. He got us a rental house on a large cattle property north of town."

Gary asked, "Is this the Huron Street address in Broomfield?" Lori said, "That's the one. We lived there with Kaysi—she bounced in and out of that home with CB."

"When I came home from working at the salon one evening in August (2003), Scott pointed to a baggie that was lying on my couch. It was obviously drugs and I guessed aloud that it must belong to Kaysi and CB. I'd warned both of them that I was gonna call the cops if they used drugs in our house. But before I could call, Scott convinced me not to turn them in—that *he* would get to the bottom of things. Scott took off to find Kaysi and I stayed at home, still upset.

"Scott put CB and Kaysi up in the Motel 6 at 84th and I-25, a few miles away from us, but he didn't tell me where they were. I found out later from CB that he told them, 'Don't call Lori, or she'll turn you into to the cops!'

"About a week before all this happened, Scott told me that he was going to scout for elk and that his phone would have no service. I said, 'Fine. I hope you have fun.' On August 23rd, late in the afternoon, he told me that he was leaving on this scouting trip. I asked, 'Scott, do you have to leave right now?' He said that one of his taillights didn't work and he had to get to the mountains before nightfall because he didn't want to get pulled over. I said, 'But the mama goat's pregnant and I don't know how to help it give birth.' Scott got really frustrated, took out his knife, and slit the goat from neck to tail. The baby came out and he said, 'There you go.' Then he took off in his truck."

A few hours later, the Subway manager called and told Lori, "Kaysi didn't show up to work."

Lori continued, "CB and I called both of them for hours, but neither of them answered. The next day, Scott answered his phone as he was driving back from the mountains. He said he'd been elk hunting and had no idea where Kaysi was. CB ran through the trailer attached to his truck when he drove up, yelling for Kaysi. Scott asked him what he thought he was doing, then CB accused him and said, 'I was there at the motel! You took her!' Scott turned to me to confirm that he'd planned this scouting trip for weeks and I told CB, 'Yes, he had.'

"Scott turned to CB and asked, 'Did *you* do something with Kaysi?'

"CB looked like he didn't know what to do. He just walked quickly down the driveway and off the property. Scott told me that afternoon, 'I'll use all the resources of the FBI to find out what happened to your daughter. If it's not CB, then she just ran away. We'll find her.'"

Scott took Lori to CB's house and other suspected drug houses around Denver over the next few days. He seemed intent on finding Kaysi. Lori leaned on him heavily for support and direction. During this search process, he proposed to Lori. "Marry me. If I need to, I'll use the resources of the FBI and devote the rest of my life to get you back together with Kaysi. I love you and want to be with you."

Lori told us, "My world was upside-down. Scott was my only hope of finding her. I said 'Yes' and we got married in Vegas. This was about ten days after Kaysi went missing."

For weeks after Kaysi's disappearance, Scott would tell Lori that Kaysi had "just been at the house," and encouraged her to keep watching for Kaysi because she was coming back home. On one occasion, Scott told Lori, "Kaysi was just here!" He showed her proof in the form of the gold necklace that CB had given to Kaysi when she disappeared from the motel. Lori saw the necklace hanging on the handle of the doorknob of Kaysi's bedroom. It *did* convince her for a while that Kaysi might be alive and simply hiding from them. Lori was further confused when their landlord, Dale, called her a few weeks after Kaysi disappeared and told her that he had seen Kaysi and CB driving CB's car past Dale's house.

I'll take a quick break from this interview with Lori and jump into two areas of information that opened up to us from her interview—Dale, and my research on Kaysi's disappearance.

## DALE'S BAD DAYS

Detective Gary and I found Dale the next day and asked him about his sighting of Kaysi. He confirmed that during 2003 he was Scott and Lori's landlord for the residence in Broomfield. Dale said he *did not* see Kaysi as he had told Lori. Instead, Scott asked him to "make up a story that he'd seen Kaysi and her boyfriend on their property."[59] Scott convinced Dale that Kaysi was alive, that she had just run away and Lori "simply needed some hope." As Dale told Lori the story about seeing her missing daughter, he felt extremely awkward and uneasy when he saw her eyes widen and relief settle in. After Scott was arrested years later, Dale apologized to Lori for fabricating such a pivotal puzzle piece of information. It had slowed her journey to finding out the truth.

Dale also talked about the day *he* got arrested in 2004, thanks to Scott, after Scott had stolen an air compressor from his garage.[60]

Dale told us, "For months, items had been disappearing from my house and garage and I suspected that Scott was responsible. On the day my air compressor disappeared, I told Scott, 'That's the last straw and I'm calling the cops.'

"The cops responded with a SWAT team, bullhorn, and snipers. Except they didn't respond to arrest Scott. They arrested *me*!! Though I'd called in the theft, they told me they were *expecting* that call after they arrested me. Can you believe it? Scott was the thief and they were scared that I was the one who was gonna kill them! The cops went into my house, down into my crawlspace in the basement, and found a rifle that I wasn't supposed to own because I'd been convicted of a financial crime. I went to jail for almost a month. I still thought Scott was my friend at the time, because he called to check on me and pretended like he was mad at the cops for treating me like that. He offered to watch my house and drive my cars around while I was in jail."

I had been reading over the police report of the response to Dale's house that day as we spoke. I figured he should know what had happened behind the scenes:

---

59 State of Colorado, County of Boulder v. Scott Lee Kimball. Warrant for Arrest Upon Affidavit. 2009-CR-0001626. Signed October 5, 2009. Received July 26, 2024, p.9
60 Personal journal

From the incident log of Dale's arrest, *before* Dale's call got through to the sheriff's office, Scott had called FBI Agent Carle and told him, "My landlord's about to call the sheriff's office and report me for stealing something or some such nonsense. His name is Dale. The real story is that he told me that he's going to commit suicide-by-cop today! Dale has a rifle in his basement that's illegal for him to possess. This is all a trick to draw the cops to his house. If they respond, please warn them! It's gonna be a shootout!'"

Scott knew how Dale would respond to the stolen air compressor. He knew how Agent Carle would respond to the warning that Dale had a rifle and was summoning law enforcement to the house. He knew how law enforcement would react to Agent Carle's call and rightly guessed they would disregard any objections by Dale that this was about Scott stealing. Finally, he knew he could befriend Dale afterwards because the call to Agent Carle insulated him as the informant. This would allow Scott to drive Dale's cars while Dale was in jail. Scott never graduated from high school, yet his ability to read people and predict their behavior, to deceive multiple people at the same time, and to befriend his victim after he had taken advantage of him, completely floored me.

I listened to a podcast about Kimball the other day as I was writing this section. The podcaster was in total disbelief that the FBI, inmates around Scott, his wives, and his neighbors were so naïve, and, yes, just simply stupid, to believe a known con man and thief. I almost called in to say, "None of this was public knowledge in 1985 or 1997 or 2004. Scott was so completely effective at downplaying his crimes, getting sentences deferred, and currying favor with law enforcement that even you, Mr. Podcaster, would have fallen victim. FBI agents are people, just like yourself, who were at one time either teachers, police officers, or businessmen like me, who just wanted to do something that had a greater purpose. Most of us give people the benefit of the doubt, and this man definitively knew how to overcome all doubt. It was as if he got a new dry-erase board every day, and any past sins, crimes, or lies were relegated to trivial matters. Whoever was in front of him was in trouble, and that person was going to lose something."

## PREPARATION. YOU HAVE TO PREPARE.

Years later, after Scott had been sentenced for multiple homicides in 2009, Harold Dow, a correspondent for CBS News, asked him about being a con man. Though Scott normally dodged direct questions, he looked Harold directly in the eyes and took his question straight on. "Yes, I'm a con man, and I've been one for over twenty-eight years."[61] (That would put Scott at fourteen years old when he began his adult life of cons.)

Harold replied, "You seem like an intelligent man, like you could've been anything you wanted to be in life."

"I'd agree with that."

Harold asked, "What made you a successful con man?" Without blinking or pausing, Scott flatly and pedantically said, "Preparation. To be successful, you have to prepare."

Thanks to Lori's interview, I learned that Scott prepared weeks in advance for Kaysi to disappear.

I was curious to see when Scott had applied for his hunting tags and how that correlated to Kaysi's disappearance. I contacted the Colorado Division of Wildlife and learned that on August 12, 2003, *eleven* days before Kaysi vanished, Scott was issued a Resident Deer License, valid for the Colorado area, east of the town of Oak Creek and west of Kremmling.[62]

I knew the date of August 12th was close to something else I had seen earlier, but it took me a while to find it. I went back to my timeline of significant events in the case. Scott was issued a Colorado driver's license under the alias "Joseph Lee Scott" on August 14, 2003. I had already confirmed this through a computerized check of the Colorado Department of Motor Vehicles (DMV) and by viewing a printout of Scott's alias identification in the FBI investigative case file. In 2003, Scott had convinced Agent Carle and Carle's superiors that he needed an alias to get Jason to confide in him. Scott had reported that Jason

---

61 https://www.cbsnews.com/news/serial-killers-life-of-crime/Updated on: June 16, 2024/ 1:07 AM EDT/CBS News, Downloaded on July 19, 2024

62 State of Colorado, County of Boulder v. Scott Lee Kimball. Warrant for Arrest Upon Affidavit. 2009-CR-0001626. Signed October 5, 2009. Received July 26, 2024, p.10

said, "I need fake documents to get out of the country because of my involvement in Steve's drug case."[63]

If Scott could show a fake document to Jason, then Jason might believe Scott had the connections to get him an alias ID too. Scott would use that trust to get Jason to tell him where Jennifer's body was buried. It makes sense, right? But I did not see anywhere in the file that Scott actually used this alias to talk Jason into anything. I did a national query on it, but the name was so common it became impossible to know for certain if he had been using it regularly. The timing of receiving this ID was highly suspicious though, right after the deer tag. It was also highly unusual—undercover agents could get those for covert assignments, but handing one out to a criminal informant? I would bet that has not happened much in the FBI since this case.

Also, on August 21, 2003, two days before Kaysi's disappearance, Scott was issued another elk license for the area from the Colorado town of Wellington to Cameron Pass and north.[64] These remote areas were almost a three-hour drive northwest of Denver. Because of the mountains, you either have to drive up through Wyoming and back down into Colorado, or west in Colorado on I-70 and then head north.

I also wanted to see evidence of Lori's and CB's frantic calls to Scott and if the towers had picked up Scott's phone anywhere. I served a subpoena to AT&T and learned that on August 23, 2003, Kimball's phone logged sixty-four calls, with a majority of them being the unanswered ones from Lori and CB. One call was Scott dialing the Motel 6 where Kaysi and CB were staying at 9:56 a.m.[65]

On the next day, August 24, 2003, Scott's phone was using a cell tower in the Steamboat Springs area, a mountain town even further away from Denver than Walden, where he was supposed to be hunting. The first call that day was incoming from Lori at 4:38 p.m.[66]

---

63 State of Colorado, County of Boulder v. Scott Lee Kimball. Warrant for Arrest Upon Affidavit. 2009-CR-0001626. Signed October 5, 2009. Received July 26, 2024, p.10
64 State of Colorado, County of Boulder v. Scott Lee Kimball. Warrant for Arrest Upon Affidavit. 2009-CR-0001626. Signed October 5, 2009. Received July 26, 2024, p.10
65 State of Colorado, County of Boulder v. Scott Lee Kimball. Warrant for Arrest Upon Affidavit. 2009-CR-0001626. Signed October 5, 2009. Received July 26, 2024, p.10
66 Although Scott's phone most likely means "Scott," we normally describe the phone's movements because we know those movements with certainty. We fill in the blanks other ways that Scott's phone was in Scott's hands.

Until that call, Scott's phone received no incoming calls and made no outgoing calls for almost a twenty-hour period—after sixty-four calls on the previous day. As the phone returned to Denver, five calls went to and from Lori.

Based upon this data, I could substantiate CB's claim of the Motel 6 interactions with Scott. CB would never testify to such in open court though, with Scott sitting across from him and staring at him. He still thought Scott was with the FBI, holding the same investigative status as I did. We were going to have to find out what happened to Kaysi while Scott's phone was turned off.

## VOMIT, THE STRIPPER & THE LOTTERY

Returning to our interview with Lori in April 2007, I asked if she would be willing to provide a DNA sample, so if we found Kaysi we would know for certain that it was her. I told her that Jennifer's DNA was already entered into the system by Agent Carle, but she had not been located as of yet.

This conversation prompted Lori to say, "That reminds me! When Scott and I were driving to Vegas to get married, we passed a road sign for the town of Rifle, Colorado. Scott pointed at the sign and said, 'That's where Jennifer's body is!' He told me he was working for the FBI on a case that involved the murder of a drug dealer's girlfriend named Jennifer."[67] Scott told Lori that the drug dealer's friend, Jason, had killed Jennifer and was willing to pay Scott to find her body in the mountains and remove her breast implants and IUD.

I asked Lori if she remembered anything else Scott said about Jennifer. Lori had met Agent Carle on a handful of occasions when he came out to the house to speak with Scott. Scott and Carle always stepped away to talk in private, and after the talks Scott would tell her that Carle was his boss. Lori had seen Agent Carle's government car, and his badge and gun, and had been to his FBI office downtown, so she had no doubt that he was a legitimate law enforcement officer. So,

---

[67] State of Colorado, County of Boulder v. Scott Lee Kimball. Warrant for Arrest Upon Affidavit. 2009-CR-0001626. Signed October 5, 2009. Received July 26, 2024, p.4

when Scott said, "I'll use all the resources of the FBI to find Kaysi," she had no reason to question his access.

I asked Lori, "Is there anything else?" The question is a simple technique used to prompt further conversation to add details on a topic or speak about something entirely different. (I came within seconds of skipping this question in a critical interview a few months later. And that slip-up would have kept us from exploring an entirely new line of investigation into Scott's murders.)

Lori said, "I know I told Detective Gary, but I don't think I told you about Uncle Terry disappearing." I agreed that Gary had mentioned it and asked what she remembered.

She continued, "While Justin was in the hospital recovering from almost being killed, Uncle Terry parked his Tahoe and trailer in our drive and made himself at home. He came here right after his divorce and was fat, lazy, and *disgusting* (she shook her head and grimaced) because he walked around in his underwear about half the time. He did nothing all day but sit on my new, white couch. After about two weeks, I came home from working at the salon and the couch was sitting on the front porch with a huge pile of vomit on it! I asked Scott, 'What happened to my couch!?'

"He said, 'Uncle Terry's dog threw up on it.' I told him, 'That's human vomit, not dog vomit!'

"Scott said, 'Oh yeah, Uncle Terry must've done it.'"

Lori added, "When I asked Scott where his uncle was, he said that Terry met a stripper named Ginger and that he won the Ohio State Lottery. I again asked, 'So, where's Terry now?' and Scott said, 'He took his things and moved to Mexico.'"

Gary and I stood there for a moment, waiting for Lori to say she had confronted Scott with the outlandish story or that Scott had said he was just messing with her. Nothing.

I asked, "Where's Uncle Terry now?"

Lori replied that he was probably still in Mexico as far as she knew because he sent Scott's Dad, Virge, an email a few months after he went down there, asking that no one bother him. "Frankly," Lori added, "I was glad he was gone and I didn't ask too many questions. But once

I learned that not only Kaysi, but Jennifer, was last with Scott, and now Uncle Terry, it's not a coincidence."

Lori provided her DNA to me without reservation. I gave her a Q-tip, and she dutifully scraped it around the inside lining of her cheeks. Then, with latex gloves on, I placed the Q-tip in a small box and closed it. I placed evidence tape over the openings and put it inside a paper bag that I labeled with her name, and the date and time, so the FBI Lab could enter her DNA (and thus a comparable profile of Kaysi's) into the system. If any unknown female remains were recovered with any DNA left inside, and the DNA matched what Lori provided, we would know if those remains belonged to Kaysi.

## PRICELESS TRASH

Before we left, Lori pulled out two trash bags from a closet in the second bedroom. She said that she had held onto the bags from the week Kaysi disappeared. Lori explained her actions, saying that although she felt like she had to trust Scott to help find her daughter, she never completely discounted CB's story that Scott picked her up from the motel. So, Lori saved his trash from that week in August 2003, in the event that one day investigators like us came looking for evidence. Scott had turned his cell phone off during those critical days, so saving his trash was a logical long shot to determine his hidden activities.

I have a handful of other cases that involved people holding on to critical evidence, hoping that one day an agent like me would find *them*. These people were not coming to me. They were hoping that law enforcement would follow the clues.

Gary and I placed a mat on Lori's kitchen table and emptied the bags. We pulled out any items that showed a date, time, and place for Scott: gas receipts, restaurant tickets, speeding tickets, etc. Some of the receipts had food or drink stains on them, while others were crumpled and torn. We laid them out, took photos, and then placed all the items into an evidence bag. One of the receipts stood out: it was from a grocery store in the mountains on the morning after Kaysi disappeared—August 24, 2003. We knew Scott was supposed to be in the mountains that day, and this receipt listed the mountain town of Walden, which was in the hunting area for his hunting license. It matched Lori's story.

If Kaysi had been recovered in that Walden area, though, we would/should have known about it because the FBI had missing person notices sent out nationwide on our three victims. However, I needed more context to see if any items from the four-year-old trash bags were worthwhile.

Before we left, Lori said, "Oh, and I thought of one more thing—someone you really need to talk to—he's a good friend of mine and his name's Bryon. He knows things about Uncle Terry and Kaysi that I didn't know. Here's his number." She handed us Bryon's contact information, then Gary and I thanked her profusely and left.

## BRYON DATHE

Bryon Dathe is one of the only characters I'll mention with a last name because, well, you'll see why when I'm done with his story. Gary and I went to see this disarming, very gentle and friendly man after talking to Lori. Unfortunately, Bryon's personality made him the ideal prey for Scott.

Bryon told us an odd story about him observing the interactions between Kaysi and Scott when Kaysi was accused of stealing Bryon's credit card. The thief had fraudulently charged almost $3,000 worth of purchases in March 2003.[68] Scott asked the officer who was dispatched if he could talk with Kaysi separately for a while, and the officer allowed it. When they came back into the room, Kaysi told the officer that she "was the only one involved" in the fraud. No one got arrested, but Bryon thought at the time that Scott must have talked her into taking the blame for something he had done.

In May 2004, ten months after Kaysi disappeared, Bryon was in the backyard of Scott and Lori's home in Broomfield, Colorado, while Scott and his two sons were inside the camper-trailer. This was the same white trailer that Scott was driving the day he had picked Kaysi up in August 2003 from the Motel 6.

---

68 John Aguilar, "Chapter 5: Misplaced Trust," *Daily Camera*, March 11, 2010 (Archived from the original on January 11, 2020. Retrieved June 29, 2024.)

Bryon told Gary and me, "Scott told Justin and Cody to go inside the house and he'd be there in a minute. I saw him walk out of the camper a few seconds after them and he told me, 'Let's head to the basement.' We all went in the house and walked downstairs. While we were down there, the camper caught fire—and by the time we managed to run back outside it was completely in flames. Scott said, 'One of the boys must've accidentally opened the curtains over the stove fire,' but I didn't buy it. I think Scott set fire to the camper and was distracting us while it started burning. I never called him on it though, 'cause I didn't know for sure."

I asked Bryon what he knew about Uncle Terry.

He said, "Scott talked me into helping him with his Rocky Mountain All Natural Beef business and I lost a lot of money investing in that. I also lost money to Scott twice on Uncle Terry's Tahoe. I only met Terry once because he was only around for about a week. Scott told me to write him a check for $2,000 and then he'd sell the Tahoe for five or six thousand and split the profit with me and Terry. He said he'd give Terry $2,000 for get-out-of-town money. So, I gave Scott a check for $2,000 and the Tahoe sat in front of my house for a few weeks.[69] Scott told me to keep it on my property because it would upset Lori if he kept it at their place. I asked Scott, 'Where'd Terry go?' And he said, 'He won the lottery and was traveling around the country with his new girlfriend.'"[70]

Scott returned to Bryon a few days later and said that he wanted to sell half of the Tahoe to Bryon for $2,500, asserting that it was worth well over $5,000. Bryon gave him another $2,500. The Tahoe later disappeared and so did the $4,500 Bryon had paid to Scott.

Gary, Profiler Art, and my boss, Phil, and I agreed that it was finally time to interview Scott. I notified the Montana warden that we were coming, and he said that he would be happy to set things up for us. I had six months to study for this big "test." As the date approached, I felt that I was as ready as I could ever be. I certainly should have been prepared for nearly any interview after all this prep work—but not this one.

---

69  Personal journal
70  State of Colorado, County of Boulder v. Scott Lee Kimball. Warrant for Arrest Upon Affidavit. 2009-CR-0001626. Signed October 5, 2009. Received July 26, 2024, p.18

# 8

# THE DANGEROUS VACUUM

I FORGOT to ask Lori about Scott's affair with Melissa, who bought the rifle for him in December 2005. Through Gary's earlier interviews with Lori, he had learned that Scott had an affair with a waitress from Perkins named Melissa, just before Scott took off for California. I called Lori and asked if she was willing to talk about it before I headed off to interview Scott.

With a deep sigh, Lori started with, "You're gonna think I'm a horrible, stupid person, but okay. By August 2005, Kaysi had been missing for two years and my marriage to Scott was on the rocks. I knew something was going on with his unexplained late nights, him throwing his clothes in the laundry and doing a load at midnight, him smelling like perfume that wasn't mine, and his explanations that always made sense at the moment until I thought about them later."

It all finally came down to a hairbrush.

On an afternoon in August 2005, Lori opened the passenger door of Scott's pickup and was greeted by a hairbrush that had slid down between the passenger seat and the door. Long, highlighted female hair was tangled in the brush that definitely did not belong to her. Lori had suspected for months that Scott had been cheating on her (much like Larissa had known he was cheating years before in Washington), and the hairbrush clinched it. Lori told the following story:

"When I found the hairbrush, I completely lost it. I started screaming uncontrollably at Scott, hitting him in the chest, crying, yelling—I went bananas. Scott was yelling at me, 'Calm down! Hey! Let's talk about this!' But I wouldn't stop. He threatened to call the cops and I dared him to, so he did. I was still hot when they got there. The male cop went to Scott and the female cop came to me. She asked me what happened and I told her the story. She asked if there was any physical altercation and I said, 'Yeah, I slapped his chest a few times, but that's it.' I could see Scott pulling up his pant leg and pointing to some deep scratches. I told the woman cop, 'If he's saying I did those (scratches), he's lying! He got those from working on our barbed wire fence.' I asked the police officer to look at the fence. I must've been yelling because she told me to calm down and lower my voice.

"The two cops talked between themselves for a few minutes, then both came over to me and asked if I threw a vacuum at Scott. 'Threw a what?!' I asked. 'We have one vacuum in the shoe closet and it's buried under piles of clothes. Go look for yourselves!' They both told me to lower my voice. The female cop said, 'You're not telling me how to do my job. I don't need to go look in a closet to see what happened here.' I was beside myself now and asked them, 'You're seriously gonna believe *him*—the man who I just found out is having an affair on me—that I threw a vacuum at him?!? This is unbelievable!!'"

The cops handcuffed Lori and took her to jail. Scott got a restraining order against her, which she found lying on their bed when she was released. She called him and he admitted to being at Melissa's house. He told Lori that he loved her but she needed to get ahold of herself. He told her that she could stay on their property, but if she started fighting him again he would have her arrested for violating the order.

And this is where the Adams County Sheriff's Office report 05-12269 picks up:[71]

"On 08-09-05 at 2342 hours, as a result of a radio call, I contacted Scott Kimball via telephone. He kept referring to me as 'Brett' even though I identified myself as Deputy Smith of the sheriff's office. Mr. Kimball finally said, 'Good, she's gone.' He explained that his wife, Lori, is the restrained party of a No Contact bond and he is the protected party. Lori was recently arrested for domestic violence against him.

---

71 John Aguilar, "Chapter 10: Unraveling," *Daily Camera*, March 16, 2010 (Archived from the original on November 3, 2018. Retrieved June 29, 2024.)

He explained that he called me 'Brett' because she was sitting next to him in the car. Mr. Kimball said, 'Brett's my brother and I didn't want her to know I'm talking to the cops. She may have weapons in her car and may harm me if she knows I'm talking to the police.'"

The report continued with Scott speaking, "Lori waits for me routinely to show up at my property at 14701 Huron Street and I expect her to be there any minute. She drives a gray Jeep Cherokee, license plate #288INP. She's blowing up my phone right now."

The deputy confirmed the No Contact order and told Scott to stay in his car while he dispatched deputies to the Huron Street address. Deputies responded and found the gray Jeep parked outside. Scott allowed deputies into the house and they found Lori sitting on the bed in the master bedroom.

The deputy next wrote, "I asked the female if she was Lori and she said she was. I then took her into custody." He added, "She was very agitated and argumentative. She shouted at us that we were out of control and that we were falsely arresting her. I explained that the only person out of control was her and she needed to calm down. She was placed in the back seat of the patrol car."

Lori told the deputies that her heart rate and blood pressure were racing. An ambulance was called and they cleared her and then transported her to jail.[72]

Lori told me that same story of her second arrest as I took notes. She said, "Scott took off for California shortly after this whole ordeal to start his life with his *next* girlfriend. What a fool I'd been to stay with him."

I simply shook my head in disbelief and almost felt ill as Lori related this maddening series of events. I assured her I probably would have reacted the same way she did. I told her that I did not think she was stupid or a bad person, but that she had survived being married to possibly the most manipulative and dangerous human being I knew.

---

72  Scott knew how the cops would respond to his call, how Lori would respond to the cops, and how the cops would respond to her agitated state.

## 9

# LAPTOP, LOTTERY & LEFT HOOK

I INVITED Gary back to the FBI Safe Streets Office and asked if he was up to calling Uncle Terry's ex-wife with me to ask about the Tahoe, the vomit, the lottery win, the stripper named Ginger, and Mexico. Of course he was.

On April 24, 2007, I called Terry's ex-wife, Karen. She was eager to talk because there were so many questions circling around what had happened to Terry three years ago. She told us the following:

"I was married to Terry for thirteen years, until he moved to Colorado in 2004 to work with his nephew, Scott Kimball, in a cattle business venture. I wasn't excited about him working with Scott again because they'd gotten into arguments before, involving Scott's questionable business deals. Terry was in the habit of taking off for months at a time without much explanation, so I filed for divorce. After he arrived in Colorado, I called Scott and asked if I could speak with Terry. Scott said that he'd have Terry call me back, but he never called. I eventually spoke with Scott's wife Lori, who told me that Terry and Scott had talked about going into business together against her wishes. I sent divorce papers to Terry at Scott's address, but they were returned to me.[73]

"Lori told me weeks later that Terry had won the Ohio State Lottery. I thought it was highly unlikely he would win anything, especially a

---

73 John Aguilar, "Chapter 7: Uncle Terry," *Daily Camera*, March 13, 2010 (Archived from the original on November 3, 2018. Retrieved June 29, 2024.)

lottery, but I sent a letter to the Ohio State Lottery to see if he actually did. I never heard back from them, either.

"I figured that Terry had found another woman to live with and was living off of that woman's income. I never heard until much later that he'd moved to Mexico with a dancer—there's just no way that happened."

I asked Karen who, besides her, would be in touch with Terry or know how to reach him.

"No one that I know," she responded. "I can tell you this. Terry would never leave without his two dogs, nor would he leave the country and his Tahoe behind—his social security payments are his lifeline and he's not the type to have a steady job."

I thanked Karen for her time and told her that I was sure we would be in touch.

No one, other than Uncle Terry's ex-wife, was interested in what had happened to him. Returning to the profiler's training on victim selection, Terry was "available" because he was living with Scott at the time he disappeared. He was "vulnerable" because he had cut his lifelines with family, friends, and workplace associates who would know or care if he disappeared. But the bigger question was why would Scott *want* to kill his uncle who just came to town? At this point, I was thinking Jennifer and Kaysi's disappearances and likely deaths were tied to something sexual. Scott's attempts on his sons' lives were financially motivated. The "desirable" piece for Uncle Terry was still a mystery. I decided to give him a few days of attention, even though nobody was knocking on the FBI's door to find him.

## THE LAPTOP

In January 2006, ten months before I got the Kimball case, Gary had seized a trailer that Scott had stolen from another one of his former Colorado cellmates, Dr. Alderman. The doctor trusted him to care for his property while he sat in prison. Dr. Alderman did not just lose his trailer to Scott; he lost his pickup and over $10,000 from his bank account thanks to two of Scott's fake oil money checks. The trailer's contents had not been fully searched yet because Gary's investigation was focused solely on the trailer theft and the check fraud against the other doctor in the story, a family friend named Dr. Cleve. Lori told Gary that Scott kept a lot of his personal things inside the trailer, but there was no reliable information that gave Gary probable cause for a search warrant into missing people or homicides.

The same thing held true for Scott's Toshiba laptop. It sat in the police evidence locker after Gary searched it for check fraud in April 2006, then stopped the search because it had images of women being tortured and raped. Gary's warrant did not allow for those types of images—possible evidence of different crimes—to be seized and reviewed. By April 2007, after the interviews we had completed, the jail calls I had listened to, and the three missing people we had identified—Kaysi, Jennifer, and Uncle Terry—I hoped that we had enough evidence on the laptop for a search warrant to look for signs of missing or kidnapped people.

The challenge, as AUSA Dave told me, is that you normally have a person who could testify that someone had indeed been kidnapped, or some other evidence, like video, to prove a crime had happened. We only had missing people. He told me to go ahead and draft an affidavit anyway, so I wrote up my best effort. My foundation was built around Scott's report to Agent Carle on July 15, 2003, that he "took a trip to the mountains in Craig, Colorado between February 17–20, 2003." Scott said this in response to Agent Carle telling him that Scott's cell phone was using a tower in Vernal, Utah on February 20th, around the same time that Jennifer's phone made ten short calls after having been turned off for three days. Scott told Carle that he had taken a route through Wyoming to get to his "spot" in the mountains.[74]

And that trip provided the federal hook. Scott traveled interstate on the day Jennifer disappeared against her will, which I asserted as best I could, and his phone used an out-of-state cell tower.

I used Larissa's stories of kidnapping and assaults supported by the Spokane police reports, CB's and Lori's eyewitness accounts of Scott taking Kaysi, the receipt for furniture that Scott had Jennifer sign the day before she disappeared, the transcript of the recording between

---

74 State of Colorado, County of Boulder v. Scott Lee Kimball. Warrant for Arrest Upon Affidavit. 2009-CR-0001626. Signed October 5, 2009. Received July 26, 2024, p.5

Jennifer's mom and Scott when he said he wanted to reenact Jennifer's murder on an escort, the recovery of the guns in the desert, the interview of Gamblin about "digging up implants and an IUD from a dead body," Uncle Terry winning the lottery and moving to Mexico, and a brief summary of Scott's fraud and misdirection of law enforcement.

I had sworn to a handful of bank robbery affidavits to request arrest and search warrants in front of Federal Judge Watanabe. Each time, he read them quickly and, without looking up, told me, "Please stand. Raise your right hand and affirm that this affidavit is true and correct to the best of your knowledge." I did so, and he signed each affidavit and warrant and off I went to arrest the guy or search the house. Not today. With a furrowed brow, Judge Watanabe read and reread the affidavit and then told me, "It's like a science fiction novel." He advised, "You're almost there with probable cause. Just give me a couple more facts to support your case."

As he handed my paperwork back to me, I felt like I was back in college and my professor was grading my exam before asking, "Are you sure you're enrolled in the right class?"

I called Lori and Larissa, hoping to fill in some holes on the three disappeared people and Scott's statements—I was back in front of the judge three days later. This time, the judge nodded, had me raise my hand to swear, and then signed the new and improved affidavit in June 2007. Judge Watanabe remarked that he had "never seen a case like this in his twenty years on the bench." I immediately took Scott's laptop and headed to our computer lab.

In my search of the laptop, I found at least ten photos of younger women (twenty to thirty years old) whose faces were unfamiliar to me. Also on the laptop were creepy photos of houses or cabins in wooded areas, as if Scott was doing surveillance on these addresses. Scott saved news articles as he followed trial updates on serial killer Dennis Rader's court cases and body counts. Rader was known as the "BTK," a nickname given for his propensity to bind, torture, and kill his victims. Most disturbing (and something that continues to live in my brain today) were almost three hundred images and videos of women being brutally raped and tortured. They were nude and bloody, often with knives to their throats, tied to trees or beds, assaulted in all sorts of violent ways and always crying or screaming in fear and pain. Finally, I found Scott's attempts at forging driver's licenses, letterheads, and court documents as he represented himself to be an FBI agent or a probation officer. He even practiced using FBI Agent Carle's signature. One of the photos was of an unknown young woman with long, blond hair who would play a significant role in the case six months down the road.[75]

## NO LOTTO

Also on that June 2007 search day, I reviewed the contents of Scott's Dell desktop computer. I found the login for a Yahoo! account under the name of Terry Kimball (Uncle Terry) on August 5, 2005, almost a full year after he disappeared.[76] This date corresponded with the approximate time frame in which Lori commented to her family, "No one's heard from Terry in a while!" A folder in the Yahoo! account contained an email sent to Virge (Scott's dad and Terry's brother) from Terry stating, "Hi, just checking in. I'm down in Mexico with Ginger, who doesn't like company, so please don't bother trying to come visit. Everything's going great. Terry."

Virge confirmed in a phone call with me that he had in fact received the email, supposedly coming from Terry in late 2005 after Terry had been missing for months. The family did not give it much thought, though, since Terry was known to travel and be off the radar for long stretches of time.

I called the officials at the Ohio State Lottery who informed me that Uncle Terry had never won any lottery proceeds. Shocker, I know. I also checked with the U.S. Social Security Administration to see if he had been receiving his benefit payments. There had been no payments since his July 2004 move to Colorado.

So, I ran another query for Terry Kimball and found that a credit card company reported Terry kiting $23,083 worth of bad checks

---

[75] U.S. District Court, State and District of Colorado. Application and Affidavit for Search Warrant, Search of Toshiba laptop and Dell computer tower, Case 07SW-05116, Affiant Jonathan Grusing, signed June 1, 2007. Received July 3, 2024.

[76] State of Colorado, County of Boulder v. Scott Lee Kimball. Warrant for Arrest Upon Affidavit. 2009-CR-0001626. Signed October 5, 2009. Received July 26, 2024

between July and November of 2004. Justin's "accident" was on July 15, 2004, and Uncle Terry was in town shortly afterwards. I also was able to confirm that Terry had no prior arrest history for writing bad checks, or fraud, in his sixty years of existence.[77]

Based upon my study of Lori's datebook, the fraudulent checks, and interviews with people who encountered Uncle Terry in Colorado, I was doubtful that he lived past August 1, 2004.

Additional bad checks were cashed in Alaska to cover hotel charges and rental cars in September 2004. Lori had previously told Gary and me that Scott took her, and her alone, on a trip to Alaska that month and had paid for their hotel and rental car. Checks had been written by *someone* using Terry's name at the Red Lion Colonial Hotel and a gas station in Helena, Montana in October 2004. I called Lori to ask about those Montana charges. She remembered that Scott had a court date in Montana and she traveled with him to stay at the Red Lion. She was highly certain that Terry did not accompany them. While she was on the line, I asked about the two dogs that Terry's ex-wife, Karen, told me he would never leave behind. Lori said, "The dogs disappeared the same day he did. I've asked Scott about them and he says he has no clue."

## LEFT HOOK

The biggest piece of the puzzle that I needed to find in order to get the FBI and U.S. Attorney's Office in a position to prosecute Scott was finally obtainable—thanks largely to AUSA Dave's disregard for what was good for his career. His bosses, understandably, wanted nothing to do with this case. The U.S. Attorney's Office had been influenced by Agent Carle in 2003 to allow Scott to work on the murder-for-hire case, without supervision by U.S. Probation, because Scott was Agent Carle's informant. Now in June 2007, Scott was a suspect in the disappearance and deaths of three people, had been caught in a high-speed chase with the U.S. Marshals in California, and had pending fraud cases in many states. Yet, largely because of my friendship with Dave,

---

[77] State of Colorado, County of Boulder v. Scott Lee Kimball. Warrant for Arrest Upon Affidavit. 2009-CR-0001626. Signed October 5, 2009. Received July 26, 2024, p.19

but also because of his innate drive to seek justice, he stuck with me. He put me in front of a federal grand jury on June 4, 2007, in an effort to formally indict Scott for violation of Title 18, U.S. Code 922(g), Felon in Possession of a Firearm. My testimony lasted all of fifteen minutes as I told how we found the guns in California, Scott's lengthy arrest record for check fraud and forgery, and how we knew he was carrying the handgun around from 2003 to 2006. For those unfamiliar with grand juries, there are no defense attorneys to cross-examine the testimony given. The only people present are the prosecutors, an investigator, a court reporter, and thirteen civilians. These are people who are randomly selected to listen to federal crimes, presented day after day, to determine if probable cause exists for an arrest warrant. If they asked me any questions after my testimony, I don't remember them. They returned with a "true bill" and federal arrest papers were served on Scott the same day, as he sat in his Montana jail. Seeing that stamped, official federal warrant should have hit Scott like a solid left hook to the jaw—this charge meant we could bring him to Colorado to stand trial. Maybe we could bargain with him about what had happened to the missing people. Also, it was my warning shot that the FBI was involved and was considering him as a suspect, not an informant. Gary and I were headed to Montana to interview Scott. It was my first interview with a suspected serial killer.

## 10

# SCOTT WINS

GARY, PHIL, and I flew in the FBI jet to Missoula, Montana. Our headquarters wanted this thing resolved before the media got wind of Scott being our informant, and before it could be broadcast to the world that we were paying him to save lives while he was secretly killing people. Not a good look. On June 30, 2007, I met Scott for the second time (the first being a witness to his informant payment with Agent Carle at the Starbucks in 2003) at the Cascade County Detention Facility in Great Falls, Montana.

I had been working on my introduction and opened with, "Hi, Mr. Kimball (I did not want to be too familiar by calling him Scott and hoped to appeal to his sense of importance), I'm Agent Jonny Grusing from the FBI in Denver—I met you briefly a few years ago with Agent Carle. We need your help on a few things: to help us figure out what happened to Kaysi, Jennifer, and Uncle Terry, and I need to talk with you about some of the things that happened while you were our informant as well."

Scott was not happy or impressed, as he replied, "Agent *Grusing*? Did you say? Do you know what *my* morning was like? I got woken up at 5 a.m. out of a deep sleep, not allowed to brush my teeth or shower, put on a bus, and when I asked the guard, 'What's happening? Where am I going?' there was no answer. And then I wind up here, in this jail, with you in front of me. I am NOT happy! Not happy at all."

"Scott, those were not done at my direction. I'm sorry. That is not at all how I wanted this day to start or how I wanted you treated before this meeting."

I asked him if he was still willing to talk and, with a dramatic eye roll, he muttered something about "things better be getting a lot better from here." As we walked past an interview room with a lie detector machine and chair, Scott said, "Hey, there's a polygraph room. Why don't you take me in there and ask me if I've ever shot anyone in the head?" He added, "Or, just shot anyone, ever?"

This was going to be a bigger challenge than I had anticipated. I whispered to Gary, "Then he must've used a knife or a rope or something? Just not a gun to shoot them? Or he shot them somewhere besides the head?" The future version of me, after spending years with this man, looked back and laughed and said, "You had no idea what you were walking into did you? Or what his first assertion of 'not shooting someone in the head' actually meant?"

Within the first few minutes after sitting down in the small interview room as Phil and the sheriff observed through the one-way glass, Scott asked me, "Can we order a pizza?" I responded, "Okay, we'll get something to eat in a little while and we've only got so much time—" He flatly interrupted, "I'd like a pizza *now*. Extra meat and cheese."

Who was in charge here? The inmate or the FBI? As I glanced toward the one-way mirror, hoping for guidance from Phil but forgetting that I could not see him or the sheriff, I knew the answer. Scott was in charge. Traveling there on the company dime made us *feel* important, but it made him *know* his information was worth gold. He was the reason that the plane, hotel, and rental car were all paid for. His information caused us to drop what we were doing in Denver and travel to meet him in this tiny jail. We would simply have to hope he was willing to share just a piece of what he knew. We bought the pizza.

After Scott waived his Miranda rights like they were simply a nuisance, I asked him about the three missing people and how he could help us, trying to play into his apparent affinity for being an informant and avoiding direct confrontation as we began our new relationship. Scott replied, "Kaysi's not dead. She's alive. I've talked to some of her friends in Arizona and Colorado who've seen her since she went missing. I know Uncle Terry's alive because my brother, Brett, saw him in California after he came to stay with me in Colorado."

Scott said that he could "provide information to help us find Jennifer," but only if we gave him immunity for the white-collar crimes. I argued that the check fraud crimes did not compare with the urgency of dads missing their daughters. He didn't budge, saying, "This is my life that we're gambling on this, Agent Grusing. Not yours. I need immunity for check fraud and forgery crimes before we talk about missing people."[78]

I tried another angle, "Look, Scott your two kids are about the same age as my two. We're both dads who care about our kids. These dads have been missing their daughters for over three years. How would you feel if that happened to Justin and Cody?"

Scott gave me a puzzled look as he asked, "Why would I care what other dads are thinking about?" Empathy simply did not register with this man.

Throughout the six-hour interview, Scott had to go to the bathroom just when Gary and I thought we were making headway. Or he would say, "Don't make me say those three words you don't want to hear." I knew the forbidden words he was referring to were, "I want a lawyer." I really wanted to correct him with a snarky joke of some sort about those being *four* words. But I had already been a smart aleck once (I do not remember about what) and he had not enjoyed that at all—he just gave me an unimpressed look that said, "Try that again and I'll head back to my cell."

I asked Scott about the three hundred images on his laptop of rape and torture of women and he curtly said, "Those were Uncle Terry's." When I challenged that Terry had already disappeared by then, he said with finality, "Those aren't mine. If you mention those again, we're done."

About three hours in, Scott said, "Jon, you can't take a guy who's lied all his life and get him to tell the truth in a day. It doesn't happen. It just doesn't."

Gary and I received coaching and encouragement from Phil during restroom breaks and we kept questioning Scott as best as we could. At one point, the warden got so frustrated with the way Scott was

---

78 I learned later that he was using this chess-like move to put us in "check," as he knew we could not give him immunity. It gave him some cover to hide behind—until he had to go face-to-face with my buddy, AUSA Dave.

ducking, redirecting, and rewording our questions that he asked us to step aside so he could take a run at Scott. Gary and I went behind the glass as he and Phil entered the small, white-walled arena with Scott. The warden asked him pointedly, "You want me to transfer you to Haver?" (I learned later that Haver was the most undesirable prison in Montana.) Unruffled, Scott asked, "Is that a threat, Warden?" Next, Scott wondered aloud how his court-appointed attorney would react when he was transferred because he was not giving law enforcement the answers they wanted. The warden sat in silence for a second.

"Sub, Ref!" I imagined the words from my basketball days. The warden and Phil were out and Gary and I were back in, learning the rules of engagement with Scott as we sat across from him. Scott's unspoken rules included: no sex talk, no struggle to control the interview, do not refer to him as an inmate, very limited sarcasm, no threats or veiled threats from us, and no direct accusations that he had caused anyone to disappear or die. We were there to seek understanding from him on what he knew. As long as we asked clarifying questions and treated him with the level of respect we would treat a fellow detective or agent, he would talk all day.

Scott asked us, "Do you really expect me to tell you everything the first time?" After six hours of sparring with this very complex man in the tiny space with his assertions of, "I can't incriminate myself any further," and "I wish I could be honest with you," I finally told him we were leaving. His most unforgettable jab came when we stood up to escort him out: "Agent Grusing, I thought you said you cared about bringing these girls home to their fathers. And you're giving up now?"

I replied, "Scott, if I can do more productive work in Denver trying to find them than talking in circles with you when you admit that you can't be honest, I think I'll head back there."

He snorted derisively and said, "Alright, if that's what you think you should do . . ."

I wrote this in my journal after my first interview of Scott, "He was very upset about us having him moved. Lies came quickly, easily, and convincingly. He got upset with any confrontation by us early on and threatened to leave. I felt calm and focused but completely exhausted after the interview. God did not grant my prayers for a confession."

I called Jennifer's dad, Bob, and Kaysi's dad, Rob, when we got back. They were not surprised that we came away mostly empty-handed, but they seemed appreciative that we were trying to find their daughters by taking a run at Scott. "Trying" would be the recurring theme, with multiple meanings, for my work regarding Scott. I have always worked out as hard as my body will allow for a brief period at least once a day. I use it to purge myself of the stress and angst people like Scott introduce and to provide an outlet for my energy. However, no workout compared to being in the tiny jail room, battling wits with that man for six hours. I was completely spent—a new form of exhaustion.

A month after our return, AUSA Dave filed the writ to transfer Scott to Colorado, based on the indictment. Scott was now our prisoner, and he was physically moved to custody in Denver by October 2007. We formed an alliance with Gary's friends at the Boulder County District Attorney's office, who had filed the check fraud and forgery cases against Scott.

Scott's court-appointed federal public defender, Lynn, and state public defender, Megan, were competent attorneys. They represented Scott's interests well, despite having possibly the most dangerous and difficult client to come through our system in recent years. Megan, a very fit, pragmatic, and savvy attorney, quickly grasped who and what Scott was, while Lynn more often than not gave him the benefit of the doubt, logically assuming that he must be telling the truth because it would benefit him to be honest with her.

The Boulder prosecutors assigned to us were also intelligent, highly motivated women who wanted to bring Scott to justice after he was able to escape charges for his attacks on his son, Justin. These two attorneys, Katharina, an outgoing hard-charger, and Amy, a quiet case-builder, would play critical roles in forming what will stand in history as the most unique plea agreement in Colorado. It had to be so, because we were dealing with missing people, not murdered ones, and this ingenious madman who stayed three moves ahead of us.

Once Scott had settled into federal custody in Colorado by November 2007, the attorneys—including AUSA Dave Conner representing the Department of Justice—met with Gary and me to learn what everyone wanted out of all the charges against Scott. After briefing them on our three missing people, they spoke to Scott and the bargaining process began. This process consisted of shipping him from a local jail over to the U.S. Marshals office in downtown Denver, then bringing him up the back elevator into the courthouse and walking him into a large conference room where the seven of us sat. I removed his handcuffs, gave him a bottle of water, and the talks began.

# 11

# SECONDS AWAY

IN TRUE crime TV, a search of a suspect's property or residence almost never fails to give law enforcement the evidence they need. Also, the detectives possess the necessary brilliance to get the killer to confess during their first or second meeting. Neither of those happened for me. After our June 2007 visit, Scott had whispered to an inmate, "I sure hope the feds don't look at our family property near Rifle, Colorado, where I grew up hunting, because it'd be a great place to hide a body." By that time, I had become friends with Barb, Scott's mom, so I asked her about the land. She told me about hundreds of acres on a family property very near Rifle, the supposed burial place of Jennifer.

Scott and Brett grew up going to this scenic place because Kay, Barb's life partner, had family property there. The mountain town of Collbran lay in a picturesque valley with a river running through the middle with steep, colorful canyon walls. When the seven of us arrived for a site survey, we were in awe of the bright green grass and the quiet sounds of running water and chirping birds; it felt like we were in a fairy tale. Barb had introduced me to Craig, the property owner, who was more than happy to show us around the eighty acres where Scott grew up hunting. Craig, a true cowboy with a broad smile and weathered hands, took us to a hunting cabin. Our evidence tech turned on the blue light to search for blood. The entire inside glowed brightly, a positive result, but that did not mean Scott killed anyone there. Craig explained that scores of animals had been quartered and downsized there over the years. We searched through the river and creek beds that were flowing heavily but saw nothing that would conceal a body. Craig said that he would have been surprised if Scott had been able to slip into their valley and leave a body there knowing that Craig and his family spent a lot of time outside. They would have eventually come across any human remains if Scott had left someone there. We thanked them and started our drive back to Denver.

As we swerved through the mountain passes, I explained to George, the FBI intern who had helped me listen to Scott's prison calls, that Scott had a *reason* to ask his former cellmate Gamblin at the Sonic that day to cut out Jennifer's breast implants and IUD—I did not yet understand why he would involve Gamblin in her homicide. There had to be some kind of evidence left with Jennifer that pointed to Scott as her killer, and he was not willing to take the risk himself to go back and remove identifiers that would last much longer than her fingerprints. Yet, Scott was very shrewd when it came to such criminal elements. He knew that saying anything about "the drug dealer's girlfriend" to someone like Gamblin opened another avenue of risk, one he could not manage when Gamblin was out of his control. That is why I liked the Collbran property as a viable search area: it was near Rifle, it had creek beds, and if Jennifer were to be recovered on Craig's property the sole suspect would be Scott Kimball. After seeing it firsthand, though, I was sure she was not there—especially after talking to Craig. At least we could cross it off the list of possibilities.

## STEVE IN SEAGOVILLE

On October 30, 2007, I took Gary with me again in the chartered FBI plane to speak with Steve, Jennifer's former boyfriend, who was incarcerated in a Seagoville, Texas, prison. Steve had been housed with Scott inside the FCI Englewood prison back in July 2002 when Scott concocted the murder-for-hire plot involving Jennifer. Besides reviewing the file and talking to Steve's friend, Jason, I'd listened to twenty-five recorded prison calls between Jennifer and Steve. I had digested most of the recordings during a three-day surveillance, waiting for an out-of-town group to rob some jewelry stores in Denver.

I learned these truths from Jennifer's calls to the prison: Steve loved her—he was crazy about her and very explicitly expressed his unending infatuation in terms that were never intended for someone like me to overhear; Jennifer thought Scott was "a little creepy," but she put up with him because Steve was confident that Scott could get her out of stripping; Steve never spoke about killing witnesses or even holding a grudge against the two people that Scott told Agent Carle he "wanted dead"; and finally, Steve was completely clueless when Jennifer disappeared as evidenced by his calls to his dad that were filled with curiosity and bewilderment.

The Seagoville prison guard brought Steve out to meet Gary and me as we sat in the empty cafeteria. I introduced Gary and myself and said, "Steve, we're here because we're investigating what happened to Jennifer. I've listened to the prison calls between the two of you. I know you really cared about her, and I think there's something you might know that could help us find her."

This former bodybuilder and now five-year inmate started tearing up and could barely speak. When Steve finally got control of his emotions, he said, "When I was in that cell with Scott and he offered to get my Jennifer out of stripping, I believed him. He was so convincing. When he and Jennifer didn't show up to meet my parents in Seattle to start her new life, I didn't know if she left me for him, for someone else in New York, or if she just vanished—and I still don't know what happened to her. I still love her, but I think she's left me for good."

I asked Steve how much Scott knew about his drug case and if Scott had offered to help him take care of witnesses who might testify against him. Steve vaguely recalled talking to Scott about his case, but by now Steve was completely focused on losing Jennifer and wanted to know how we might find her. He circled back to being convinced that Scott was okay for Jennifer to be around, but then she never returned his calls. More tears came to his eyes as he concluded that she must have left him for someone else.

Steve had no clue whatsoever about all of the hiring-a-hit-man and murder-for-hire stories that Scott had been selling to the FBI, Jennifer's parents, and Lori.

I tried to approach Jennifer's disappearance with him a few other ways, mentioning that her car had been abandoned at the Denver airport and that she hadn't been seen in almost five years. Steve could not think of anything new that would help us. I was deflated that I had wasted the government's time and money, along with Gary's, as I called for the guard to take Steve back to his cell.

As we sat there waiting, I asked him, "So, anything else going on? Outside of the Jennifer situation?"

I was just making small talk to pass the uncomfortable time.

Steve lifted his head and said, "Oh yeah, another inmate also named Steve lost *his* girlfriend to Scott, too, right after Jennifer disappeared."

The guard appeared in the doorway to the cafeteria to take Steve back as this statement sank in. I asked the guard to please hold on for a second. "What? Another inmate?" I asked Steve.

"Yeah, I don't know the other Steve's last name or the girlfriend's name, but he was thrown in the hole right when Scott was released. When he got out of the hole he was super-pissed and told the rest of us that he lost his girl to Scott. When we asked what happened, he wouldn't talk about it, except to say that he was stupid to trust Scott in the first place. I didn't think much about it after that."

I probed Steve for more details but he did not have any, except that the other Steve, hereafter "Steve 2," was in for bank robbery. Steve 2 was also balding and seemed a little scary. He knew that Steve 2's girlfriend was younger and blond, but that was it. As the guard took Steve away, Gary and I agreed that this timely answer to a random question I had asked for no other reason than to fill an awkward silence only seconds before we left, never planning to talk to this inmate again, might just end up handing us another homicide victim of Scott's. It had to be an act of providence.

## GIRL #3

Before I got back to the hotel I called the federal prison in Englewood, Colorado, where Scott, Steve, and Steve 2 had spent time. The prison lieutenants identified Steve 2 as the bank robber within minutes. When they told me his name I remembered helping with his arrest three years earlier. I had interviewed the cab driver who had taken him to rob his last bank in Lakewood, Colorado. The driver had no idea he was assisting in a federal crime until Steve 2 walked out of a bank inside of a King Soopers grocery store and nearly bumped into a police officer. Steve 2 pulled a gun out of his pocket, put it to the head of a woman beside him, and screamed at the cop to back away as he carjacked a third person who was watching it all happen. The cop radioed his fellow officers for backup, and they arrived as Steve 2 was driving away in a truck he had stolen from the parking lot. A shootout took place, with police officers emptying their rifle rounds into the cab of the pickup—Steve 2 only suffered cuts from the broken glass. Then he was arrested. Yup, he was a little scary like Jennifer's Steve had said he was.

When I got back to Denver, I asked the prison lieutenant to look through the visitor logs of Steve 2. He found only one female who might be a girlfriend, LeAnn Emry. Through records checks, I learned that in 2003 she was twenty-four years old when she was visiting the prison, and listed her home address in Aurora, Colorado.[79] The Aurora phone number was disconnected, so I tried a number in Idaho that was listed to her parents. A man picked up and I identified myself. I asked if I could speak to LeAnn.

The man said, "Well, I'm LeAnn's father and I haven't heard from her in over four years. I hope you can tell me where she is."

My heart sank as my mind scrambled with activity, piecing together the events of the past few days and thumbing back through all of Scott's prison calls and statements to us. Nope, he had never mentioned or even hinted about someone named LeAnn. My next thought was one that still haunts me today: *how many more like LeAnn are out there?!?*

LeAnn's dad, Howard, told me that he called the local sheriff in Aurora back in late January 2003, when he learned that her car had been located in Utah, just across the Colorado state line. The sheriff's office told him to work with law enforcement in Utah. He then called Steve 2 at the prison, who told him, "LeAnn is gone and she's probably not coming back. I know who took her, but I can't tell you."

Howard asked, "What are you talking about? Tell me what happened to my daughter!"

---

[79] State of Colorado, County of Boulder v. Scott Lee Kimball. Warrant for Arrest Upon Affidavit. 2009-CR-0001626. Signed October 5, 2009. Received July 26, 2024, p.13

"The man who took LeAnn would kill you in half a second, Mr. Emry. Call the FBI and tell them that 'Hannibal' took your daughter. Then tell them to come see me 'cause I'll tell them who Hannibal really is. Don't go trying to find this guy on your own because he'll kill you."[80]

Steve 2 refused to give any more details, so Howard hung up and called the FBI.

When Howard told the FBI operator about his daughter's disappearance and what Steve 2 had said, he was transferred to Agent Rick. Rick was another agent on my Safe Streets Violent Crime Squad, who was handling the investigation into Steve 2 and his string of bank robberies. I knew Rick well—he was an excellent golfer and SWAT team leader who would give you the shirt off his back. He was not a strong investigator. I didn't know anything about the February 2003 call from Howard to Rick until I heard about it from Howard on this day in 2007. I continued listening to this third dad, my stomach turning upside down.

Howard continued, "So I spoke with Agent Rick and told him that Steve 2 told me to speak with him and say, 'Hannibal took my daughter and you need to go talk to him (Steve 2).' Agent Rick simply told me, 'Steve 2 is a liar and I wouldn't believe anything he says.' I asked Agent Rick if he was going to follow up on the Hannibal thing. He said, 'No, I am not.' That same week in February 2003, I learned from the Utah sheriff that LeAnn's abandoned car had tons of bottled water and dried food, like she was preparing to be on a long road trip. From the tire tracks around the car, a truck or Jeep had pulled up beside her car and a man's set of footprints had been found going to and from the passenger door. The sheriffs told me that the Book Cliffs north of where her car was abandoned consisted of almost infinite horseshoe canyons and dirt roads. The deputies drove down the roads close to her car but saw no sign of LeAnn or anyone else. I know that area because I used to take LeAnn rock hunting there."

Over the next few months in 2003, Howard got calls from bill collectors saying that LeAnn had written fraudulent checks in Wyoming, Utah, Oregon, and Washington. He was incredulous, telling

---

80  State of Colorado, County of Boulder v. Scott Lee Kimball. Warrant for Arrest Upon Affidavit. 2009-CR-0001626. Signed October 5, 2009. Received July 26, 2024, p.14

me, "LeAnn had never stolen money from anyone that I knew of, especially our family." He sent me emails of his research into her last known whereabouts and included photos of her from high school into her early twenties. I thought about calling Rick at the FBI office in Albuquerque to see what he remembered but held off for a while to learn more about LeAnn.

LeAnn disappeared on January 29, 2003. Before Jennifer. Before Kaysi. Before Uncle Terry. And before Justin's awful day. Did I blame Rick? Not really. Very few investigators would take a call from someone like LeAnn's dad with the message, "A violent bank robber said that Hannibal (a fictional villain from a movie) took my daughter." Everyone on our squad had important cases that took more hours to work than we had in a day. For Rick to push his other cases aside to investigate such a fantastic claim would take both perspective and experience with criminals like Scott. None of us had that. Instead, the FBI gets complaint calls daily that we have to handle and push aside, such as, "Someone's put a chip in my brain and I need you to take it out," or "The Secret Service is following me everywhere I go and you need to tell them to stop."

Instead of dwelling on what could have been, I told Howard that I would work with him to find out what had happened to his daughter. I told him Hannibal's true name: Scott Kimball. I informed Howard that we thought Scott was responsible for other missing people and that we were taking LeAnn's disappearance very seriously.

# 12

# SCOTT AS HANNIBAL

MOST PEOPLE may have heard of the well-known movie *Silence of the Lambs* starring Anthony Hopkins in the role of fictional serial killer Hannibal Lecter. It has become one of his most acclaimed works, winning him an Oscar for Best Actor. If you have not seen the movie, I highly recommend it—his portrayal of the serial killer provides significant context for this story. The irony, however, is that in this story, Steve 2 looks more like Dr. Lecter than Scott does.

On October 31, 2007, fittingly,[81] I drove Gary to interview inmate Steve 2 at the United States Penitentiary in Florence, Colorado. This desolate prison houses the most dangerous inmates in Colorado. The drive south from downtown Denver takes over two hours and is uninviting to sightseers. Upon arrival, we identified ourselves and the guards took us to Steve 2's cell block. I explained to him the reason for our visit, adding that I had spoken to Howard, LeAnn's dad, and that we were intent on finding his daughter. I noticed that Steve 2 was missing his pinkie finger, a new development since we had arrested him a few years ago during the bank robbery shootout, so I asked him, "What happened to your finger?"

With a toothy grin, he held up his hand. Gary and I glanced at each other with raised eyebrows. Steve 2 was not playing with a full deck.

---

81 Fittingly, because Gary and I were meeting this inmate who shot it out with police to tell us the Hannibal story on Halloween. What better day for the road trip?

He explained, "So, I have life-upon-life sentences for all the things I did, and I figured that to escape this place I'd need to get placed in the infirmary. There's only one guy back there, an old doctor, and there's a guard who stands outside the door while you're in there. On the other side of the infirmary there's a door that leads to the prison yard. The doctor has a set of keys and there's an exit not far away. I planned to get sent to the infirmary, overpower the doctor by knocking him out or killing him, and once I take his keys I have a chance at escape. To get to the infirmary, I slammed my cell door as hard as I could while sticking my pinkie inside. That broke it pretty bad. I got down to the infirmary, but the guard stayed in the room while the doctor worked on me. So, I did it again a few weeks later. They took me on the same trip down to the infirmary and this time no guard was inside. I thought my plan was gonna work until a big old U.S. Marshal walked inside and said, 'We know what you're up to. I'm going to remove temptation for you.' He was holding a pair of snippers, took my hand, and he just lopped off my pinkie. The doctor sewed it up and here I am."

Dangerous person. Check mark. I asked him what had happened to LeAnn.

Steve 2 began his story. In December 2002 he was on the same cellblock in FCI Englewood as Scott. They often walked the prison yard together and dreamed aloud, but quietly, of how they would escape. They chucked rocks at the fence, watching the routine and response of the white trucks with guards circling the exterior. Scott said he was getting released in two weeks and that he "was hired as a hit man" against a witness in a drug case. Because of his undercover role in this case, people on the outside could not know his true name.

Steve 2 told Scott about his girlfriend, LeAnn, and their plans to move to Mexico before he was arrested for the robberies. Scott proposed a plan. "Here's the deal. You let your girlfriend know that I will protect her until we break you out. We've seen the routine of the guards. All we need are rope ladders to get you over the fence. LeAnn and I will rent a van that looks just like theirs and I'll create a diversion to draw the guards to the other side of the prison. We'll load you in the van and off we go. LeAnn will help me get the cash to get you two down to Mexico, but you have to promise me something in return."

"Name it. You know I'm good for it," Steve 2 replied.

"You have to torture and kill my ex-wife, the mother of my children. She's screwed me over at every turn and I'll need an ironclad alibi when she's dead because everyone will suspect me," Scott explained.

Steve 2 told us that he and Scott worked on details for how he would not simply kill Larissa. He would torture her with a blowtorch and cauterize the wounds he would inflict to keep her alive and prolong her suffering. Before Steve 2 gave LeAnn's cell number to Scott, Scott told him, "She can only know me as Hannibal because I'm working on a case for the FBI." Steve 2 called Scott one sick bastard, but he agreed to introduce Scott as Hannibal to LeAnn.

"Why did he choose the name Hannibal?" I asked.

Steve 2 explained that while they sat at the prison lunch table, Scott's cellmate, Dr. Alderman, would often join them. Steve 2 heard Scott ask the doctor, "How do I keep people alive longer when they're dying?" The inference was clear to everyone at the table except the naïve doctor. Scott was talking about torturing someone. Without hesitation, Dr. Alderman discussed how quickly blood clots, airway restrictions and deprivation, death by exposure, and other ways to die. Later, Steve 2 asked Scott, "What was that all about?"

Scott just smiled and said, "I've been called Hannibal in other prisons because of my interest in how people die."

Scott was released from prison, walking out with LeAnn's phone number and a promise to help Steve 2 escape to Mexico. Within two days of his release, Steve 2 was thrown in the hole (solitary confinement) and had no access to a phone. He had no way to warn LeAnn or her dad, Howard, about what was coming.

"Scott must've told the cops about our escape plans—there's no other reason to lock me down with no phone privileges," Steve 2 told us. When he was finally out of the hole he wrote a letter to Howard and told him about Hannibal. Steve 2 knew that he had been conned by Scott; he knew that LeAnn was most likely dead and he was fairly certain that if he gave Howard the true details about the man who took his daughter, Howard would be dead too.

I showed Steve 2 a photo of a young girl with long, brown hair that had been retrieved from Scott's laptop. He did not hesitate, "Yep, that's LeAnn, except her hair was blond, not dark brown." The girl in the photo resembled the girl in the photos LeAnn's father had provided, but I wanted to be absolutely sure that it was LeAnn on Scott's computer. Her dark hair effectively made her look quite different.

Gary and I thanked Steve 2, but we were happy to leave the uninviting prison and hoped to never see that man again.

When I got back to the office I looked once again in the case file of the murder-for-hire investigation into Jennifer, but I saw nothing about an escape plan for Steve 2 and LeAnn. I searched LeAnn's name in our records and found two references in what we call a "zero file." These files capture miscellaneous potential criminal activity that is not part of an ongoing investigation. Zero files were designed for such an occasion as this—to catch something that otherwise would fall through the cracks. In the file I read that on December 27, 2002, Scott reported to Agent Carle that Steve 2 was "planning an escape from FCI Englewood with the assistance of LeAnn. (No Last Name Given)." Additionally, on January 28, 2003, Scott told Agent Carle that he was "leaving for California to visit his brother."[82]

I would later learn that Scott made a third reference in early February 2003 to LeAnn's disappearance that made it to the zero file. He told Agent Carle, "LeAnn may have got a speeding ticket in Utah."

The January and February 2003 reporting documents were breadcrumbs from Scott, left five years before, knowing that someone like me would see it someday and say, "Oh, shit. This guy was simply toying with the FBI." His calls to Carle were designed for the express purpose of the agent writing down something related to the murder he had just committed. Killing had become too easy for Scott. He needed a challenge.

Based upon what Howard had learned about LeAnn moving around the western states, I turned my investigative interest to LeAnn's transactions before she vanished: the check fraud activity and any references to Scott, or Hannibal.

---

82 State of Colorado, County of Boulder v. Scott Lee Kimball. Warrant for Arrest Upon Affidavit. 2009-CR-0001626. Signed October 5, 2009. Received July 26, 2024, p.14

## TRACKING LEANN

With the help of AUSA Dave, I served subpoenas on the phone records, banks, and credit cards associated with LeAnn and Scott during the time period around January 2003. The subpoena returns provided me with uncanny amounts of activity. In January, Scott was calling LeAnn's cell phone from ten to seventeen times every day. They were writing bad checks and charging up credit cards not only in Colorado but in many other western states. I was in awe of the amount of time Scott had spent with LeAnn that January, because during that exact time frame he had also been setting the table to make Jennifer disappear. "Nobody has that much time in a day," I thought.

Then it hit me.

That's why Scott, upon his release from prison, told his mom, Barb, that he was "working a snuff film ring involving prostitutes." He was giving himself an excuse if she ever saw him with either one of these women who were about to disappear—his story to her was that he was *saving* them from being killed, not killing them. And Scott knew Barb would never tell Agent Carle about the snuff film thing because those two didn't like each other, and the informant piece kept them from talking anyway. Evil genius.

I called the store manager of the Best Buy store in Lakewood, Colorado, regarding a purchase made with a debit card from LeAnn's TCF Bank account. The manager found that on January 10, 2003, LeAnn purchased a Toshiba laptop computer, model 1905-S301. This was Scott's laptop! The same laptop I had searched a year earlier, after having to fortify the affidavit for the judge with cause that Scott might have kidnapped Jennifer, Kaysi, and Uncle Terry. The photos of LeAnn, photos of other unknown young women, and Scott's fascination with serial killer BTK were on the computer that LeAnn had bought at Scott's direction.

With the records of fraudulent checks and credit card charges, I tracked LeAnn and Scott as they had moved around the Denver area after his release from prison in December 2002 through January 16, 2003. I saw them together in the states of Oregon and Washington from January 17–19, 2003, and then in Wyoming from January 24–25, 2003.

LeAnn was in Grand Junction, Colorado, near the Utah border, from January 28–29, 2003. Scott left Denver on January 28, 2003. (Remember that breadcrumb number two from the zero file was Scott's email to Agent Carle informing Carle that he, Scott, was "leaving Denver and going to California to see his brother.") Finally, the subpoena returns put Scott in Las Vegas, Nevada, by January 30, 2003.[83]

The dates on receipts from purchases made in Oregon and Washington exactly matched the time frame when Scott's silver handgun had been purchased at the gun store that later burned down. Scott could not buy the gun because he had felonies on his record. So, it had to be LeAnn. The FBI in Seattle had been working with Scott at that time to debunk his claims that he knew who killed AUSA Thomas Wales. Yes, the FBI paid Scott to travel from Colorado. However, the Seattle agents were skeptical enough of the murder-for-hire story that they quickly polygraphed him and moved on to other leads. Scott, though, took full advantage of the trip by meeting up with LeAnn and convincing her to drive the gun back to Colorado because he could not carry it on the plane. I had no insight on how that conversation might have gone, because LeAnn never mentioned it in her texts to her cousin, Heather. (From further cell phone returns that I received from subpoenas, I learned that just days before LeAnn disappeared she had emailed Heather: "My orders come from Hanable (sic) and he's a dangerous person to f*ck with. If Hanable knew I was talking to you he'd have me killed in a second. Plus, he'd have you killed too."[84]). The dates connected to that time near the Utah border matched the dates when LeAnn's car was abandoned across the state line. My best guess was that she gave Scott the gun during this clandestine meeting in Utah, just before he used to it kill her.

I looked back at my report of our interview of Scott's brother, Brett. He told us that on February 2, 2003, Scott had paid for an "escort" at the Esmerelda Hotel in Indian Wells, California. Scott told Brett that the girl's name was Athena and that he, Scott, had received calls from her

---

83 State of Colorado, County of Boulder v. Scott Lee Kimball. Warrant for Arrest Upon Affidavit. 2009-CR-0001626. Signed October 5, 2009. Received July 26, 2024, p.15
84 Jace Larsen, "Suspected Serial Killer Could Get Plea Bargain." December 11, 2008. https://www.9news.com/article/news/investigations/suspected-serial-killer-could-get-plea-bargain/73-341335589. Downloaded July 4, 2024.

after he left town. I found Agent Carle's records of calls to Scott's phone from an unknown cell number with a 760 area code that occurred for the next few weeks in February 2003—the phone was likely Athena's.

Three separate purchases had been made with LeAnn's credit card in the Los Angeles area on February 4, 2003, by a female who was *not* LeAnn. I confirmed this fact by asking her dad, Howard, to review the signatures on the three receipts. At my request, FBI agents in Los Angeles canvassed the local strip clubs, hoping to find an "Athena" who might be able to shed light on why she was using LeAnn's credit card. After three solid weeks of visiting these establishments, they found Athena and showed her photos of Scott and Brett.[85] The investigators reported that Athena said, "They look familiar." When asked about using LeAnn's credit card, she said it "wouldn't be unusual for a client to give me a credit card" in lieu of payment for services, but she didn't recall using such a card. The agents noted that Athena's mental faculties and recollection had likely been impacted by heavy drug use.[86]

## TRACKING SCOTT

As stated, from December 27, 2002, to January 27, 2003, Scott called LeAnn's cell phone ten to fifteen times every day. From January 28–29, 2003, Scott went dark—he had turned off his cell phone, so there was no record of any incoming or outgoing calls. The next call he made was to the Mandalay Bay Hotel in Las Vegas at 1:13 a.m. on January 30th. As Scott later told Harold Dow during the *48 Hours* documentary about the Kimball investigation, Scott was indeed "smarter than average people," and the key for him to evade arrest for so many years boiled down to one word: "Preparation." Scott added, "To be a good con man, you've got to prepare."[87] Scott had prepared to take LeAnn weeks in advance. He had made her believe she was stealing money

---

85 You might think that's a pretty cool job benefit to get paid to visit strip clubs. However, I visited my share trying to find fugitives and bank robbers and they were not as glamorous as you might think.
86 State of Colorado, County of Boulder v. Scott Lee Kimball. Warrant for Arrest Upon Affidavit. 2009-CR-0001626. Signed October 5, 2009. Received July 26, 2024, p. 15
87 "Serial killer Scott Kimball on his life of crime." *48 Hours*. Updated on: June 16, 2024/1:07 AM EDT/CBS News https://www.cbsnews.com/news/serial-killers-life-of-crime/

for herself and Steve 2, when it was actually for Scott. He had the forethought to let LeAnn know him only by an alias and managed to leave no trail for her family. He severed her communications with her boyfriend, Steve 2, who knew Scott's true identity. He left no digital footprint of himself while making her disappear. His final step was to give her credit cards to a hooker to make it appear she was alive and well in California, while Scott headed back to Colorado. LeAnn's disappearance defined the word preparation.

Impressive. If he had only used that intelligence and perception elsewhere.[88]

After a handful of meetings with Scott and his defense team at the federal courthouse without much progress noted, we met again on February 1, 2008. I do not have any details of the meeting from my journal notes. This was the first time we had been face-to-face since learning about LeAnn. The prosecutors and Gary agreed with me that we shouldn't let him know *we knew* about his fourth victim—we would listen to his demands, denials, and assertions of truthfulness to see if anything pointed to LeAnn or any other unknown victims. AUSA Dave was present for all of these meetings, along with the Boulder DA prosecutors, Katharina and Amy, and Scott's defense attorneys, Lynn (federal, gun charges, kidnapping) and Megan (state, check fraud, forgery). The two recurring themes that manifested during these meetings were: (1) Scott wanted immunity for all check fraud crimes, and (2) his claims that he knew what had happened to Uncle Terry, Jennifer, and Kaysi, but he was not the killer. His attorneys attempted to speak for him, but he brushed them aside like mosquitoes because HE was in control. He chose his words carefully and examined each of us for nonverbal cues that we might not be buying what he was selling. Any eye roll or prolonged exhale from just one of us prompted defensive and accusatory moods. He often said, "I can see you've already made up your minds," and "It's obvious to me that this meeting's not going to be productive." After a few hours of this we agreed to adjourn and meet again soon.

---

[88] Jace Larsen, "Suspected Serial Killer Could Get Plea Bargain." December 11, 2008. https://www.9news.com/article/news/investigations/suspected-serial-killer-could-get-plea-bargain/73-341335589. Downloaded July 4, 2024

In situations like this, Scott would inevitably wait until the prosecutors and defense attorneys had vacated the room and Gary and I were waiting for the U.S. Marshals deputy to arrive. Scott would say things like, "Jon, we need to talk. I know you want to find out what happened to Jennifer and Kaysi. These attorneys are just getting in the way. Just give me ten minutes." I could just see the knowing frown on the U.S. Marshal's face as he sensed that I was once again going to put the Marshals off. I hated doing that, because the FBI had a reputation as a prima donna, but I was hell-bent on finding any information Scott might have.[89] Scott would throw out teasers and tidbits during these brief sidebars, but only enough to keep us wanting more—nothing we could use as evidence to prosecute him or find his victims.

## THE PROFILERS

In March 2008, I was ecstatic to go for a one-week training conference with the profilers in Stafford, Virginia. A few times during the conference Art and I met for lunch, a treat for me after hearing just his phone voice for over a year. I learned about how and why serial killers act like they do, what rapists say when they're caught, and about pathways of violence and statement analysis. I couldn't take notes fast enough as I absorbed all of the experience and wisdom of these very seasoned agents and former detectives, trying to apply every principle I could to learn how to deal more effectively with Scott.

I learned the basic guidelines, definitions, case studies, and warning signs of dealing with serial killers versus one-time murderers. "Violence happens in two primary ways," one of the profilers taught. "Predatory violence involves planning and premeditation, along with careful victim selection. Affective/emotional violence stems from an established relationship between the victim and the offender, and the violence often occurs in a 'he just snapped' event, with little planning or premeditation. Serial killers, mass attackers, and spree killers are *predators*."

---

89  I knew by now that Scott's information was going to be circular and deceptive, and that he would get more information from me than I would get from him. However, we had direct access to him for a limited time and I figured the inconvenience was worth the longshot that we would get something valuable.

Serial killers, like Dennis Rader, who gave himself the nickname BTK (bind, torture, and kill), are above average in intelligence and possess an uncanny ability to maintain their public-facing lives as non-threatening, helpful members of society. One of the profilers said, "Just like you and I have hobbies or passions like golfing, surfing, or painting, a serial killer's passion is murder. He dreams about it all the time. When he's not planning a murder, committing one, or covering one up, he's thinking about his next one. His private family life is his cover so he can keep killing without being arrested."

The same profiler said, "Some common myths about serial killers are that they *want* to be caught. They don't. They know that would be the end of their killing. Another myth is they kill the same way every time. Most don't. The majority of serial killers are not reclusive, social misfits who live alone. They are not monsters and may not appear strange. They look just like you and me, everyday human beings. Many serial killers hide in plain sight within their communities. Serial murderers often have families and homes, are gainfully employed, and appear to be normal members of the community."[90]

He continued, "They select victims who are Desirable, Available, and Vulnerable (he drew a triangle on the dry erase board with these three attributes at each corner). The killer will wait until he has access to the victim (Available), and until he knows he can *win* against the victim and the victim won't be missed for a while (Vulnerable). How they're attracted to the victim (Desirable) can vary greatly. Common themes are sexual desire, money, or the victim offending the killer in some way, often unknown to the victim."

One of the FBI agents asked the instructor, "What are common personality traits of serial killers? And are most of them men?"

"Good questions! Let's start with the definition. A serial killer is someone who kills at least two victims (used to be three) with a cooling-off, or dormant, period in between the killings. Spree killers have no cooling-off period and will continue on their rampage until caught or killed themselves. Mass attackers are more single-event predators who consider, plan, and prepare for a larger-scale attack with

---

90 They handed us a book titled, *Serial Murder: Multi-Disciplinary Perspectives for Investigators*, that is now available online: https://www.fbi.gov/stats-services/publications/serial-murder

the goal of high body counts. About ninety percent of serial killers are male, falling in line with the percentage of violent crimes committed by males. The race distribution of these killers in the United States closely mirrors our national numbers and percentages. Common personality traits are high scores in psychopathy, narcissism, and Machiavellianism. These people are very charming, have a grandiose sense of self-worth; they are pathological liars and expert manipulators. They can fake remorse and guilt, but they lack true empathy and compassion. They rarely accept responsibility for anything, but they excel in effectively blaming others."

I scribbled notes as fast as I could in the margins of the book they gave us, writing, "This is Scott!" beside almost each personality characteristic and case study.

I met separately with Art and one of the instructors after the sessions. Although I am rarely expressive, I couldn't contain my excitement at what I was learning. "This is exactly the case I'm working on! You guys are amazing! My big question is how do we prosecute someone like this?"

Art told the other profiler, "Jonny and I have been on speed dial for a while now and I've told him about the critical piece of turning this investigation from a missing person one into a homicide. I know that sounds impossible from where you're sitting now (looking at me), but you've done the other groundwork."

The instructor asked, "Have you entered the DNA from your missing people into CODIS?"[91]

"Yes, thanks to Art's direction," I responded. "And I'm working closely with each of the local jurisdictions to look through any queries about Scott or our victims or other suspicious activities while he was in their counties."

We discussed future interview strategies for Scott and the victim's families. The other profilers pledged to continue their support through Art, and they encouraged me not to give up because it would continue to be an uphill battle. I thanked them profusely and got on the plane back to Denver.

---

91 Combined DNA Index System is a computer software program developed by the FBI that supports a national DNA database for forensic analysis. CODIS allows local, state, and federal law enforcement to exchange and compare DNA profiles to identify suspects, solve crimes, and identify missing persons.

I do not remember if one of the profiling instructors handed me this next bit of wisdom during the conference, or if I came to my own conclusion after absorbing their experience for four days: Scott was the only one who knew what had happened to our victims. Scott's behavior and decision-making do not function in the same manner as 99 percent of other humans. Using the right tools, and approaching him with supernatural humility and persistence, I now had some confidence that eventually I would get him to tell me things about what he did. But that was not going to come without a high cost.

## A SETBACK

I returned home from Virginia, looking forward to playing Wii golf with my eight-year-old son, Ben, and ten-year-old daughter, Bethany. But April, my wife, was forced to ask what was wrong with me when I was short-tempered and nasty after missing some easy virtual putts. I should have been ecstatic to be home with my incredible family. I had an idea of what my problem was but did not want to say it out loud. Living and breathing the depraved mind of this evil serial killer was getting inside of me. I was having weird dreams and found myself pushing violent thoughts out of my head. I would wake up every two hours with the revelation of a new clue to run to ground or a different question to ask the next time I was with Scott. It is not easy to go back to sleep with a buzzing brain that refuses to shut off. It would not be the last time.

Two weeks later, on April 7, 2008, I was in our driveway shooting baskets with Ben. He intentionally rolled a ball under my feet as I was going up for a dunk (yes, the goal was lowered) and I lost my temper again. Anger that was senseless and very unlike me spilled out as I yelled at him and scared myself. I threw the ball hard at the garage. Ben's unspoken question was written on his face: "What's wrong with you?" I later told April that I was deeply concerned because this was not me. I love my wife and children more than anything else on earth. I prayed earnestly, asking God to deliver me from the ugliness that was beginning to consume me. I decided to do the worst thing possible to punish myself to make my soul "right." I was going to fast for a day. I'm not a big guy but I eat all day every day. This was going to hurt, but I needed a deep soul cleansing.

The next day, on the no-food day, we met again with Scott and all of the attorneys.

## APRIL 8, 2008

Because of what happened during the meeting I still have a vague memory of where I was sitting—along the side of the long conference table nearest the door. Scott was at the head of the table as he continued to talk in circles about what might have happened to our victims. He insisted that he was not talking himself into more prison time but was willing to cooperate if we put something on the table. My prosecutor buddy, AUSA Dave, was having none of it.

Scott asked Dave, "What about federal prison? Is serving out my time there an option?"

The salty federal prosecutor peered at Scott over spectacles that sat low on his nose and dryly shot back, "For *what*, Mr. Kimball? Did you commit some crime on federal land that we need to know about?"

I will never forget Scott's question, "What if one of these girls is on national forest land?"

The question should not have meant as much to me as it did. Colorado itself has millions of acres of national forest. Scott was relatively safe throwing that on the table because it was not really a hint to where one of the girls could be hidden. Except, thanks to Lori, Kaysi's mom, it was a hint.

"How many of you like homework? Raise your hands. What? No one?" I ask this question in my presentations to students. No hand has ever gone up. No one ever tells me they like homework. I tell them that, unfortunately, homework is not only part of school, but part of our jobs. Big cases might get lucky breaks, but more often the difficult cases are solved because the investigator does the little things that do not seem significant at the time but still must be done. In baseball, it is going for the base hit every time you step up to bat, not swinging for the fences and missing. Whether it is a terrorism case, check fraud, or a serial killer case, *details matter.* You will never know which detail will matter the most. Run (investigate) each lead or tip to ground. Leave nothing undone as far as it depends on you. I am not saying be perfect, because I certainly was not. But, when I walked away from twenty-five years of doing this stuff—working the extremely challenging cases that came with heavy consequences riding on the outcomes—I was able to say I had learned as much as I could and done the best I could. I tricked myself into liking homework because the rewards of doing it consistently provided me with the best chance to succeed. So, homework became play. At least I told myself to treat it that way.

As for the national forest land question from Scott, it triggered a memory of the first conversation I had with Lori (Scott's second wife) as I searched through her two bags of trash at her apartment. Gary and I had collected all the receipts with dates and time stamps and I had made copies of the wrinkled, dirty documents when I got back to the office. A single receipt stood out from the others. It was from the day after Kaysi disappeared, August 24, 2003. Scott had been at the North Park Super's in Walden, Colorado, where he bought some meat, lighter fluid, SF Rotini, and Ragu Cheese at 10:35 a.m.[92] Walden was a tiny mountain town about two hours from Denver—in the middle of national forest land.

If Kaysi had been murdered—or otherwise died there and recovered—I should have been notified. I had entered Lori's DNA into the CODIS database. That entry laid out for any law enforcement entity who wanted to know whether the DNA inside their unknown recovered skeletal remains ("Jane Doe" for females) belonged to a known missing person, like Kaysi. All they had to do was enter the victim's DNA profile into CODIS to learn their identity. Before I made the call to the U.S. Forest Service near Walden, Colorado, to ask if any female victim had been recovered, I knew the chance was almost zero it was her. If Kaysi had been recovered, I would know already. But I called anyway, doing my homework on my no-food day. All the prior FBI

---

[92] State of Colorado, County of Boulder v. Scott Lee Kimball. Warrant for Arrest Upon Affidavit. 2009-CR-0001626. Signed October 5, 2009. Received July 26, 2024, p.12

agents on the case had told me, as well as AUSA Dave's assessments, "It's probably a waste of time, a fool's errand, Jon-Jon." And most of the time, they were right.

A receptionist from the U.S. Forest Service near Walden answered my call. I identified myself and said I was looking for a missing person who may be in their territory. I asked if they could send me a forest service map of the area. She put me through to an agent who told me, "You need to send in eight dollars to pay for the map." With as much politeness as I could muster, I told the man that sending him eight dollars of federal money would cost me two days of filling out multiple forms and justifications. He did not budge, however, and transferred me back to the receptionist. With polite resignation, I told her that I was looking for a young woman who had disappeared and might be on national forest land. She responded, "Well, right before the snow hit last season, they did find that female hiker, but that's all I know of."

The blood rushed to my head. I asked for any details she might have about this hiker. She told me the Jackson County Sherrif had collected the remains, but she did not know what had happened afterward.

The receptionist at the Forest Service had offhandedly given me the biggest puzzle piece of all.

Before saying goodbye, I had already found the number for the sheriff and called as soon as we hung up. I introduced myself and Sheriff Rick told me that a hunter had found a skull on a small mountain in a remote area south of Walden. An anthropologist named Dr. France confirmed it was female, but that was as far as they had gotten.

My mouth was dry when I asked the critical question, "Did you test the remains?" When Sheriff Rick asked, "What do you mean?" I knew from his question there was a chance that this hiker might be Kaysi. I asked if Gary and I could visit him and we arrived at his office the next morning.

To get there, we had to drive north into Wyoming, then west, then south through the mountains to reach the densely forested town of Walden. The sheriff's entire office was a single-office throwback to the early 1900s. There were very few computers, if any, with lots of paper on the desk, a few radios, and some rifles. Sheriff Rick, wearing a cowboy hat and sporting a handlebar mustache, was very cordial as he explained that his deputies normally dealt with mountain lions and bears, not missing persons. He handed me the report of his deputies finding the hiker. I thanked him and asked him where the remains were currently located. He replied, "The cranium was sent down south to the Jefferson County Sheriff's Office to be examined and the other parts of the skeleton were with Dr. France." Dr. France, the anthropologist who had confirmed that the victim was female, further told the sheriff that the hiker was a Caucasian female likely in her early twenties, who had been dead and exposed to the elements for about two to five years. Thus, the estimated time frame placed the years of death for this "Jane Doe" between 2003 and 2005.

Kaysi disappeared on August 23, 2003.

Before we left, the coroner, who was also the town farrier, showed us a clay shell molded from the cranium of the female "hiker" to recreate what Jane Doe's face might have looked like. It was displayed on a small table in his living room. His plan was to eventually put the image on a missing person flyer. We learned from Sheriff Rick after our odd visit that the coroner had tucked the hiker's cranium away for a short time before starting his project. I believe the coroner had good intentions but was unaware of modern advances like dental identification and DNA. Gary and I felt we had gone back a hundred years in time.

I quickly got Sheriff Rick's permission to collect the remains of the hiker and send them to our lab. The next day Gary and I drove north to Ft. Collins, and it was our privilege to meet Dr. France, a gray-haired, spectacled woman in a white lab coat who exuded intelligence and curiosity. She showed us her reconstructed skeletons taken from a civil war submarine recently recovered just outside of Charleston, South Carolina. The American History Museum in Washington, D.C. asked her to examine the bones and provide her conclusion on how they had died to help them figure out how to arrange the former sailors in an exhibit. We worked our way back through her lab to the female hiker's remains, where she showed me her report. Her conclusion was "no cause of death determined. The hiker was missing her hyoid bone." Dr. France didn't write this in her report but told us that she wondered if the young woman had died by strangulation.[93] I gave her a receipt for the bones, then drove with Gary to the FBI office. I dropped him off, then headed down south to the Jefferson County Sheriff's Office and checked the hiker's cranium out of their evidence room. The sheriffs were housing Scott in their jail at the time, and I thought it ironic that I might be solving one of his homicides with evidence sitting a hundred yards, if that, away from his cell.

This was a first for me, driving around with human remains in my Bureau car, or any car for that matter. Usually our Evidence Response Team (ERT) handles any collection of evidence since they have specific training and all the proper packaging. I was racing against the clock, though, and wanted to find out if this was Kaysi. We were coming down to the wire on how long Scott would cooperate.

The next morning, I asked our FBI evidence room to FedEx the skeletal remains, along with the buccal swabs of Lori's DNA, to our lab. The DNA examiners wanted to do a one-to-one comparison instead of relying on the CODIS profile. I was hopeful, but not positive, that the results would come back confirming this was Kaysi. As Profiler Art said from the start, "That will change everything." It would instantly move the investigation from a missing person case to a homicide. DNA lab results normally take months to process and I was hoping and praying the process would move quickly. These samples were competing with the most important cases in the U.S., all needing to be processed, so my boss made some calls to expedite the request.

---

93 As you learn more about Scott, consider if he would have the experience, wherewithal, and willingness to accept the risk of returning to the scene and removing the hyoid (if he was responsible, if that bone would provide details of how she was killed, and if this was Kaysi).

# 13

# A FRIGGIN' MIRACLE

WHILE WAITING for the lab, I reviewed the report from Sheriff Rick on how exactly this hiker had been found in the middle of nowhere. I learned that just before the snow began to pile up in the mountains of Walden in late September 2007, a male nurse named Lou from Denver went elk scouting with two friends. They parked a few miles away from a remote mountain named Dennis Hump, and Lou split off from his buddies. In his written statement, Lou indicated that he wanted to scope in his rifle and head off the beaten path. He wove in and out of the dense trees that stood on the side of the small mountain as he enjoyed the perfect weather and his new scope. A few hours in, Lou looked up and saw what appeared to be a perfectly round, white rock directly in front of him. In a subsequent interview he told the media, "If I hadn't been at that exact spot at that time of the morning with the sun glinting off the skull, I would not have seen it. Something happened. Somebody wanted me to find it."[94] As Lou neared the object, he could tell it wasn't a rock because it was too smooth and round. When he turned it over, he had no doubt it was a human skull and thought about what he should do—he had no cell service and didn't know his location.

Lou decided to put the skull[95] in his backpack and tied colored ribbons on the tree beside him to mark the spot. He continued mark-

---

[94] https://web.archive.org/web/20190118041634/http://scottleekimball.com/2007/09/29/hunter-finds-human-bones-in-routt-national-forest/ (Downloaded on 07/20/2024)
[95] Lou called it a skull; it was technically the cranium because it was missing the mandible.

ing the trees on his way back to the trail and on to the car. He and his friends called the local sheriff and guided him back to the spot just as the snow was starting to come down.

To summarize this piece of the investigation: Scott's question prompted this entire quest with, "What if one of these girls is on national forest land?" Lori's unlikely keeping of trash bags in a closet for five years had enabled us to explore the context of his statement. Even more unlikely, knowing Scott's intelligence, was the possibility that he had left behind a pertinent receipt with the mother of a girl he supposedly took (and likely killed).

By now, I was on a first-name basis with Elise, the lead technician at the FBI Lab. After I submitted the DNA of our three missing people, I asked her questions like, "How do we identify these victims if they're found? How long does the process normally take? What's the best way to get you a familial sample? Will the lab techs testify in court if we get that far?" Thanks to the likelihood of bad press and widespread criticism of my agency unknowingly operating an informant who was going around killing people, I didn't have to wait long for the lab's results.

On April 24, 2008, Elise called to say they had retrieved mitochondrial DNA from the femur of the hiker and that the DNA was determined to be the same mitochondrial DNA Lori gave me. It was irrefutably Kaysi. From a missing person to a homicide.[96] We had it!

Gary and I had kept Lori and Rob in the loop about our investigation into the hiker and our suspicions she might be Kaysi. While they also guessed these remains were those of their daughter, such confirmation is never easy to deliver or receive. Gary and I called Lori and Rob separately and delivered the news the best way we knew how.

We also informed our prosecution team and bosses about the new development and asked everyone to please keep the news quiet. We were trying to figure out how to tell Scott in such a way as to elicit a response that might help us with what was now Kaysi's obvious murder. Maybe he would slip and give us a clue about his other victims. We invited Lori and Rob to accompany us and our evidence team to

---

96 State of Colorado, County of Boulder v. Scott Lee Kimball. Warrant for Arrest Upon Affidavit. 2009-CR-0001626. Signed October 5, 2009. Received July 26, 2024, p.12

explore the entire mountainside where Kaysi had been found. We were looking for other skeletal remains and evidence that pointed to Scott's involvement in her murder.

## MAY 16, 2008

We schemed as a team on how we might use the recovery of Kaysi and the identification of LeAnn as Scott's fourth potential victim to our advantage in our next meeting with him. Our plots were an exercise in futility. I had written multiple affidavits that contained all the juicy details of this investigation in order to access Scott's laptop, some old trailers, and a former residence. We kept the documents under seal in the U.S. District Courts because they included the names of Scott's family and cellmates who wanted to remain confidential. We also needed to protect the integrity of the investigation into an FBI informant and the ever-changing status of the missing persons surrounding him.

I was in Grand Junction, Colorado, four hours west of Denver, teaching a course to local police officers when this investigation made the front page of the *Rocky Mountain News* on May 16, 2008. Luckily for the FBI, the journalist from the *Rocky Mountain News*, Sara, reached out to us before she published the article. She had gotten her hands on my affidavit that outlined the investigation to get into Scott's computer. It had been sealed, but a year had passed since we executed the warrant, and Sara was always combing through recent court filings. My affidavit about Scott's supposed involvement in not one kidnapping, but three or four, had lost its sealed secrecy; it was filled with details about the now-suspected homicides. Sara called our office and said she was going public with the details whether we commented or not. The FBI Special Agent in Charge came to Phil and me for advice. We advocated, "Maybe the media can help our case. Instead of fighting them by saying 'We can't comment on an ongoing investigation,' what about turning it into an article that asks for the public's help?"

FBI executives far above me in the food chain worked with me to help frame our statements as, "We can't discuss a lot of things, but we can say that people who have been around this man (Scott) are missing and we need the public's help finding them."

That angle was far better than an article solely focused on, "Scott is an FBI informant who's going around killing people on the taxpayer's dime. And the FBI doesn't have anything to say about it." We released a request to the public, asking anyone with information about Scott or our victims to please call the Denver FBI. I waited until I returned to Denver from my training in Grand Junction to call the twenty-five or so people who had contacted the office with information after reading the article. Most of the callers were old colleagues of Scott's, who talked to me about how he had stolen money from them or their girlfriends. Others provided tips on our missing persons, though none of those revealed any earth-shattering information.

## SCOTT KNOWS

The big hiccup for us was the fact that LeAnn's photo had been published in the newspaper article, along with the story of her disappearance. That meant we would not have the opportunity to surprise Scott with our knowledge about her. Even though he was in prison, front-page news spreads quickly. Even so, luck was on our side. Scott's mom, Barb, called him on the recorded prison line before he read the article. The conversation was truly priceless. I could not stop grinning from ear to ear as I listened to them go at it:

Barb: "Scott, did you see the news today?"

Scott: "No, Mom, what's up?"

Barb: "You're on the front page. With pictures of Uncle Terry, Kaysi, and Jennifer. And some girl named Lynn or Lisa or something."

Scott: "Wait, an article? About me? With whom? I don't know anything about where Kaysi... and I don't know any Lynn or Lisa."

Barb: "It started with an 'L'—it's some twenty-five-year-old girl with blond hair. The paper says you were last with all these people. It looks really bad, Scott."

Scott: "Mom, we've already been through this. And we shouldn't be talking about this on this phone. It's a recorded line. Anyway, I didn't hurt anyone. I know what happened to . . . wait, you think the other girl is named Lynn?"

The conversation continued for another couple of minutes while Scott tried figure out how much damage control would be in his immediate future. Barb's head was spinning. She was wondering what she was going to tell her friends, family, neighbors, the press, and the rest of the state of Colorado who were seeing the headlines. Despite Scott repeating over and over that he was innocent, Barb's final response to her son was, "You've been judged in the media and found guilty."

The resignation in Barb's voice was hard to dismiss. She was quickly accepting the reality that Scott's lifetime of cons and lies was just a small peek into the rabbit hole hiding his much darker nature. The newspaper article broadcast her worst fears to everyone she knew. And she would never recover. She would forever be the mom of a serial killer. Barb would always see the judgement in the faces of her friends. "She must've known. What a horrible mother." Looks of disdain and disgust were waiting for her in the grocery store, the mall parking lot, even when she walked to the mailbox.

## MORE HANNIBAL

Almost daily, Scott's picture was posted alongside our four victims on TV and in the newspapers. Local reporters continued to uncover facts about Scott, the FBI, and the backstories of those who had disappeared. A former Jefferson County inmate named Hans saw the news and asked to speak with me, asserting that he had spent six months incarcerated with Scott. Hans had been paroled, so he met Detective Gary and me at a secluded picnic table in a west Denver park area surrounded by trees that afforded us some privacy.

Hans was a large man who exuded confidence and humor. When Scott had been transferred into Hans's cell block he was able to quickly determine that Hans was the leader of the unit. Scott turned on the charm. He told Hans, "I'm a hit man and willing to kill anyone if the price is right." Scott spoke of owning multiple businesses and having too much money to worry about bothersome things—like his small-time white collar charges.

"Scott wanted to impress me," Hans told us. "He talked about being engaged to a bartender in Alaska who only knew him under his brother's name. He bragged that he could get people to do things that they'd never do otherwise. I called bullshit when he said that he pistol-whipped his ex-wife's boyfriend within an inch of his life in front of her and never got charged with it."[97] Hans told Scott, "There's no way you got away with something like that with a witness present." Scott just smiled and said he was getting out of jail soon because he was only serving time on a bogus check fraud case.

Hans continued, "When we watched movies at night in the jail, Scott sat by me and talked about how the murders on the screen weren't how things really happened. When a man in a horror show was run through a woodchipper, he told me, 'I've used a woodchipper just like that one and that's not what happens to a human.' When one of the Hannibal Lecter films had a scene involving pigs eating a person, Scott said, 'Pigs don't do that. I've seen pigs eat a person. You have to cut their head off and smash the skull for them to eat everything.' He told me how pigs attack a dead person and they'd completely devour a body if they've gone without food for a few days."[98]

Scott told Hans, "My second wife cheated on me. Then she divorced me. We had two children together, so if anything happened to her, I'd be the first person the cops would suspect. Since I couldn't kill her, I took her from the house to an abandoned place near a dumpster and pretended like I was gonna kill her. I left her there, naked. I knew the cops would never believe her if she told on me, and they didn't."

When Gary and I asked Hans if there was anything else, he added that Scott had bragged, "I enjoy both of my female attorneys. I love the way they smell."

I never told either of the attorneys about Scott's comment. If they read this book, they will be properly appalled.

---

97  Ed Coet, *SLK Serial Killer* (Publishamerica, Inc., 2010), 312 (From my interview of Hans)
98  Ed Coet, *SLK Serial Killer* (Publishamerica, Inc., 2010), 313 (From my interview of Hans)

## DETECTIVE BURNS & CAT

The news article did not just bring inmates to speak with me. Detectives in Colorado, as well as some in surrounding states, wanted to see if perhaps their unsolved homicides might be linked to Scott. Two detectives from the Denver suburb of Westminster came to the FBI office. I knew Detective Bernard through working previous bank robbery cases, but I did not know the other detective. Bernard said he was working on the brutal homicide of a local prostitute named Cat, and he had run down every lead or tip without success. Cat was twenty-five years old when she disappeared from a 7-11 store on East Colfax Avenue in Denver in October 2004. Her body was found two days later. Hands missing. Naked. Brutally beaten. Discarded near a dumpster in a commercial parking lot. She was displayed as if the killer wanted her to be found.

Hadn't I just heard that story from Hans? Left for dead beside a dumpster? Except that story was about Scott's ex-wife, Larissa, and Scott did not kill her.

The East Colfax Avenue reference in the fall of 2004 jogged my memory. That was the same time frame that Scott's son Justin was recovering from his near-fatal head wounds. Scott had been skulking around Children's Hospital while Larissa and her family guarded Justin. This particular 7-11 was only two blocks away.

Cat was severely beaten by a variety of objects and had trauma in places that I cannot mention, as I must preserve the integrity of the case. The most noteworthy piece of her puzzle was that the killer had removed both of her hands. They had been expertly severed and had never been located. She was not killed at the dumpster scene, but more than likely transported there after she died. Whoever killed Cat was inhumane, sadistic, and had some skill at dismemberment. That is not a skill most people acquire.

Detective Bernard knew from his investigation that Cat used illegal drugs and stole from people here and there, but she had not ripped off or offended the people who knew her. The people who were last with her had no reason to want her murdered—especially in such a horrific manner. Bernard asked if I thought Scott could be responsible. I told him about the Larissa dumpster story and what I could say about our four victims.

"However, Bernard, nothing about Cat has surfaced during our investigation—but I didn't know anything about LeAnn until Steve told me about her going missing from Steve 2."

I added, "If Scott ever says that his cellmate killed Cat, then Scott did it."

When my kids were young, we used to watch the traffic lights at intersections. While waiting for a red light I would predict when the light would turn green, even before the crossing lights turned yellow. I would count down to one and every once in a while I got lucky and the light would change. For a brief time, my three- and five-year-old kids believed I was magic. It did not take them long to figure out my shenanigans.

However, I got lucky with *this* guess to Detective Bernard about Scott. It was about three years later when Scott told me and an FBI polygrapher that he knew who killed Cat. This former cellmate of Scott's knew details only the killer would know, and he knew them because he supposedly killed Cat. The statement placed Scott squarely in the middle of the murder investigation. On this day in 2008, though, I thanked Detective Bernard for coming and promised that I would keep him in the loop if anything came up about his investigation.

## KAYSI'S KILL SITE

From June 29 through July 3, 2008, Gary and I, along with thirty members of our Evidence Response Team, searched the remote mountainous area between Kremmling and Walden, Colorado. I recall our parade of dark FBI Suburbans driving into the tiny town of Walden and seeing the locals in the coffee shops pause for a second, then stare open-mouthed at the mysterious feds who were invading their community.

So as to not get lost on the winding, branching, and pothole-filled mountain roads you had to know where you were going, so Sheriff Rick guided us on the forty-minute drive over dirt roads to the area where Nurse Lou had found Kaysi's cranium. Mosquitoes the size of moths greeted us, pounding audibly against our car windows as they waited for their next meal to step out of the vehicles. I watched in true awe as the undersheriff allowed one of these monstrous bloodsuckers to feast on his forehead while he briefed us about the hillside where Kaysi's initial remains were located. I used enough DEET on my neck and arms to erase the face of my digital watch.

Our victim witness coordinators stood with Kaysi's mom and dad, Lori and Rob, as they cried quietly on the side of that mountain. Rob remarked to me, "There's no reason for Scott to take her to someplace *this* remote except to kill her. She had to be terrified."

Gary and I had come to the same conclusion during our first trip up here. This place was scenic and spectacular, while also horrifying and depressing because of our mission. We spent three days walking side by side, up and down the eastern face of that mountain. We recovered a few more skeletal remains and found evidence of campfires along with shards of broken taillights and shotgun shells, but nothing else of significant evidentiary value.

Spending time at the scene taught me several things about Scott. He had been willing to drive a significant distance in order to find a remote location for this victim. This was consistent with the profiling unit's training: if an intimate relationship exists between the subject and the victim, the victim will likely be hidden. We knew that Scott grew up hunting in Montana and Colorado and was very familiar with tracking animals, camping, scents, and navigating remote areas. Finding other victims would be challenging to say the least. Although Scott's misdirection and circular talking often led us nowhere, he was narcissistic enough to drop hints that actually led somewhere if we just did our homework.

The most disconcerting piece of information we gained during this search happened on day two when we were with Lori. She remarked to Gary and me that this place seemed familiar to her and she could not figure out why. When she woke up the next day, she had remembered. Scott talked her into marrying him one week after Kaysi disappeared, reasoning that he loved her and could use the FBI and all its resources to find her daughter—so why not do it together?

Lori told us, "We were back in Colorado from the Vegas wedding for a few days (in early September 2003) when Scott said, 'Let's go for a honeymoon! You work hard all the time. I'll drive you up into the mountains, let you relax with a nice bottle of wine in an unbelievably gorgeous and scenic spot, and I'll test out my new four-wheeler while you unwind.'"

Guess where Scott took her? A mile or so from this spot where we set up our base for the searches for Kaysi. Scott took off on an ATV for a day while Lori sat in a folding chair, having no idea she was extremely near her recently murdered daughter. We drove Lori to different dirt and gravel pullouts along the logging roads until she found one that looked familiar. We stopped there, got out, and walked around for a few minutes. She told us that in retrospect she thought this *was* an odd way to spend a honeymoon—taking in the beauty and quiet of this remote mountainous area while Scott was out four-wheeling.

We decided that Scott must have used the honeymoon trip as an excuse to revisit and manipulate the crime scene, check to see if Kaysi's remains had been disturbed, and to remove any evidence he might have inadvertently left behind. But he did not have to bring her mom up there, did he?

When I teach this part of the story, I cite sadism as one of the dangerous personality characteristics of the Dark Tetrad; the others being narcissism, Machiavellianism (manipulation), and psychopathy. Sadists enjoy the pain of other people. Scott could have easily disappeared one day, as he routinely did, and handled this "clean-up" by himself. But instead, he not only manipulated the mother of the daughter he had just killed into marrying him, but he took her under false pretenses to the murder scene. For what reason?

Did Scott take Lori up to the mountains for love? Concern for her being overworked? Absolutely not. There were lots of places to go on a honeymoon besides this one. Had he brought her here to spend time with her? He had left her *alone* for the day.

I can think of no reason for Scott to take Lori to this site except as a clear manifestation of him satisfying his deep-seated sadistic bent. It wasn't much different from him leaving breadcrumbs in the FBI file about LeAnn or asking Steve's parents to meet Jennifer at the Seattle airport when he'd already killed her. At this point in my relationship with Scott, I did not know how he could achieve any higher marks in these four Dark Tetrad categories.

# 14

# CIRCLING AROUND

IN JUNE 2008, our prosecution team met with Scott and his two attorneys. They had previously been informed of our recovery of Kaysi, so we now formally told them about LeAnn, and that we knew she was another one of his victims. There was no great "I gotcha" moment, simply a resignation that LeAnn would be included in whatever plea agreement we would eventually hammer out. The two Boulder prosecutors, Katharina and Amy, had been working with AUSA Dave over the past few months to file charges against Scott for check fraud and forgery (state habitual offender) and felon-in-possession of firearms (federal). Scott was looking at forty-eight years of prison time for the state charges and an additional seven years of federal time. Scott and his defense team were finally willing to bargain with us. They knew we could file a stand-alone case on Kaysi's homicide if we had to. They asked us to draw up a global plea agreement that addressed Scott's known crimes and the missing/murdered people. As the attorneys continued to negotiate, I collected Scott's DNA and fingerprints while Gary stood beside me.

Scott whispered to me, "Jon, I can get you to Jennifer, LeAnn, and Uncle Terry. It wasn't me but I know who did it. I was there." I just listened as I continued to roll his chubby fingers into the ink and smash them on the correct spaces on the white paper. He continued, "Who told you about LeAnn? Did you find her car? You know she was trying to break Steve out of prison. I didn't kill Kaysi. If you have her remains examined, you'll see that she overdosed and fell into a fire. I tried to save her. I'm guilty of not reporting a death, but that's really it."

Dave heard Scott whispering to me, so he raised his voice and called us into the conference room. Dave said, "Mr. Kimball, since we know Kaysi is dead and we found her, the time for figuring out what, if any, talks and negotiations might occur are going to happen *right now*. I'm willing to aggregate the prison time between the white collar crimes in Boulder and the current federal gun charges and wrap them up into one big deal. However, you have to tell us where the other women are. Now."

Scott started to speak, but Dave quickly interrupted him and spoke more loudly, shutting him down. Scott leaned over to me and said, "I want to talk now. I think this is productive."

I was sorely tempted to tell Dave to please shut up and let the man talk. However, I was also having way too much fun watching someone steamroll Scott and not allow him to dominate the conversation just because he had knowledge we wanted. Scott interjected, "Mr. Conner, you're being rude! I have something to say."

Dave shot back, "That's because I *am* rude, Mr. Kimball!"[99]

Dave proceeded to tell Scott he had already had his chance to talk about Kaysi, but he instead chose to jerk us around. So, we went and found her anyway. Close enough to the truth, I thought. I left the meeting smiling, telling Dave how grateful I was to have a prosecutor with a backbone made of steel who was willing to wrestle in the mud with Scott. If a serial killer like Scott says he is finally ready to say something, most prosecutors would never dream of talking over him and shutting him up like Dave did. However, Dave and I both knew that the man could not help himself; he would continue to lie until it benefitted him somehow not to.

The prosecutors and defense attorneys began to make some progress over the next few weeks. Scott's mom, Barb, talked to me almost daily, trying to find a way she could help us figure out what had happened to our missing victims. She spoke with Scott often and asked me for advice on what to say to him. I advised her to simply be herself—Scott would know immediately if she was being coached. Added to that, he

---

[99] Personal journal

was incarcerated and had legal representation. I could not have her offering any questions that came from me, unless his attorney was present. Barb was very understanding and said she would just try to get her own questions answered. I already knew she was going to be frustrated and disappointed. Every time she asked Scott about Uncle Terry or Jennifer she would get fantastic stories about who was responsible, such as the Sons of Silence, elaborate drug rings, and deep undercover operations that Scott claimed he could not discuss with her. I told her that Gary and I had coined the term "pixie dust" a few years ago. Scott's ability to circumvent the truth and make whatever fantastic tale he was spinning sound legit to anyone in earshot, was nothing short of a magical mist compelling people to suspend logic and believe him. Barb said the label was as good as any she could come up with considering the forty-plus years she had tried to parent him.

## SCOTT'S CHILDHOOD

During the summer months of 2008, Gary and I visited Barb and Kay a handful of times. We mutually benefitted from these visits. I learned more about Scott than anyone else would or could tell me, while Barb and Kay got to question the lead investigators looking into the murders Scott had possibly committed. After battling MS for decades, Barb was confined to a wheelchair. We shared glasses of lemonade or ice water at her kitchen table overlooking the lake behind her house. One day, Barb told us the following as Kay listened and confirmed her story:

"After the divorce in 1976, Scott attended elementary and middle school in Lafayette, Colorado. He visited Montana to stay with his dad, Virge, and his second wife, Barb 2, who had children of her own. Scott would've been about eleven years old when he first met his stepbrothers up there. Within the first day, he came running into the living room holding a brand-new $20 bill and exclaimed, 'Look what I found down the block, just lying in the alley!' His dad congratulated him on the lucky find and Scott announced to the family that he was putting it in his room. That evening he started crying and screaming, 'Someone stole my $20 bill!!' Virge knew it wasn't himself or Barb 2, so he started in on her kids, accusing them of stealing from Scott. After they sorted everything out, his stepbrothers and stepsister had nothing to do with it. He'd set them up. And it just got worse from there."

"Eleven?" I asked incredulously.

"Scott was contrary almost from birth," she replied. "He might've been only five years old when he looked at one of the walls in our house and said, 'Mom, that wall's gray.' I said, 'No, Scott, that wall isn't gray, it's blue.' He came right back with, 'Nope, it's gray.' He believed his lies at a very early age and became better and better at lying. I truly believe that he doesn't know today when he's lying or telling the truth because his lies have become truth to him."[100]

(If you recall from Chapter 7, in Scott's interview with Harold Dow from *48 Hours*, Scott said he had been "a con man, and a good one, since he was fourteen.") Barb continued:

"He bounced back and forth for a few years between Montana and Colorado. Scott was fifteen when he moved with his brother, Brett, to Montana to live with his dad and new family for good. He dropped out of high school after a few years and went to live with his grandmother, Ruth, in Missoula, Montana. He stole from her for years, writing bad checks on her accounts until she had to declare bankruptcy."

Barb told us that by the time Scott turned seventeen or eighteen, he was unwelcome at both his dad's and grandma's homes, so he moved to Canada and started swindling people up there. Within a year, Barb got a call from Canadian authorities saying they were deporting Scott to her home in Lafayette, Colorado. She reluctantly agreed and told Scott upon arrival, "You're enlisting in the military."

Scott was in the Marines for six weeks, until a knee injury sent him back to her home once again. When Scott was twenty-one, a rifle blast went off while he was sitting in a pickup in Montana. Barb did not know the details, but most accounts agreed it was a suicide attempt. She told us, "The blast from the rifle was strong enough to take off the front part of his forehead. He survived, but they had to use some bone from his leg to patch up the hole. Dr. Cleve thinks it took out some of his frontal lobe, and it affected his judgement and decision-making."[101]

---

100 Personal journal
101 Personal journal

I separately asked Scott's brother, Brett, about the gunshot and the resulting crater in Scott's forehead. Brett said,

"We were shooting pool in a hotel in Montana and Scott was drinking hard, bottle after bottle, and getting madder and madder with each drink. He was so pissed that his girlfriend broke up with him. Next thing, he grabbed the keys to my truck, stormed out of the hotel, and said he's gonna kill himself. We ran after him, but I couldn't get to the truck door before he closed and locked it. He grabbed the rifle from the rack, put the butt on the floorboard, and pointed the barrel to his forehead. He was crying, and I was screaming and grabbing a rock to break the window.

"At the very last second, I saw Scott tilt the rifle so it was pointing straight up instead of at his forehead, then he pulled the trigger. It's funny, 'cause I was more angry at Scott than anything, because my first thought was, 'This is all just for attention!' I broke the window and pulled him out. There was blood everywhere. If he'd really wanted to kill himself, though, he would've pointed the gun right at his head."

I separately confirmed with Brett that this incident was what kicked off the accounts of Neighbor Ted molesting Scott. He said, "It did. And I'm not discussing what happened between Ted and me."

I had heartburn over the Neighbor Ted story for multiple reasons and those reasons would continue to multiply. My most insightful run at Scott to test the validity of these claims would not come until 2011, when I brought the profilers down to meet with him in prison. Scott asserted that Uncle Terry, his stepmom, and two different babysitters had also sexually abused him from ages nine to sixteen. We will revisit this Neighbor Ted rabbit trail in the next chapter. For now, I had to refocus on finding out what had happened to Scott's victims.

## HEARTBREAK HOTEL

Following the release of the newspaper article, LeAnn's dad, Howard, called me. He was coming to Denver to meet with a true crime documentary producer about doing a story on Scott making his daughter disappear. The production company was putting him up in downtown

Denver at the Hotel Monaco. Howard asked if I would have breakfast with him. "Of course, I'd love to meet you," was my answer.

In the restaurant of the boutique hotel, I shook hands with this grieving, silver-haired father wearing large, square glasses. As we sat in the booth he slid a folder toward me. It contained photos of LeAnn from birth up until the last picture he could find before she disappeared. Howard shared with me how she was a straight A student and graduated a year early from Aurora High School. She wanted to go to physical therapy school at a local community college, but they would not take her until she turned eighteen. LeAnn's mom had suffered an aneurism at the same time, and LeAnn had to take over the family finances for a few months. She met a guy named Kevin, who was heavy into drugs, and he talked her into moving to Dallas, Texas. Within a few months, LeAnn was dancing at a strip club and living in a fleabag motel.

This father's heart was crushed at LeAnn's downward spiral. He had never recovered from his trip to Dallas three years later when he had planned to grab her things and bring her home. He was crying as the waiter asked, "Would you like coffee refills?" I nodded my head and Howard continued with his story. LeAnn's next boyfriend after Kevin was Steve 2. Things went from bad to worse.

Howard once again walked me through the sequence of events, moving from his daughter's disappearance to his calls to law enforcement and his unfruitful search to find her. I told this despondent, desperate man that we were doing everything in our power to find his girl. I told him about my own daughter, who was only ten at the time, and that she meant the world to me. I was a fellow dad who would do everything I could to resolve this nightmare for him and others like him. I wanted him to understand that I knew how much LeAnn meant to him.

He asked me, "Agent Grusing, I really want to know what you think, and I want you to be honest with me. Is there any chance my LeAnn is alive?"

As compassionately as I could, I told him, "No."

## SHERIFF WHITE

For a month now I had been talking with the Utah Grand County Sheriff, Steve White, about LeAnn's abandoned car. They had recovered it five years prior, just across the Colorado-Utah state line. Sheriff White said they had scoured the area back in 2003 trying to find LeAnn and had located a fragment of a human skull in a dry creek bed about five miles away from the car. The bone fragment had been tested, but there was no viable DNA available to use to identify whom it might have belonged to. The sheriff explained that this was high-desert area, an endless maze of canyons and cliff faces that was extremely hot and dry during the summer. He invited me to come out and walk around to see what he was seeing, so I took Gary and some members of our evidence team. We met them on a hot July day, and I got to shake hands for the first time with the sheriff and his top deputy, Darrel. Darrel's skin, baking in the sun with no hat, looked like well-worn leather. As we stood on a tall rock outcrop, scanning the landscape, Deputy Darrel explained the terrain around us. The dirt roads leading from the main highway into the Book Cliffs were used by sheep ranchers and oil drilling rigs. Few people came to this stark and desolate area of Utah, compared to the more scenic and populated Moab County south of I-70. Darrel had grown up in the area and knew most of the sheep ranchers who worked near where the car had been abandoned. We followed him down several creek beds to where they had recovered the skull piece.

I thanked Sheriff White and Darrel for their time as we all agreed that we could only *guess* where LeAnn might be. Only Scott actually knew. I told them I was confident we would be in touch soon. I could not know at the time how closely we would work together through most of 2009 in those arid canyons and dry creek beds.

## INFORMANT BEGINNINGS: ALASKA & MURDER

While I was somewhat stuck, waiting on the next puzzle piece to click into place, I decided to go back in time and see if the informant file from Alaska matched what Scott's cellmate recalled about the murder-for-hire plot to kill the Alaska judge. Seven years had passed since Scott's cellmate, Wes, was trying to hire Scott to murder the judge, but Scott had managed to save the day. I decided to ask for forgiveness instead of permission from the Alaska FBI agents, who probably did not want me poking around into this sensitive issue. On July 30, 2008, I found a phone number for the now-free inmate, Wes. I called and introduced myself.[102] When I was met with silence, I told him that although I did work for the same agency that in 2001 had believed Scott's story over his, I had more than a few doubts about Scott's veracity. I said, "I think Scott's a very dangerous person, Wes, and I'm wondering if he told you anything that can help us in our investigation into him." Over the phone, I could sense the tension subsiding, and Wes started his story.

"When Scott got placed into my cell, he was talking about being a hit man within the first few hours. He said, 'I've killed all sorts of people for money—men, women, even priests, as long as the price was right.' He also said he killed people who owed money to his employers."

Scott told Wes a story of taking two men on horseback down an isolated trail in the snow in western Montana. Wes said, "There was a bounty for the two men and he pretended to be a hunting guide. Once he got them deep in the wilderness, he pulled his gun on them when they weren't suspecting anything, disarmed them, made them strip to their underwear, took their horses and gear, and left them to die of starvation and exposure to the cold."[103]

Scott told a few other stories about being paid to murder, and Wes told me that he was convinced that this man was a killer. Scott asked Wes if he "needed anyone to die."

Wes told Scott that he and his girlfriend simply wished the key witness against him had told the truth. They wanted the witness to amend her statement to the cops about him (Wes) writing bad checks so he could get out of jail. Scott said, "Look, I've got some people who can look into your case, possibly get it thrown out. Who's your judge and prosecutor?"

Wes told him the names of the U.S. District Court Judge and Assistant U.S. Attorney who were assigned to his case and Scott replied, "I'm a horrible speller. Please write them down and I'll see what my

---

102 Personal journal
103 Personal journal

friends can do." Wes wrote them on a slip of paper and handed it to Scott. Scott asked Wes two questions: "Is your girlfriend willing to help? Does the witness need to die?"

Wes replied, "Absolutely not! She just needs to tell the truth. Please don't have anyone hurt or kill her!"

Scott came up with a plan. "Alright, here's how we'll get you out. I have a friend on the outside who can meet up with your girlfriend and convince the witness to change her story. No one's gonna get hurt or killed. He'll research your case first to see what the evidence is and make sure her story matches the truth. How's that sound?"

Wes could not think of a downside. He thanked Scott for wanting to help him out. Wes and his girlfriend made a few calls to Scott's outside contact, Ron, who agreed to convince the witness to tell the truth. Scott told Wes what he already knew—the calls from the prison were monitored, so Wes had to talk in code to initiate the plan. At Scott's instruction, Wes told Ron, "The fish is fat." Ron needed to know that it was okay to convince the witness to tell the truth by using the "fish" statement, and Wes would reimburse him for his work.

Wes did not find out what Scott actually did to him until he was in court two years later on murder-for-hire charges. "Ron" was actually an undercover Bureau of Alcohol, Tobacco and Firearms agent who was working alongside the FBI. Scott had provided the Alaska FBI agents with the handwritten names from Wes and told them, "Wes asked me to kill these two people."[104] To prove the murder plan to the investigators, Scott convinced Wes to call Scott's guy on the outside and ask him to say, "The fish is fat," to initiate the plan.

What Wes did not know was that Scott had explained to the investigators that "the fish is fat" meant "kill the judge" who presided over Wes's check fraud case. Once Wes said those words on the recorded line, the FBI had proof that Wes wanted people killed and would pay Ron to do it. Ron testified that he had been hired by Wes to murder the judge and prosecutor on Wes's case.

Once investigators had proof of Wes's intent to kill a judge on a recording, they threw him in solitary confinement. Wes would wait there for almost two years until his trial for attempted murder.

---

104  Ed Coet, *SLK Serial Killer* (Publishamerica, Inc., 2010), 185

Wes told me that his defense attorney was fantastic during the trial. Wes had one thing going for him—before he made the calls to Ron, he was so excited about getting his case overturned that he told twenty-two fellow inmates about the plan. To be clear, this was the plan "for the witness to tell the truth," not to "kill the judge." Wes explained to his buddies how Scott was going to get Wes's girlfriend and Ron to convince the witness to alter her testimony. Could she be intimidated not to testify? Maybe, and that was a crime. But was Wes planning or attempting to kill anyone? Especially the judge? The other twenty-two inmates, one after another, told the Alaska jury that those words never came out of Wes's mouth. Finally, Wes took the stand and testified that yes, he was an idiot for asking Scott and Ron to intimidate the witness. But he never wanted anyone killed. The jury believed him and cleared him of the murder charges, convicting him only of witness tampering.

That aligned with what I had seen in the files. Agent Carle paid Scott $18,000 in August 2003 on behalf of the Alaska FBI for his assistance in saving the life of the judge and prosecutor.[105] When I read the case summary the first time I suspected that Scott had fabricated the murder plot in Alaska. Now I knew it. Wes shared even more details with me about the extent of Scott's deceptive capabilities and provided me with more homework on possible homicides in Montana that had taken place in the 1980s and 1990s.

I glanced back at the last line of the search warrant affidavit that Agent Carle had authored for Jennifer's abandoned car. Regarding the Alaska informant reporting, he wrote, ". . . information originally provided by CW-1 (Scott) resulted in the indictment of the two suspects. However, it should be noted that the individuals were acquitted at trial."[106]

Scott told me and the press after his conviction that his purpose behind this first murder plot in Alaska was to get transported back to Colorado because his family and his mom were there.[107] On his way from Alaska to Denver he spent several weeks in a detention facility near Seattle. That was plenty of time to launch a second scheme.

---

105  Ed Coet, *SLK Serial Killer* (Publishamerica, Inc., 2010), 186
106  John Aguilar, "Chapter 4: Catch and Release," *Daily Camera*, March 10, 2010 (Archived from the original on January 12, 2020. Retrieved June 29, 2024.)
107  Ed Coet, *SLK Serial Killer* (Publishamerica, Inc., 2010), 186

# WES PART 2

After speaking with Wes, my guess was that the Seattle murder-for-hire plot was also bogus. I knew that Scott failed a polygraph in March 2003 because the Seattle FBI agents were starting to see inconsistencies in his story that his former cellmate, Jeremiah, had killed Thomas Wales, an Assistant U.S. Attorney, in October 2001.[108] I called the lead agent in Seattle to ask what happened with Scott. He told me, "Once Scott told us that Jeremiah had killed AUSA Wales we took it very seriously because it's a Major Case. We called FBI Alaska and they confirmed that Scott was a reliable informant who had saved the lives of a U.S. District Judge and an AUSA, which is why he was in the jail—to protect him from being killed as an informant. Scott's story seemed believable at first. Scott said Jeremiah bragged that he had sneaked into Wales's backyard, shot him through his sliding glass door, and took a 'token' from the scene to prove he did the homicide to those who'd hired him."[109]

The Seattle agent continued, "After Scott was transferred to Denver, we paid to fly him back and forth in January and February 2003 to meet with Jeremiah because we didn't have any solid leads on the murder and needed to run this to ground. Scott never stayed with our talking points, though, and it seemed like Jeremiah was clueless about the whole murder deal."

I did not interrupt the Seattle agent, but a bunch of gears started clicking into place when he named January 2003 as a month that Scott was up there in Seattle. I knew from Howard's research and my subpoenas that LeAnn was in Oregon and Washington during the middle of January 2003 when she agreed to drive up there and meet Scott. That was when they bought the Firestar .40 caliber handgun in northern Oregon that Scott had hidden by blackmailing his brother after the chase in California. I returned my focus to the Seattle agent, who was wrapping up.

---

108  Jordan Michael Smith, https://magazine.atavist.com/the-snitch-fbi-scott-kimball-informant-killer-colorado/May 2021. Downloaded July 13, 2024. p.14
109  The "token" was bogus but I'm not disclosing it, sorry.

"So, we gave Scott the polygraph in March 2003 and he failed. We were completely pissed that he wasted all of our time. We called him a liar, put him on a plane to Denver, and called Agent Carle to tell him what happened. When I wrote Agent Carle an email saying, 'Scott is untrustworthy,' he flipped out. He said, 'What the hell are you doing? Don't put it in writing!'[110] Agent Carle said that calling Scott unreliable would hurt his case, but I didn't back down."

---

110  Jordan Michael Smith, "The Snitch," *The Atavist*. No. 115. (2021): 14 (Retrieved June 29, 2024)

# 15

# DEEPER DECEIT

From August 17–19, 2008, I did my homework and put in the time listening to Scott sprinkle the pixie dust on a news reporter during recorded calls and visits to the jail.[111] Scott had been reaching out to a few news stations by mail and phone to spin his own versions of what was happening between him and the FBI. Jay was the local NBC investigative reporter in Denver who had covered our searches and family interviews for several months. He and Scott had been corresponding by mail, and apparently Scott had agreed to be interviewed. Within the first fifteen minutes, Scott sensed young, vulnerable prey. He quickly used the "poor me, I'm an innocent victim" angle, and it was very effective. I even caught myself wondering if we had the right guy and almost dialed the warden to demand Scott's immediate release—okay, no, not so much. Maybe I wasn't buying what Scott was selling, but I was truly in awe of how convincing he could be when motivated.

I listened as Scott told Jay, "I helped the FBI solve crimes for the past decade, and I've never failed a lie detector test. I'm the whistleblower the FBI is afraid of and they know they need to silence me. This is how they're doing it—by framing me for killing people who are just missing." His crescendo into the final argument included that the FBI was a family-wrecking-corrupt-lying-truth-concealing-blackballing organization that only wanted to frame him because they could not prove who really took these girls.

Scott's outright lies competed well, I thought, with the known facts of the case. He disregarded common knowledge and substituted his own reality which made complete sense to him, and which seemingly made sense to Jay.

Scott told Jay that he should feel privileged that he had chosen him to be the reporter receiving these deep, secret truths. Scott said he refused interviews with *48 Hours*, *Dateline*, and with Paula, another NBC investigative reporter, who had "totally betrayed his trust." Jay responded that he did feel honored, but he wondered why Scott had chosen him. Scott explained he wanted to believe in humanity and give someone a chance to get the story out. When Jay did not laugh out loud at that one, I knew he was under the spell. Scott directed Jay to listen to recordings of him talking to Jason, Steve's hit man, because Jason was the one who had killed Jennifer.

"Jason confessed to killing her on these tapes, but the FBI's hiding that evidence from the public and from my attorneys," said Scott.

"Why are they doing it?"

"Because, Jay, the FBI has to destroy me as the whistleblower. They are lazy and incompetent and know that I'll tell all of their dirty secrets."

Before Jay ran the story, he reached out to the Denver FBI PIO (Public Information Officer) and asked for a fact-check of Scott's claims—the pixie dust was wiped from Jay's eyes after he spoke with the PIO.

Listening to this visit did not provide me with any evidence to use against Scott in the missing person case. However, it reinforced the veracity of AUSA Dave's opinion that Scott "doesn't have it in him" to ever plainly reveal what had really happened to Kaysi, LeAnn, Jennifer, and Terry.

## ANOTHER SCOTT DUEL

Following my July 2008 call to Wes, we called for another status meeting with the prosecutors, defense attorneys, Scott, Gary, and me. AUSA Dave offered Scott a deal that involved immunity for all of his check fraud crimes *if* he told us where LeAnn, Jennifer, and Uncle Terry were located. Scott was bristling that day. He was very defensive and unwilling to admit to anything. Scott insisted, "There can be no homicide agreement because I didn't commit any homicide. I did *not* kill anyone. What we're talking about here are conspiracies that started out of the prison. Yes, I can help, possibly a lot, in finding out what happened, but I'm not pleading guilty to *anything* that has the words 'murder' or 'homicide' in the agreement."

After the meeting Dave privately told me, "I'm losing my patience with this man, Jon-Jon. My bosses aren't happy that I'm still working on this case. No one comes out looking good when they tangle with this guy, trust me. You've done a great job to get us to this point, but I'm not seeing progress here and don't know how much longer I can hang on."

On August 19, 2008, Dave called me and said, "Jim (Dave's supervisor) doesn't want this case on my plate any longer. I'm not seeing any actual charges we can file on him either now or in the near future. Jim formally declined the kidnapping case against Scott today. You know that I'm willing to see any case through to the end, but this one doesn't have any legs on it."[112]

I asked Dave to please hang in there with us. Gary and I were close to making a deal on the check fraud and forgery side. Gary and the Boulder prosecutors had been shoring up the habitual offender charges that would give Scott a forty-eight-year sentence. He would probably serve half of that time if convicted. The federal gun charges would add another seven years if we could convict him on those counts.

Gary and I had some confidence that Scott would accept the label "serial killer" if he thought it would somehow benefit him. We had not yet figured out how to get him there.

## NAUGHTY NEIGHBOR TED

In September 2008, I took Gary to meet Neighbor Ted, the man who supposedly had molested Scott from age ten to age eighteen. I needed to learn if these assaults really occurred, and if they shaped Scott into the person he had become. I also wanted to find out if Scott had manipulated the Colorado justice system like he did in

---

112 Personal journal

Alaska. Scott's cousin, Ed, gave me a tip on Ted that required follow up—more homework.

I called Ted and he agreed to meet us at a Starbucks outside of Boulder. Gary and I found him to be a small, wiry, intelligent, guarded, and inscrutable man. We sat outside on the patio at a metal table in Colorado's cool, sunny fall weather. Ted passed me a handwritten timeline of every occasion Scott and his brother came to his house. The pages and pages of information were very helpful, but the neat handwriting, along with specific dates, times, and details of the visits felt a bit creepy.

Ted adamantly denied Scott's allegations of the sexual assaults. He asserted there was absolutely no evidence to support any of the claims to begin with, and no evidence had been presented in court. According to Ted, Scott made up the entire tale and convinced a few relatives to go in on the story and claim that Ted assaulted them too.

"This was all about Scott going after my money," Ted said. "I never touched any of those kids in an inappropriate way and they know it." This bald, elderly soul was looking hard into my eyes as he spoke, almost daring me to contradict him. I did not. I just listened. Gary and I thanked him for his time and his detailed notes. Before we left, I promised to return his original timeline to him once I made a copy for our file. During our ride back, we agreed that very few people would admit to sexually assaulting a child—conviction or no conviction.

When I returned to the office I began going through Ted's logs. They recorded in detail the specific dates, along with activities, of the visits made by Scott to Ted's cabin. The dates ran from the mid-1980s into 1990 when Scott would have been in his twenties—a strong young man in his prime. Unless Scott had undergone a personality lobotomy, and I knew he had not, he would never have allowed a small, frail man like Ted to sexually assault him. Scott, as an adult male, was almost twice the size of Ted, and possessed a much more predatory, Type A personality. I could not rule out that something odd had happened between them, but it smelled more like the Alaska con. Scott's behavior after the supposed assaults and his varying assertions of torture also resembled his behavior in the other cons I had found in Colorado. If this was a deception, Ted had spent seven years in prison for something he did not do.

## COUSIN ED

Scott's defense attorneys sought permission from AUSA Dave and me for Scott's cousin, Ed, to visit him in prison and help broker a deal to recover the victims. Ed was a former military guy whom I'd met only briefly. He seemed to have a decent moral compass and, though sympathetic to Scott's family, he wanted to bring justice to the victims' families. I figured we had nothing to lose and were looking for anything that might help, so we okayed it.

Cousin Ed called me after visiting Scott and said, "I'm going to be Scott's spokesperson in this matter to the media. I'm also thinking about writing a book. I'd like to give you information when I can but not betray Scott's trust. For starters, Scott just told me that Ted confessed to him that he killed a young girl in Nederland and buried her behind his house. You should check it out."

I asked Cousin Ed, "What do you think about the whole Ted-molesting-Scott deal? You think it happened?"

Ed replied, "I'm writing about it in my book. Scott's brother (Brett) just told me that Ted got him drunk when he was five years old and molested him also. He said he did much worse to Scott, though. Ted only touched Brett a few times, but he molested Scott for years."

"I just don't see it, Ed. Scott is a predator, not a victim. Especially with him being eighteen years old? I think he was *hunting* people by then, not being victimized by them."

Ed replied, "Brett was believable and Scott told me many more details. Brett said, 'We never told our parents about it because they liked Ted. Except for the molestation shit, he was friendly, kind, and generous with us.'"[113]

Cousin Ed continued, "I think Scott's close to making a deal with you guys on the missing person and check fraud agreement. He's

---

113  Ed Coet, *SLK Serial Killer* (Publishamerica, Inc., 2010), 94

saying he'll do twenty-six years, maximum. You think you can get to that number?"

I told Cousin Ed that I'd check on the Ted tip and see what the prosecutors wanted to do about Scott's proposed number of years in prison.

I owed Ted a visit anyway to return the notebook. This time, Gary and I went to his cabin outside of the mountain town of Nederland. It sat up high off a winding dirt road and was built of polished golden pine trees. The property was welcoming because of its picturesque setting, neatness, and attention to detail. He invited us in and I began telling him about the report of Scott seeing him bury a small girl in his backyard. Ted smiled quietly and asked us to walk out back with him. He pointed to the rocky slope with pine trees surrounding his cabin and asked how anyone could possibly dig to bury anything or any person under those rocks. We couldn't argue with him.

Ted said, "I'm certain that Scott tricked the justice system into getting upset that some young, local boys, including himself, were supposedly molested."

I asked him, "Why didn't you take it to a jury trial? You said there was no physical evidence except for their testimonies."

Ted said that his attorney had told him, "You will lose, and if you lose, you'll never get out of prison. A plea deal's the only way to go."

Ted believed Scott walked away with about $50,000 as part of the settlement. Scott's cousin and brother received less because they only supported Scott's story; Scott was the primary complainant. Ted said the police searched his house and found no evidence of the supposed crimes because "none of it happened." I looked around his living area, dining room, and kitchen as we sat around the dining table—Ted was OCD on neatness and cleanliness. I didn't disbelieve his assertion that no evidence was found by police. He compellingly protested a couple of other seeming impossibilities of Scott's accusations and again proclaimed his innocence.

Gary and I left the cabin and during the drive back we rehashed our visit with this odd little man. I would see Ted once more just before he died. And I would ask him why he was writing to another inmate in the early 1990s about a woman in Ft. Collins named Peggy Hettrick, a widely-publicized unsolved homicide from 1987. I was especially curious because Scott became a person of interest in the case for a short time. Scott would mention Ted to me periodically over the next few years, but he never blamed Ted as his reason for becoming a serial killer. He saved that blame and responsibility for his mom and his victims.

I struggled with Scott's claims of molestation. I had too many unanswered questions and too many facts that did not fit, even considering Scott's twisted logic. Scott never tried to kill Ted, yet he tried to kill both of his young sons for life insurance money? He tried to have his mom killed because she was gay? He contracted to have an inmate kill Larissa because she divorced him? He killed Uncle Terry for no apparent reason? Yet, he did not attempt to kill the man who lived alone on an isolated hill in the forest, the man who molested and tortured him as a child? Whether he was molested by Ted or not was immaterial to helping me find our other three victims. The truth about the molestation story was something I would probably never know and needed to simply let go.

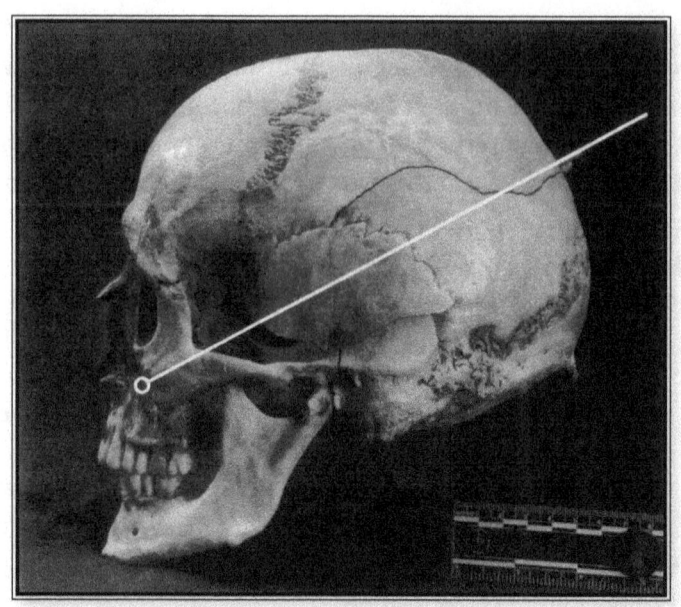

*Book Cover (Uncle Terry)*
*Permission from Dr. Diane France*

*Kaysi McLeod*
*Permission from Lori McLeod*

*Jennifer Marcum*
*Permission from Bob Marcum*

*LeAnn Emry*
*Permission from Howard Emry*

*Uncle Terry*
*Permission from ABC News*

*Personal Photo of LeAnn's Marker*

*Jennifer Lynn Marcum*

*Dave Conner*
*Permission from U.S. Attorney's Office (Denver)*

*Jonny and Dave*

# 16

# DEAL WITH THE DEVIL

I BLINKED twice and was then back in the conference room seated around the table with Scott, Detective Gary, and all the attorneys. It was time to try once again to get answers.

AUSA Dave offered Scott his second deal, which would involve immunity for any check fraud and forgery in exchange for providing us with the locations of Jennifer, LeAnn, and Uncle Terry. Scott's response to Dave's proposal was that the reason the four people disappeared involved a conspiracy. He added, "I wasn't the killer, but I can help find them."

After the meeting, Dave told me his bosses did not want him to be involved any longer in negotiating with Scott Kimball. The Denver U.S. Attorney's Office did not want to take on the risk of entering into an agreement with him because they could not verify if he had ever been truthful in federal court in the past. I was beyond discouraged. This was a major blow to prosecuting Scott. Dave had always pushed my cases through to the bitter end. His bosses gave him latitude because of his terminal cancer, and he fought tooth and nail to send dangerous people to prison and keep them there. Our only hope to forge a homicide deal with Scott rested with the two Boulder DAs and Detective Gary.

The Boulder DAs, Katharina and Amy, had been working furiously on a global plea agreement that would include all of the affected counties involving Scott and our four victims. These other counties did not simply include places where these people had disappeared *from*, but also where they might have disappeared *to*. Scott's attorneys supplied us with a list of districts we had to convince to buy into our deal before we could recover Uncle Terry, LeAnn, and Jennifer. The counties included Grand and Uintah Counties in Utah, along with Boulder, Adams, Summit, Eagle, and Mesa Counties in Colorado. Katharina told me that *all* of these county district attorneys had to agree that Boulder would represent their county in the global plea deal. All of the DAs would have to answer to their constituents that giving Scott a deal was in everyone's best interests.

It is often difficult to convince DAs from differing counties to agree on something, even when it appears simple and straightforward. Each elected DA has a slightly different interpretation as to how the law should be applied and what proposed actions (or inactions) should be accepted in their jurisdictions. Anything involving Scott was far from straightforward. These decisions involved missing people, murder, and a possible serial killer being set free in a few years.

We scheduled a meeting with the families of the victims, with Katharina taking the lead. Gary and I were there to assist in determining what outcome the families were hoping to see from the investigation and any subsequent plea agreement. Uncle Terry had no one speaking on his behalf. An inside joke had developed during the investigation: "No one cares about Uncle Terry."

The parents and siblings of Kaysi, Jennifer, and LeAnn had formed their own breakout group during this horrific ordeal and appeared to have formed a consensus. Because Kaysi had been recovered, Rob and Lori deferred the justice decisions to the other parents. Jennifer's mom and her dad, Bob, both wanted their daughter to be found regardless of the prison sentence Scott received. Whatever Scott received on the justice end was secondary. LeAnn's parents agreed with Jennifer's parents: "Bring our daughter home. We don't care what bargain you need to make with this horrible man."

Normally, the parents do not get to dictate plea deals. But in truth, these parents had been ignored by four or five different law enforcement agencies and prosecutor's offices, and each would be justified in bringing lawsuits against the agencies if they so desired. On the other hand, they recognized that they, too, had been fooled by this exceptional con man and needed these same agencies to prosecute him. Some families met with us in person and some over the phone as we sat in the historic Safe Streets Task Force building where we had interviewed Scott's son Justin. Boxes of Kleenex waited on the table. The long, emotionally heavy days were filled with a combination of crying, anger, and relief. We all sensed a resolution was coming, but no one was naïve enough to think the plan would sail through. No one around the table had any level of confidence that Scott could speak the truth and get us to resolution. Katharina was a great listener and communicator, balancing compassion with the demands of the law, while never promising anything we could not deliver. After two long days in that room around the conference table together, we came to an agreement we hoped might work for Scott and his team, the families, and something all seven DA offices could possibly stomach.

If it worked, though, Scott could possibly be free at age sixty-five, maybe years earlier.

And he would absolutely start killing people again.

But if we didn't offer him some sort of incentive to cooperate he would never come on board and lead us to LeAnn and Jennifer.

In October 2008, we had a face-to-face meeting with all of the affected DAs except for the ones in Utah, who attended by phone. No Scott, no defense attorneys. Katharina and Amy allowed me to present the facts of the case to date and they summarized the results of our meetings with the parents of the victims, Scott's attorneys, and the status of all the charges pending against him. Most of the DAs expressed complete gratitude for taking on this major headache and offered any support that Boulder needed. A few asked clarifying questions such as, "If LeAnn's recovered in my county, who is going to process the scene? Who notifies her family? Who talks to the media?" We answered these questions as best we could.

One DA, however, would not commit to *anything*. We figured from the start that he would be a problem and discussed days prior how we might manage him. Though we ended with a positive tone overall, we knew that this one holdout could derail everything.

In November 2008, AUSA Dave's office flatly stated that they were not participating in any of the negotiations moving forward because the Capital Crimes Unit (CCU) would not agree to bargain with someone like Scott nor give him any leniency on his sentence. The CCU in Washington, D.C. reviews all potential death penalty cases and even though the feds were not prosecuting these murders, federal charges were possible and had to be discussed. So, as we anticipated, the ball was solely in the court of Boulder County to move forward with homicide charges.

The one DA who held out on our global deal let us know that he "didn't want to be any part of a deal that lets a serial killer free." We tried to get him to see this from the families' perspective. Our position was that this was the *only* way we could even prove he was a serial killer. The DA did not budge, though, saying his constituents would hate it.

I wrote in my journal, "This case looks like it has little or no hope."

Scott called me from prison in late November. He was frustrated because he had heard the deal was not going through. Scott said, "I'll plead to aiding and abetting, but no homicide charges." His federal defender, Lynn, was on the call with us and she agreed—they would not allow him to plead to anything involving murder. I explained that the Boulder prosecutors would not move forward with a deal if he did not plead to something that included murder, because he was clearly involved. I found myself smack in the middle between the defense and the prosecution. I was not able to help either side budge, so I prayed desperately for guidance.

Instead of guidance, I got so mad while playing Mario Kart with my son and Doug, my close friend from childhood who was visiting, that I dropped my controls and walked away. Working so intently with Scott and watching this case going down the toilet was directly affecting me as a dad, a husband, and a friend. This case was consuming my nights and weekends; I could not foresee any positive outcome.

A hearing was scheduled in Boulder County Court for December 17, 2008. Scott's attorneys were supposed to persuade him to plead guilty to two second-degree homicide charges. Scott would say he simply "aided and abetted" in the deaths of Uncle Terry, LeAnn, Jennifer, and Kaysi. In exchange, the Boulder DAs would allow him to serve a forty-eight-year prison sentence, with parole possible in twenty-four years. The hurdles facing the deal included that Scott was not ready to do it, and the one rogue DA was still holding out on the global agreement. The Boulder DAs called a final meeting during the week of December 10th, hoping to push *all* of the DAs to agreement.

Dave was working with his connections behind the scenes, pressuring the problematic DA to agree to the deal. This DA had longtime allies who had climbed to their elected official positions. Our hope was that they would be the ones who could exert enough influence on this dissenter to convince him to cooperate with us. We all met one last time. Right before the six other DAs were about to give their consent, the disagreeing DA started to walk out of the room. But, a perfectly timed question arose from Amy, our very quiet Boulder DA. It hit him squarely between the eyes, and stopped him in his tracks when Amy asked, "So, (first name of the DA), are you with us or not?"

It was the way Amy worded the straightforward request. The tone. The delivery. The brevity. It was all perfect. She had correctly couched her query with the understood parentheses that he would be going against his fellow DAs. And they were the only ones who presently mattered in this decision. He paused. Then, he looked around the room and said, "Fine, go ahead! I won't oppose it." And he walked out of the room.

It was done. We were stunned and grateful. Now, Scott had to plead to murder, something that so far he had refused to do.

## THE DAY OF THE DEAL

Heavy white snowflakes were landing on my hair and suit on December 17, 2008, as I walked into the Boulder County Courthouse. The courtroom was packed with media and families, so Gary, my boss Phil, and myself, along with other law enforcement, took the only seats available in the courtroom, which were in the jury box. Scott was seated at the defense table with his attorneys, and the Boulder DA team sat at the prosecution table. Everyone was on edge. We did not know if Scott was going to plead guilty to what we called Part A. We had divided his plea into two steps. That day's test was to see if he would accept responsibility for the "Big Bitch," the habitual check fraud and forgery charges that Gary had helped the DAs file against him. This plea meant he would accept a forty-eight-year prison sentence with the understanding that we would concurrently run second-degree homicide charges along with that sentence *if* he cooperated in leading us to Uncle Terry, LeAnn, and Jennifer.

All that mattered was that Scott pleaded guilty. If he did, he would be unable to kill anyone in the general public for a minimum of twenty-four years.

Without emotion, Scott raised his hand, agreed he was of sound mind, and told the judge he was pleading guilty. He did it. No drama. It was just a simple, "Yes, your honor," for each count of check fraud, time after time. The jailers escorted Scott back to the judge's chambers and we sat together at a table, ready to plan out Part B: Finding our Victims.

I was sitting in chambers at the table directly across from Scott—I could not tell you today where anyone else was sitting. He asked for a piece of paper and a pen. He drew a line down the middle and said, "Colorado-Utah border." He drew a line straight across and said, "I-70." He drew a small circle just left of the vertical line (Colorado-Utah border) and above the horizontal line (I-70). He pointed with the pen to the circle and said, "LeAnn."

He then moved his pen about half an inch to the left, drew a second small circle and said, "Fifteen miles west: Jennifer. I can get you to both in one day."[114]

I asked about Uncle Terry and he replied offhandedly, "Oh, he's up on Vail Pass under deep snow. That's an easy one."

Scott began reeling off all the things he would need to recover these victims: "I'm gonna need a helicopter, skis, ropes, maybe a plane, some ATVs, a Jeep or four-wheel truck, and excavating equipment. I'm also gonna need access to the internet to use Google Earth to see what's changed since 2003 to 2004." Gary and I looked at each other and suppressed smiles, knowing Scott was watching us closely.

It was not as much about the outlandish list, but the odd and unnerving vibe that settled onto all of us in the room. Everyone except Scott. He was . . . not just excited, closer to giddy maybe? Unnaturally energetic? We could sense he was *reliving* the heinous steps he had

---

114 State of Colorado, County of Boulder v. Scott Lee Kimball. Warrant for Arrest Upon Affidavit. 2009-CR-0001626. Signed October 5, 2009. Received July 26, 2024, p.5

taken to snuff out these three lives. His total lack of humanity and any sense of impropriety or remorse made us ill. I finally responded that I would take responsibility for writing up the documentation for the Department of Justice Headquarters, asking for the authority to check Scott out of jail for these "body hunts." Once we were granted authority, our team would determine what equipment would be needed.

Scott once again asserted that he could locate all three victims in one day, if we gave him the right transportation and tools. The Boulder DAs told his defense attorneys that they would work through them on any future details, while I would begin drafting the required documentation needed to check him out of prison for the trips. After Scott was removed from the room to be escorted back to his cell, we all just stared at each other for several moments. We appeared to be unable to articulate exactly what had just happened, even though we had all witnessed it. Katharina finally found the words and said what we all knew: "We just made a deal with the Devil."

After telling Phil what had happened, I was on the phone with Dave, who gave me a quick list of things to think about as we were agreeing to allow this very dangerous man to roam around with us for a day or two. Even with our SWAT team, Scott could talk anyone into doing anything and something bad *was* going to happen. It always did to anyone who was around him. Dave said, "There's no truth in that man, Jon-Jon. You've tied yourself to him because it's the right thing to do, but I don't see any good coming of it." I couldn't argue with him. I told Dave I would ask for multiple layers of security and that I would ensure I was never alone with him.

My next call was to Sheriff White in Grand County, Utah. He needed to hear that the remains of Jennifer and LeAnn were supposedly within fifteen miles of each other on the north side of I-70 in his county. The sheriff was excited and said he would provide four-wheelers, Jeeps, and trucks and be ready to go when our search party arrived. I then called Sheriff Cale who covered the Vail Pass area in Colorado. I let him know about Scott's assertion that Uncle Terry was up there somewhere, and we would be coming to find Terry. Sheriff Cale said, "Our mountains are under six to eight feet of snow right now. We can have snowmobiles and Snowcats ready to go." I asked, "Are Snowcats large animals that I should be afraid of?" and he dryly replied that they were slow-moving machines on treads that could transport us through deep snow.

I spent the next month drafting memos on how we would safely check Scott out of jail and return him each day, without anyone killing him or him killing any of us. I would accept most of the liability during this search in case something went wrong. With Scott having direct access to thirty people at a time, something *was* going to go wrong. I worked with Sheriff White toward a February 9, 2009, target date to attempt to locate Jennifer and LeAnn in his Utah county. We had Scott transported to the jail in Grand Junction, Colorado, right beside the Utah county line. Our evidence team, SWAT contingent, and teams of attorneys were set to go.

Sheriff White and I were on speed dial during the week prior to our search date. As the date got closer he said that snow was in the forecast for the canyons. He explained that the dirt roads would turn into a muddy soup, and even the best four-wheelers would not make it into the areas we would need to access. One day prior to us leaving Denver, on February 8th, Sheriff White said, "Jonny, there's no way we can do it because of the snow. We went out earlier and got stuck three times."

Reluctantly, I postponed everything. I had to make at least ten different calls, but I had no answers for the FBI agents and attorneys who were asking for a rescheduling date. Disappointment spread through our office, as I knew it would.

On February 11th, Scott called me from prison with Attorney Lynn on the line. Right out of the chute he demanded, "What happened, Jon? I thought everything was ready to go! Now I'm stuck in this prison out here by Utah without any of my things. I am not happy, Jon! You need to do something. Now!"

I had spent over two years living and breathing this exhausting man. I really wanted to unleash my sarcastic tongue on him or at least defend myself. I knew it would do no good, though, or get us any closer to finding our victims. I remained silent.

Scott was still angry and animated when my brain finished its internal argument and returned to the call. I hoped I had not missed anything important. I knew if I could weather another fifteen-minute onslaught of grievances by Scott, then address one or two grievances I could actually control, he would settle down and we could speak to each other like civil humans. When I made peace with him by saying that I would make some calls to the prison about his things, he extended his peace offering:

"LeAnn is in a mountainous area and is secure and bundled. She's masoned up in rocks, like a cave."

I thought, "What does that even mean?" I pictured a baby tightly wrapped in a papoose, almost like a gift, tucked away in the side of a mountain. Lynn told him not to say any more.

## BARRY'S BODIES

For the past few months, a cellmate of Scott's named Barry had been calling me. He had been secretly revealing to me what Scott was saying, and that Scott's drawings indicated where our victims were located. Gary and I met with Barry at the jail on two occasions and retrieved Scott's hand-drawn maps, complete with X's marking burial sites in the Lavender Canyon area near Moab, Utah.[115] Scott had offered to pay Barry if Barry would dig up the bodies or clothing of the victims corresponding to the X's. Scott also told him that Uncle Terry was located under the cattle chute on his Lowell property in Broomfield, Colorado. Finally, Scott drew Barry a map of a few square miles around the Broomfield house, where Uncle Terry and Kaysi had last lived. He drew streets, fence lines, and landmarks, labeling them A, B, C, and on through to Z, AA, and BB. He told Barry that at least one body was buried at one of the sites he had marked with a capital letter.

I suspected Scott was testing this man to see if he was a "rat." Even more so, Scott enjoyed jerking people's chains. He knew I had to follow up on every lead, which would drain FBI time and resources and would inevitably make us look foolish when nothing turned up. Not to mention that during this time my squad mates were starting to grumble that I was not around much to help with bank robberies and fugitives. I was still devoting 90 percent of my time to this plea

---

115 Personal journal

deal with Scott. "When are you going to be done? What else is there to do in this case?" I had no good answers for them. I was beginning to feel like an outsider.

I sent the Lavender Canyon map that Scott had drawn to Sheriff White in Utah. The sheriff knew the area well and agreed it was probably bogus. Scott had placed his "landmark" on the wrong side of the main highway. Also, the area was filled with tourists. It was not a remote site like we knew Scott would patiently seek out as he had for Kaysi. Also, with assistance from the Broomfield Police Department, we spent a couple of days digging up the dirt surrounding the cattle chutes on a property Scott had squatted on. We found nothing.

Scott started threatening Barry in a very careful, veiled manner after Barry was transferred out of his unit. He said he knew where Barry's wife and kids were and hoped they were doing well. The FBI had to determine if Scott had the connections to get to Barry in another prison and/or to Barry's family outside of jail. I asserted, "Absolutely not. Scott has no friends anywhere as he's screwed them all by ratting on them, framing them, cheating on them, taking their money, or killing them. Plus, I'm watching his mail and phone calls—he's just playing Barry like a fiddle, knowing he'll call me with the maps because Barry thinks that'll get him out of jail."

"So why do it?" Phil asked. "Why would Scott take the time to scare some guy in jail to mislead us right before this huge deal, undermining everything for him and us? It's just as bad for Scott as it is for us."

"Because Scott loves playing games," I responded. "He's so addicted to exerting complete control over people and wrecking their lives that he does it just because he *can*. From stealing thousands of dollars from his brother and best friend, to taking and killing his fiancée's daughter. It's like breathing air or eating food is for the rest of us. Scott has to manipulate the people closest to him or he won't survive."

# 17

# BODY HUNTS

## TRIP 1

ON THE morning of February 23, 2009, lights began to come on early in the hotel rooms of the large search party that had been assembled. We began putting on hiking boots, multiple layers of dry-fit clothes, plenty of sunscreen and, finally, our weapons. Everyone met in the parking lot and we loaded the Suburbans and Tahoes with our gear. The first stop was to pick Scott up from the detention center in Grand Junction. The search party had to wait thirty minutes for me to sign all the necessary paperwork to check him out. When we were finally ready, we walked Scott toward the SUV where the two of us would sit in the back seat. Frank, Scott's defense investigator, and the FBI SWAT agent who drove filled the remaining seats in the SUV. Scott was in belly chains with handcuffs connected in the front and had zip ties around his ankles. I tried to put leg irons around his ankles because I had written in the Department of Justice memo that he "would always be in leg irons, at minimum." But Scott's ankles were abnormally large for someone his size, and I could not even get one of the teeth to click into the pawl of the cuff. So, zip ties it was.

Before we loaded into the SUV, Scott turned to me and asked, "Agent Grusing, did you brush your teeth this morning?"

The question was so totally out of context related to what I was focused on that I had to take a few seconds to adjust and try to figure out why he would ask such a thing. More importantly, I had to give him an answer. I went with the simple truth, "Yes, Scott, I did."

Wrong answer.

Scott responded, "Well I didn't get to, and I'm not going anywhere until I get to brush my teeth."

I have told this story hundreds of times and I always ask the audience why he would say such a thing and what my response to this demand *should* have been. I had nearly thirty people waiting on me and we were already behind schedule. How would you answer him? I quickly pushed aside the initial, knee-jerk, practical answer, "You're an inmate. I'm not. You've lost some rights. I haven't."

I remembered why this team was assembled in that parking lot, what the judge had ordered, and the facial expressions of the families who were waiting on the FBI to tell them where their daughters were hidden.

We were there under court order to find LeAnn, Jennifer, and Uncle Terry, and were mandated to listen to Scott and his attorneys in order to complete our task. Once again, Scott knew who was in control, and it wasn't me. I knew that if I told him, "Sorry, Scott, we gotta get going, please get in the car," the day would be a disaster. I still don't know today if he actually brushed his teeth when they escorted him back to his cell, wasting another half hour of our time, but that was not the point. Once he was back inside the vehicle we took off for Utah.

Our caravan arrived at the I-70 highway exit where LeAnn's car had been recovered and we filed off the highway to meet with Scott and his attorneys. Defense investigator Frank pulled out a map that was marked with the canyons and dirt roads winding into the Book Cliffs north of where we were parked. On the far left side of the map was a single, large red dot. Scott's attorneys explained, "This is the spot where Jennifer was buried." Scott told them she had been placed under rocks in a creek bed. Their team was most certain of this red dot location because it was beside a large ranch gate and sheep pen.[116]

---

116 State of Colorado, County of Boulder v. Scott Lee Kimball. Warrant for Arrest Upon Affidavit. 2009-CR-0001626. Signed October 5, 2009. Received July 26, 2024, p.6.

I asked about the nine green dots and seven yellow dots on the right side of the map. Scott said, "The green dots are where LeAnn *probably* is. The yellow dots are where she *might* be."

Those sixteen dots were at the ends of dirt roads near the Colorado-Utah border. Scott explained that there was a small metal shed near a horseshoe canyon where LeAnn was hidden; he would know it when he saw it, but he was not as confident about the location of LeAnn's burial site as he was about Jennifer's.

Darrel, the Utah sheriff's deputy, told Scott, "I grew up in this area. The large ranch gate where Jennifer is—does it have a beam across the top?"

Scott said it did. Darrel asserted, "That's Spring Canyon. The gate is the Hansmire-Campbell Ranch gate. I know exactly where that is."

The red dot on the map seemed to grow in size with Deputy Darrel's statement of confidence.

We had been looking for Jennifer the longest. We felt we owed her father, Bob, the most because her kidnapping was the at the core of this whole Denver FBI murder-for-hire and informant disaster. Bob had been relentless in his pursuit to find out what happened to his daughter. Thinking about him, I offered, "Let's go to Jennifer's site first, recover her, then chase down the nine green dots." Everyone agreed, so off we drove.

The roads were still muddy from the snow and our SUVs slipped and slid around as we approached the Hansmire Gate. Scott was in the back seat with me, saying, "We should be turning left before the gate, then we'll see a sheep pen before we enter the horseshoe canyon." He explained to us that the "driver" had placed Jennifer in a "wash" after they went through a "frame-twister" creek bed and that they had been driving at an angle along the canyon wall.

Scott said, "We should find her underneath about ten or twelve large, smooth stones in the wash." His vivid descriptions and excitement were contagious, and the other three of us in the SUV became confident that something positive was about to happen.

Our caravan made it through the eleven miles of mud roads to the impressive ranch gate. Scott said, "That's it! That's the gate that I saw back in 2003. I decided not to go inside of it, so I turned left and went into that (he pointed to the left) canyon."

The SUV parade pulled over so we could talk for a minute before we entered the canyon. Scott's federal defense attorney, Lynn, was wearing high heels. We had noticed her choice of attire when we were back at the jail and wondered how she would fare in the muddy canyons. When the agents in the SUV carrying Lynn stopped at the pullout she opened the rear door, and when she stepped out of the vehicle her left heel sank in the mud up to her ankle. Her right heel suffered the same fate. Off-balance, she lifted one foot out of its shoe and took her next step into the brown goo with her bare foot. I don't remember her getting out of the vehicle for the rest of the day.

We had to use four-wheelers to get back into the canyon, which according to Deputy Darrel was called Spring Canyon. He assured us that our SUVs would get stuck if we tried to drive back in there. Several of us loaded up on ATVs and drove into the canyon. Scott was freed from the zip ties on his ankles to allow him to ride the ATVs and explore the conditions. As we entered the canyon just around the curve from our pullout, Scott pointed out an old, wooden pen and some stones piled one on top of another. He said, "Those stones used to be a cabin, and that was the sheep pen. He said he had passed both in 2003 on the dirt road to watch the "driver" bury Jennifer. We were now driving down the middle of an old, dried-out creek bed as we entered the horseshoe canyon. The canyon walls extended upward in a slope of a couple hundred feet to a rocky crest on top. We stopped and looked around the large, enclosed canyon that was about three or four football fields long and one football field wide, with brush and rocks covering the canyon walls.

Scott told us that the driver had taken their Jeep about halfway down the same creek bed we were in, then drove up the right side of the canyon wall, "button-hooked" back toward the entrance and carefully went through a creek bed that twisted the frame of the Jeep, hence the term "frame-twister." He pointed to one of two washes that extended downward from the canyon wall on the right (on the east side, facing west) and said that Jennifer should be under a pile of rocks in one of those beds.[117] He pointed Deputy Darrel to one of

---

117 Darrel taught us that "washes" describe the channels of water that flow from high points to low points, while "creek beds" are the horizontal channels for water flow.

the washes and said, "It's most likely this one, though I'm not one hundred percent sure."

We spent a few hours with the Evidence Response Team (ERT) looking at the two washes, trying to estimate how much dirt and rock had shifted in the six years since Jennifer had been buried there. The team leader volunteered to assess the area while we went to find LeAnn. Solid plan. We took off on the four-wheelers, loaded back into the SUVs, and drove south to I-70, then east, then up north toward the dirt roads that were fifteen miles closer to the Colorado border to find the first of the green dots where LeAnn might be secure and bundled.

Scott got testy on the way to the first green dot, telling Deputy Darrel as we got near the canyon that he was not seeing the metal shed that he needed to see. Darrel told him there was no metal shed in the area, while Scott confidently asserted there was. Scott was extremely agitated as he got into the back seat with me, complaining, "Jon, this is not going to work if these sheriffs won't listen to me! I'm telling them this isn't the right place! Are these the best guides you have? We won't find these girls if they don't know what they're doing!"

As calmly as I could manage, I explained that this was the best we had and we would work with them because we must. I added that I had confidence in Deputy Darrel and Sheriff White.

The roads were too bad for us to get to the first green dot canyon anyway, so we turned around and waited for the evidence team to meet us back at the recovery site of LeAnn's car. Cell phones did not work out there, so we used the sheriff's radios to communicate. Scott was crabby, blaming us, and we were not happy with him either. Our evidence team leader reported that they had turned over a ton of rocks, literally digging into the two creek beds Scott had pointed out, but found nothing.

On the way back, Scott turned his attention to something we had discussed two or three phone calls ago—my agreement that we would grab him a burger and coke while we were out. I had no idea that this meal was more important to him than any success we might have searching for victims. When I asked him if the sandwich, chips, and drink that the sheriff's office provided for lunch counted as the meal, he said, "Not even close. I need a Big Mac, fries, and a Coke. This is very important to me, Jon. I've been waiting on this meal for months."

Scott felt none of the disappointment and sense of failure that we did. His confident assertion that he would lead us to both girls and possibly Uncle Terry in one day was not even in his mind as we drove back into Colorado. I did not believe the FBI would have vouchered the meal for this serial killer if I had submitted it, so I just paid for his McDonald's meal deal out of my pocket. As Scott ate his meal in the back seat, he offered, "Jon, I'm eighty percent sure that Jennifer's in the creek bed I told Deputy Darrel about."[118]

We had a lot of things to figure out before we checked this man out of jail again. Unfortunately, that was happening again early the next morning.

Our investigative team met for a late dinner and a beer and reviewed the unusual day until about 9 p.m. Though we all felt the pressure to find LeAnn and Jennifer, at times we laughed until we cried, retelling Scott's odd statements and mimicking his mannerisms.[119] We agreed that we were tethered to this disturbing con man until we found *something*, or *someone*, and we had to apply the right kind of pressure to find our victims. Only one FBI agent, a former detective from Virginia (hereafter Agent Virginia) thought Scott was being honest with us. This highly seasoned investigator spent an hour walking around Spring Canyon with Scott, giving me a break. Scott convinced him that he was just a victim in this whole ordeal, and that the driver was really the bad guy.

Agent Virginia told us, "I don't know, fellas. I think Scott's doing all he can and there might be something to this conspiracy thing. I don't think he's the bad guy. I think the driver's the killer."

I reached over and pretended to wipe pixie dust out of Agent Virginia's eyes, telling him that he had gotten the full blast of Scott's uncanny, persuasive, and manipulative abilities without having someone there to guide him out of the fog. I shared with the team some of Scott's backstories, with the intent of setting a guardrail that no one should be alone with this man, regardless of their prior law enforcement experience. Gary seconded my admonishment, explaining that

---

118  Personal journal
119  Scott sometimes had a slight tic when he blinked. He dramatically rolled his eyes when he did not agree with something. And there was the unmistakable giant divot on his forehead we all tried *not to* stare at. Yes, we were basically middle schoolers, I know.

when he had been alone with Scott three years before, the pixie dust had been flying, and even he had been unsure if his check fraud case against Scott was really all that solid.

Before we adjourned that night, our evidence team agreed to dig up the two beds that Scott had pointed to in Spring Canyon as Jennifer's location. We would take him to the first green dot for LeAnn, then on to other green dots if that one fell through.

## TRIP 2

The following morning, February 24, 2009, Sheriff White presented Agent Virgina with a riot helmet and mask with the label "Pixie Dust Shield" on it. We were howling. Once we managed to get our game faces on, our team met with Scott's attorneys before checking him out of the jail. We passed on Scott's frustrations surrounding the metal shed that we couldn't find, and our SUVs not getting him back to the canyons where he had made green dots to indicate where LeAnn was *probably* buried. We let Deputy Darrel speak candidly with the team about the near-infinite possibilities of spidering roads leading to canyons that spanned northward. Our task of exploring that territory was all but impossible if Scott was uncertain of which initial road, then branch road, then the next branch road he took from LeAnn's car to get to the first green dot.

Scott, however, was not uncertain about anything when he hopped back into the SUV with me. He was bristling with energy—confident that he could guide our evidence team to the wash he had pointed to in Spring Canyon where he had hidden Jennifer and that they would find her there. He handed us some sketches of what the rocks piled on top of Jennifer would look like—evenly covering the depression in the wash that hid her and creating a uniform elevation across the top that was about six feet in length.

After securing Scott's seat belt in the rear seat behind Investigator Frank, I sat behind our SWAT driver. I was as ready as I could be for another long day with this highly energetic and frustrating man. While I was focused on visually double-checking Scott's handcuffs as

I climbed into the SUV, I gouged the top of my head on the angled, metal support for the emergency light that was mounted on the headliner inside the rear door. Small lightning bolts shot through my head as it started bleeding quickly. I confirmed the open wound with my fingers and felt the cool air moving inside my head. Luckily, Scott was hyper-focused on Frank as he complained about not being afforded the resources or expertise from us that he needed to be successful. I wondered, "Can serial killers smell blood? Or sense it?"

I was not afraid that Scott was going to attack me like a vampire, but my imagination did take over for a few minutes. I wondered if this would somehow make me vulnerable to him, and if it might give him some advantage during this whole body search ordeal. I was able to discretely apply pressure to the wound with my left hand, using tissues to hide the blood from Scott until the gash clotted over. It's funny how the small things that happen uniquely to you can override the required attention to the much greater and more important mission. The gash on my head consumed my thoughts that morning as we drove around looking for LeAnn's canyon. As a result, I was not listening much, if at all, to the conversation inside the SUV. We spent most of the morning in the Bryson Canyon area, driving in and out of creek beds, drill pads, and ranches.

We explored different canyon cul-de-sacs, hitting about five of Scott's green dots without success during the daylight hours. Scott, highly agitated by noon, requested internet access in order to view satellite photos. I told him, "We can get you that when we get back to town. We've got to accomplish as much as we can while we're out here—as you know, it takes us an hour and a half to get there from here." Although we were only between fifteen and twenty miles from the interstate, we were deep into a network of canyons, and the dirt roads that would get us out were winding and unmanaged and riddled with huge potholes, bumps, and twists.

After another McDonald's stop in the late afternoon, we took Scott back to the jail parking lot in Grand Junction. Before checking him in, we allowed his attorneys to review their printed maps and online Google maps with him on their laptop. The makeshift workstation was assembled on the hood of one of our SUVs. We stood by for an hour or so and let them try to figure out why we weren't getting to the right canyons. Our evidence team, completely worn out and dusty from digging up the creek beds in Spring Canyon all day, met us back at the hotel. They had found nothing. Something had to change with the search process.

## DEEP BREATH

The court order to check Scott out of jail had expired. I had no answers for Howard (LeAnn's dad) or Bob (Jennifer's dad). I had used up the days of permitted travel for almost thirty people and had zero to show for it. Scott called me almost daily from the jail with Attorney Lynn on the line and told me that it was our fault that we hadn't found LeAnn and Jennifer. He continued to demand unreasonable resources and more reliable sheriff's personnel next time if we wanted to succeed. I told him, "I hope there will be a 'next time.'"

Between those calls, and meetings with my boss and co-workers and the sheriffs in Utah, we came up with a plan:

1. Detective Gary and I would go to the jail in Grand Junction and spend the day with Scott and his attorneys. We would interview Scott until he could explain, in plain English that we clearly understood, what he was willing and/or able to say about the locations of LeAnn and Jennifer. We were going to extract whatever information from his twisted brain that we were not yet grasping to aid us in the search.

2. The FBI in Utah volunteered to fly its surveillance plane over all of LeAnn's green and yellow dots to give us the bird's eye view we would need for our next trip.

3. I called Dr. France, the anthropologist who had examined Kaysi's remains, and asked what resources she could think of to help us. She suggested that I call Dr. Jim, a forensic geologist whom she described as, "One of the brightest people I know." This colleague of Dr. France's could accurately assess the dry dirt and rocks we were digging through to determine

if we were digging deeply enough, or if the significant rains and snowfalls of the past six years had shifted the landscape through erosion. I made myself a note to call Dr. Jim to see if he would be willing to lend us his expertise.

4. We needed to take Scott back to Spring Canyon to see why we could not find Jennifer in the places he had pointed out.

5. I would write up a new memo to FBIHQ and to the Department of Justice to check Scott out of jail again if all these previous steps showed that we could be productive.

# TRIP 3

By the first week of March 2009, I once again was the proud owner of a Department of Justice court order for the temporary checkout of Scott from the jail in Grand Junction, Colorado, for the purpose of resuming the search in Utah. We had checked all the boxes on the plan outlined above and intended to show Scott the surveillance photos from the plane just before heading out.

On March 10, 2009, Detective Gary and I went to the jail and showed Scott the photos. He responded by drawing more sketches of how the Jeep was parked when "they" buried Jennifer, and how LeAnn was placed in something like a tomb inside the canyon wall. Scott got excited about an overhead photo of a horseshoe canyon in one of the green dot areas that we had not been able to access on prior trips because of the mud and snow.

The next morning, we drove Scott to the new site in Bryson Canyon. As we were nearing, he started saying things like, "I've got a good feeling about this, Jon. If we see a waterfall, I think LeAnn's gonna be there."[120] His excitement continued to escalate and he added, "We'll find her on a rock shelf wrapped up in a carpet."[121]

---

120 State of Colorado, County of Boulder v. Scott Lee Kimball. Warrant for Arrest Upon Affidavit. 2009-CR-0001626. Signed October 5, 2009. Received July 26, 2024, p. 16
121 Previously, with his attorney, Lynn, on the phone, he'd told me that we'd find LeAnn "secure and bundled."

Scott had never given these details to us, even in the day-long interview we just had with him. A carpet would stick out prominently in this light-brown dirt landscape with white rocks, versus the bleached-white sheep and cattle bones that had briefly given us false hope. On our previous excursions, Deputy Darrel weighed in on bones that we'd come upon in the other canyons. He'd say things like, "This one's a sheep leg, see the way the bone's shaped?" Or "These are coyote ribs, too small to be human."

If Deputy Darrel had been unsure of any dried bones we found during our first two trips, we took photos that I texted to Dr. France when we got back to the interstate or up on a canyon wall where I could get cell service. She was precise in her answers, giving us the formal name and classification of each bone. Almost everything was sheep or coyote.

During this trip, Scott was as giddy as he had been in the judge's chambers months earlier when he knew he would be going out on body hunts. As we piled out of the SUV inside the horseshoe canyon, he pointed to an oil drill pad and said, "That looks familiar. Let's walk down through this creek bed." We followed him down the slope to the dried bed, allowing him to lead, but not by too much. He was wearing a long-sleeved, white T-shirt and tan pants (I'm sure his attorneys brought the clothes for him so he was not wearing an inmate jumpsuit) and still strapped up with a belly chain, with handcuffs in front but no leg restraints. The box canyon walls quickly ascended vertically, so there was nowhere for him to run. With his build, he could not even remotely come close to outrunning us anyway.

When we reached an eight-foot-tall rockpile in the middle of the creek bed Scott told me, "That's a waterfall." As we faced the "waterfall" he looked down at a bone on the edge of the creek bed and said, "There's a bone."

As I stated earlier in this story, we had seen numerous sheep, coyote, and cattle bones by now and this one did not look much different from those. I asked Deputy Darrel what he thought of it, and he remarked that he didn't think it was human, adding, "Probably another sheep bone."

Scott shrugged and said, "Okay, well, let's head back the other way." Scott started walking back up the creek bed, as if he were ready to return to the SUV.

Today, I can't explain exactly why I did what I did at that moment. The best term I can use, as I stated earlier, is "serendipity." It is a scientific term that can be defined as "looking for something and finding something better." Another fitting definition is "becoming aware of the potential of something."

By that day, March 11, 2009, I had lived and absorbed everything about Scott that I could for thirty consecutive months. Add to that, my mom's little church group in Lubbock, Texas, was praying diligently for some resolution to this case. When I visited home a few times a year, I would thank them for their resolution and devotion in asking for God's intervention because I—we—desperately needed it. I gave them tidbits about the investigation, public information as reported by the Denver news, so they would feel like they were part of the case.

Finally, by now I had triangulated my assessment of Scott with those who knew him best—his former wives and his mom. Yet, with all that work, I still could not tell when he was lying.

I could tell, though, when things were "JDLR," to borrow a phrase from my boss, Phil. *Just Doesn't Look Right.*

As Scott walked back down the creek bed, I let him out of my sight and hearing for the first time during our Utah body searches. His attorneys, the sheriff, and a few FBI SWAT guys were walking along with him. I looked at the sheep bone, the makeshift waterfall, and the canyon wall that sloped upward beside the waterfall. I started hiking up the loose dirt and rocks, trying to ascend vertically from the bone, to see what might possibly be located above it. I did not know if I would find more sheep bones or a rolled carpet with a female skeleton inside. After about five minutes of hiking upward in the closest direct line I could from the bone, I saw something that didn't belong with the landscape—a gray hair clip with brown and blond hair still inside of it.

Just to the right of the hair clip was a white bone with rounded edges and grooves that differentiated it from any sheep or cattle bone.

An image from Scott's laptop popped into my mind and provided a reference. He had two or three photos of LeAnn with darker-colored hair. Her father, Howard, had given me photos of her with blond hair. This hair clip had longer hair strands with both of those colors. It *had* to be hers.

My voice cracked the first time I tried to shout, "I found LeAnn!" The words came out faint and raspy. Visual images of sitting at breakfast with LeAnn's heartbroken dad scrolled through my mind. I said the words again, louder, even yelled them, and within a few minutes the search party brought Scott up the side of the canyon wall to the area where I was standing. Instead of walking up the slope from the bone like I had, they climbed up from wherever they were along the creek bed and side-hilled across the canyon face to find me. They appeared about ten feet above me to my right; Scott and the others were looking down on the scene where I was standing.

With a disapproving and vacant look, Scott assessed me, the hair clip, and the bone and said, "That's not her. Let's keep moving." His tone was flat and without emotion. The words hung in the air for a few seconds as I remained silent. Scott just kept staring down at me.

Phil broke the silence by asserting, "He's being weird. Get him out of here." Daryl, one of our FBI SWAT guys, started walking Scott down the canyon wall. We looked more closely at the bone and hair clip and the others agreed with me. These items belonged to one of our victims, most likely LeAnn. No other human, especially one with long, blond hair in a hair clip, would choose to be in this godforsaken canyon up on the side of the canyon wall. The sheriff called the coroner as we poked around a little. We were mostly interested in a large, red rock slab that covered the loose dirt and rocks next to the bone. We figured that the slab had shifted forward from another large, flat rock that had collapsed under it from the monsoon flooding, and we hoped the remaining skeleton of LeAnn was hidden by those rocks. The hair clip and bone were the only parts peeking out at me, pointing me to her. My immediate thought was that the prayers of my mom's friends had been heard, and this was indeed a miracle.

I walked up to the top of the canyon and called my mom to ask her to pass along a message to her five or six women, "Please tell them, 'Thank you.' And please keep this quiet."

No carpet was ever found in the area, nor did Scott ever tell me what he meant by "bundled and secure" and "wrapped in a carpet."

I am confident today that he was talking about a different victim. Those statements guided me and an investigator from Utah down a subsequent two-year rabbit hole looking for his unnamed victim, a Jane Doe who was left on a rock ledge and wrapped inside of a rug.

Before the coroner arrived and started digging, we walked down to the bottom of the canyon to find Scott and our SWAT guy, Daryl. Scott's defense investigator, Frank, had a big frown on his face, and started in on us as soon as we were near, "Your SWAT guy here told Scott, 'Run and let's see how far you get.' He wanted to shoot him!!" We saw FBI Daryl's wry grin and did not have to ask if he had told Scott to run. Scott's weirdness in trying to lead us away from LeAnn, while at the same time leading us near LeAnn's burial site, had agitated all of us—Daryl just spoke aloud what all of us were thinking. Daryl apologized and Phil explained that tensions were running a bit high.

Scott had already moved on from whatever weirdness caused his misdirection and indignation, intended to hinder us from finding LeAnn. He proclaimed, "Alright, let's go find Jennifer!"

We loaded up and moved west to Spring Canyon, this time driving on the upper road that would take us through the Hansmire Gate. This was the first time we had driven this single-lane, winding dirt road to the gate, but Scott was correctly predicting the way the road would bend *before* we could see around the next hill. He was showing off, wanting us to believe that he had been here before—likely numerous times. I would wonder much later if he was just reliving what he and his attorneys had looked at on Google Earth as they prepared for these body hunts. Today, I think that is the more likely scenario, and a better reason for him to feel the need to brag about it. Remember, he is a con man in the very core of his being, and he consistently wanted us to think certain things were true when they were not.

We went through the Hansmire Gate after forty-five minutes of carefully navigating roads with potholes as wide as our SUVs. We arrived at the same pullout parking area from day one, where the defense attorney had lost her high heels in the ankle-deep mud. Spring Canyon awaited us, just around the majestic canyon wall and crest beside the impressive ranch gate. The riverbed leading into Spring Canyon had dried enough that we could now drive our SUVs back into the canyon, even as the brush scratched against the car doors.

We walked Scott to the two dried creek beds extending downward from the west-facing canyon wall that he had previously pointed out. We were impressed to find the massive digs in those spots completed by our Evidence Response Team. Jennifer was not in either of the locations that Scott was so confident he had placed her. Of course, he was still talking in his "the driver did it" terms, though sometimes he would slip and talk as if he had been the driver. None of us bothered to challenge him at this point. Scott looked at a barbed wire fence twenty-five yards south of the second creek bed and asked Sherrif White's deputy, Darrel, "Was that fence there in 2003?" The deputy considered it for several moments, studying the wood and wire, then responded that it looked older than six years. Scott pounced on his absence of total certainty and mentioned that he "could've driven Jennifer back in that direction *if* the fence wasn't there." We spent a couple of hours assessing the fence and the face of the canyon wall, not finding the frame-twister and similar dried creek beds on the other side of it. Scott reluctantly agreed that he could not have made it back into that area with his Jeep, so we returned to the areas that had been previously dug up.

Scott found another wash extending down from the canyon wall and pointed to a depressed area of dirt a few yards away. The longer he looked at it, the more certain he became that Jennifer would be just under the dirt and rocks in the wash. He stood on a particular flattened spot inside the wash and confidently proclaimed so everyone could hear, "Merry Christmas! She's right here."[122]

One of our evidence techs placed a small red flag at the spot and our team said they would start working on it. Scott then asserted that we should drive into the canyons west of Spring Canyon to check them out. I fervently asked, "Why would we do that?! You just said, 'Merry Christmas, this is the spot!' Everything points to this canyon and this spot. The gate, the sheep pen, the frame twister, the creek bed, a west-facing canyon wall, and a dirt road that goes directly to I-70, which you (Scott) said you took after burying Jennifer."

---

122 State of Colorado, County of Boulder v. Scott Lee Kimball. Warrant for Arrest Upon Affidavit. 2009-CR-0001626. Signed October 5, 2009. Received July 26, 2024, p.7

Scott replied, "Yes, I agree this is the most likely spot for her. But you've never killed anyone, have you Agent Grusing? This isn't as easy as it looks. This is probably it, but I'm not one hundred percent sure. It's been six years and a lot has changed. We're here with four-wheelers and afternoon hours to kill, so why don't we go explore our surroundings?"

I looked around to see who was jumping to my side of the argument versus the serial killer's new assertion that everything close to us was now in play. Crickets. So, we gave in to Scott's uncanny mastery of persuasion and went to explore Coal Canyon.

That was a mistake. But agreeing to use Scott to find these victims in the first place was a bigger problem that we could not circumvent or undo.

With Scott loaded onto the back of Deputy Darrel's four-wheeler, and the remaining four of us on two additional ATVs, we explored the adjacent Coal Canyon back through its two-track dirt road. Coal Canyon was larger than Spring Canyon, with horseshoe canyon walls—it seemed similar to the canyon where we had found LeAnn. This canyon also had more brush and rocks on the walls, but less dirt and fewer dry creek beds and washes than Spring Canyon. I do not remember any of Scott's remarks, but we were in and out within an hour before we explored the next canyon over. It was too dissimilar to all of his statements about Jennifer's burial site for even his creative mind to "make it work." When we finally made it back to Spring Canyon our team was still digging so we didn't bother them. We loaded Scott into the SUV and headed back across the state line where I bought him his McDonald's, once again, and then checked him back into the jail.

This time, Scott's investigator and defense attorneys joined us for dinner and drinks at the hotel. We were beginning to form an unlikely assortment of friendships through this ordeal. We learned that defense attorney Megan was a somewhat renowned aerobics instructor, featured in *Buns of Steel* magazine. Investigator Frank talked about the struggles of Cousin Ed to write a book about Scott, blending together my investigative documents and Scott's outlandish claims. Phil was always the life of the party, cracking jokes and laughing about how stressed his bosses were about this venture. He overheard our SWAT guys dreaming of unlikely ways that Scott might "accidentally" fall off one of these Utah cliffs and end this insanity. We all agreed that this was a once-in-a-lifetime mission and none of us knew how it would end.

The evidence team returned during dinner and told us there was nothing in the "Merry Christmas" wash. We weren't surprised. The Boulder DAs agreed to stay behind the next day and watch the Grand County Coroner unearth LeAnn's skeletal remains. I had to get back to Denver for multiple reasons, one of which was to inform LeAnn's dad, Howard, about our "find" before the media got wind of it and he learned about it secondhand. The FBI Lab would take weeks to confirm it was her, but no one at the table had any doubt it was LeAnn.

The next morning, I drove through the canyons to the first location where I could get cell service and called Howard. I told him that I would much rather tell him the news in person, but I did not want to leave a task so personal to an FBI agent in Idaho whom he didn't know. I said the same words that I had choked on inside of Bryson Canyon, "I think I found LeAnn." Howard immediately began crying and through his sobbing asked for the details. The buildup of anxiety, unrest, and anger that accompanied years of searching diligently for her now released like a pressure valve. Tears were streaming down my face and I struggled to keep my voice steady while I told the story of the previous day's events. I explained that the lab results would take weeks to confirm and he understood. With thank you's from both sides, we ended the call.

I would subsequently travel south to Lubbock to tell my mom's Sunday School prayer group of the miraculous finding of LeAnn. I thanked them on behalf of LeAnn's family and the law enforcement and legal teams involved. They were ecstatic that their hours of praying had moved God to intervene; the prayers had meant something to us and had proven effective in an unexpected manner. I asked them to turn their prayers to finding Jennifer, since our efforts to date had been fruitless and I didn't know how to flip the right switch in Scott's head to tell us where she was.

# 18

# THE LAST, LAST TRIP

By late March 2009, the FBI Lab had confirmed that the remains we recovered in Utah were those of LeAnn. The coroner had slowly unearthed her entire skeleton from beneath the large, red rock slab—finding all of her major bones except for her skull. Where her head should have been located was a spent .40 caliber round. Our ballistics lab compared the lands and grooves[123] on the casing to the insides of the barrel from the Firestar handgun—the gun Scott had purchased from the now burned down gun store in Oregon in January 2003 just weeks before LeAnn disappeared. These results confirmed he shot a round from *that gun* into LeAnn's head on the side of that godforsaken canyon wall. The Hermiston gun store owner did not recognize Scott from his photo when FBI agents showed it to him, per my request. The owner did, however, comment that LeAnn "looked familiar." The information from the gun shop owner was far from definitive, but we could logically surmise that Scott convinced LeAnn to purchase the gun that he later used to kill her.

No clothing was recovered at the site except for a single white sock near one of her feet. I knew from cell phone records and receipts that Scott drove to Las Vegas before he met his brother, Brett, at a hotel in San Bernardino the next day. In that hotel room, Scott took a photo of the stripper named Athena so he could someday blackmail his

---

123 The raised and recessed portions of a firearm's barrel that make up the rifling.

brother. He then gave LeAnn's credit cards to Athena to use, making LeAnn seem alive while he was driving back to Colorado.

## MORE HOMEWORK

By March of 2009, I was tired of losing to Scott in our quest to find Jennifer. I decided to write down the things I knew to be true about her disappearance and compare those with his many assertions. I learned many things during the five or ten minutes preceding LeAnn's recovery.

Scott was giddy just prior to leading us to the site. He described what the scene around the bone in the creek bed would look like before we got there. Scott added details that weren't true, like rolled up in carpet and bundled. He took us very close to LeAnn's burial site and then took us away from it—it was an "I'm smarter than you moment." He did not want us to actually find LeAnn. Finally, he didn't care about the court's consequences for misleading us.

I called Scott's investigator, Frank, and asked him to help me narrow down which of Scott's assertions we could rely on versus him playing guessing games. I asked Frank to get me a list of non-negotiables regarding Jennifer's burial site from his client. I threw out some topics like, "How sure is he about Hansmire Gate? The empty sheep pen? The frame-twister before the dry creek bed or wash? Was it a west-facing canyon wall? Does he still assert that he put large stones on top of her?"

I asked Frank to tell Scott that we could not check him out again (thus no more McDonald's) unless we had some certainties. Frank agreed and promised to work on that list for me.

All of my energy for the investigation, along with that of Gary, the prosecutors, and the defense attorneys, was focused on our three female victims. With dark but accurate humor we continued the "No one cares about Uncle Terry" comments with a bit of tongue-in-cheek. But the truth was that no one did. He was divorced, alienated from his adult daughter, and he was a drifter with no friends or co-workers. Nobody except Scott, Lori, Scott's dad, Virge, and Virge's ex-wife even knew Terry was missing. Nobody was pressuring us to look for him. Thus, we mostly forgot to pressure Scott about Uncle Terry since the quests of Bob, Rob, and Howard to find their girls were front and center in our minds.

After recovering LeAnn, I had a chance to catch my breath and remembered that Scott had told us back in January 2009 where he put Uncle Terry—Vail Pass. He had even faxed me a map! I had sent the map to the sheriff up in the Vail mountains, Cale, and he said that the X where Scott supposedly put Uncle Terry was about seven or eight miles from the Vail Pass turnoff from I-70. The body, if it was there, would be under eight feet of snow. Considering Scott's stunts with LeAnn and Jennifer, I told my team we needed some proof that Uncle Terry was going to be in the place Scott claimed.

I was on speed-dial with Dr. France throughout these body hunts and after the most recent trip she reminded me, "Call Dr. Jim." This man was a trusted colleague of hers who resembles the actor Paul Giamatti—at least I think he does. Dr. Jim was a renowned botanist and geologist who helped law enforcement find bodies that were hidden in all types of ground. He was expecting my call and pounced on the opportunity to help us find Jennifer in the canyons of Utah after I told him that we were shooting for late April to undertake one more trip with Scott.

Katharina, Amy, Gary, and I jokingly called ourselves "Team Kimball," and wondered aloud what lettering and decals should be on our T-shirts, hats, and RV. Gary had a vivid imagination that dreamed of the cross-country trips we would take, escorting Scott around the western United States to find all the people he had murdered. Phil joined in the fun but accurately advised that such a trip would extend beyond our lifespans, especially if we were relying on Scott's direction to truthfully lead us to a victim.

Returning to reality, I authored for the third and final time the memo to DOJ Headquarters requesting to check Scott out of jail. We planned to exhaustively explore the area of Spring Canyon in Utah to find Jennifer. Our SWAT and evidence teams were up for one last effort, along with the prosecutors, defense teams, and the Utah sheriffs. Sheriff White had run two sets of cadaver dogs all through Spring and Bryson Canyons, looking to find any clue to the whereabouts of LeAnn's cranium or any evidence at all of Jennifer. They found nothing on either venture.

Sheriff White and I theorized that the skull fragment his deputies had found three years ago when we first met might have belonged to LeAnn. It had been exposed to the elements long enough that there was no DNA left inside, and there were no teeth found nearby. The dry creek bed containing the skull piece was miles from LeAnn's recovery site, but with the big winter runoffs, it could have logically moved that far and in that direction. It was either that option, or the possibility a critter took it somewhere we had not yet discovered. Or . . . the possibility that Scott took it as a souvenir. We went with options one or two.

## I'M STUCK. LITERALLY.

On Tuesday, March 31, 2009, Sheriff White called me to say that Deputy Darrel had spoken with the landowner of the ranch near Spring Canyon after our search party had cleared out.[124] Darrel, I knew, was totally sucked in by this case and would not stop poking around those canyons until we found Jennifer. The landowner told Darrel that the only frame-twister creek he knew about was deep in Spring Canyon, further back inside the canyon than we had explored, of course. Sheriff White and Darrel were going to check out this secret road the following morning. My mind was in overdrive, turning over the possibilities all night. I woke up half-convinced I should just drive the five hours out to Utah early and search with them. I threw a change of clothes and my pickax in the trunk of my Bureau car—commonly referred to by the agency as Bucars—just in case I decided to go. By the time I was halfway to the Denver office, I was fully convinced I should go to Utah. I called Phil to ask permission. When he said, "Sure," I took off on I-70 West to Utah, dialing Sheriff White's number as I was heading out of town. I made it to the dirt road turnoff of I-70 in Utah by 10:45 a.m., but my GPS took me down the wrong branch as I was heading to the Hansmire Gate.

I tried to carefully maneuver my Chevy Impala over a small, shallow stream flowing across the dirt road leading to the Book Cliffs and Spring Canyon. I did not recall the stream-crossing during our body

---

124 Personal journal

hunt trips with Scott. However, back then I was in the rear seat, paying more attention to my prisoner than to the roads or directions. The steep slope of the dirt road on the far side of the creek looked challenging for the FBI's Chevy Impala, but not impossible. I thought I could make it over the stream and up the road if I went slowly. Just after I crossed the stream, however, the front bumper of the Bucar lodged into the steep dirt incline. I was high-centered and couldn't move forward or in reverse. After a few seconds of trying to decide whether I should laugh or curse or cry, I jumped onto the hood and tried my cell phone. No bars and no service. The small stream was bubbling as it flowed beneath the car—there were no other sounds in any direction. I hiked in the direction of Spring Canyon for about a mile until some bars finally appeared on my phone. Sheriff White could barely understand me. I couldn't tell if it was because of poor cell service or because he was laughing so hard. While waiting for him to come and bail me out of this mess, I took in how vast and unforgiving the area was. Small animal bones were everywhere. The earth was dry and dusty with spiny, tough, plant life. It was the perfect place to get rid of someone.

Sheriff White and Deputy Darrel arrived and were still cackling when they saw my FBI car suspended over the tiny stream. They asked, "Can we please take pictures?" I told them, "Not if I want to keep my job."

After towing my car out of the creek, I followed them deeper into Spring Canyon than we had been with Scott and the search team. No trail was visible from the area where we had been working because brush obstructed it, which was why we did not explore it earlier. Darrel had already dug up some of the nearby gullies matching Scott's description of where he had buried Jennifer. I had to rid myself of some angst and Bucar embarrassment so I began digging. I hacked my way down a wash with my pickax, cutting a small swath about twelve inches deep. No luck. Without Scott there to say, "This isn't it," or "higher up," I knew I was shooting in the dark. (It probably would've been worse with him there anyway.) I took pictures of the area for future reference. We explored another canyon or two on the four-wheelers to no avail and then I drove back to Denver. I ran into heavy snow on Vail Pass and could only go fifteen miles per hour because of slick roads with no visibility. I was exhausted when I finally got home that night, physically and emotionally spent with yet another healthy serving of disappointment.

The local newspaper from Salt Lake City started running daily articles about "Serial Killer Scott Kimball," featuring of our missing people and updates on our efforts to dig up his victims in Utah. The sheriff's office in Grand County was not used to such media pressure and one of their spokespeople talked freely about the case. The "I'm sorry, we can't comment because it's an ongoing investigation" adage is an effective rule of thumb, especially in a case like this when we were working under a sealed federal court order to get Scott out of jail. I called Sheriff White, who had not spoken to the media at all and seemed the least affected by all the attention, and asked about the recent articles. He said that he wanted nothing to do with the press and agreed none of the "Scott Kimball material" should be out there. But the stories continued because they were able to find people outside of law enforcement who were willing to add fuel to the fire.

# TRIP 4

Dr. Jim arrived at Spring Canyon on April 20, 2009, the day before we checked Scott out of jail. The geologist camped out and surveyed the canyon to determine how much soil might have moved since 2003, and which washes or creek beds might have changed significantly. He drove to find cell service and called me to report that the soil erosion might have covered up to an "absolute maximum of one-and-a-half feet" over the past six years.[125]

Also on April 20th, 2009, Detective Gary and I met inside the jail with Scott and his defense investigator, Frank, to cement the non-negotiables in hopes of giving our search a small chance at success. Over the past month, Frank had confirmed with Scott that the unique Hansmire Gate, the sheep pen, and the straight exit from the Spring Canyon dirt road to I-70, left *only Spring Canyon* as the place where Jennifer could be. Scott was adamant that we either had

---

[125] State of Colorado, County of Boulder v. Scott Lee Kimball. Warrant for Arrest Upon Affidavit. 2009-CR-0001626. Signed October 5, 2009. Received July 26, 2024, p.7

not dug deeply enough, or we were in the wrong wash, but *she was in that small canyon.*

I showed Scott the map he had drawn that would lead to Uncle Terry. It was the same one that he and Defense Attorney Lynn had faxed to me back in January. Clearly irritated that we were still interested in finding his uncle, Scott spouted out, "Look, Uncle Terry is right where I said he'd be (using his finger to point to the X on the map). You'll find him fully dressed in white tennis shoes, still wearing his eyeglasses, Walmart jeans, white socks, and underwear. Just take this logging road (pointing to it on his map) past the depression in the road, then you'll take a decline around the curve in an area cleared of trees (denoted by smaller X's on his map). Terry is wrapped in a gray tarp with about forty feet of nylon rope. He's about one hundred feet off the two-track dirt road, the body resting against a tall pine tree."

Later, our team agreed Scott could have given us details for LeAnn and Jennifer with the same clarity he provided for Uncle Terry if he had wanted to. We really did not need to check him out of jail to find any of these victims. This entire undertaking, though ordered by the court, was simply an exercise in patience and humility on our part, letting him relive how smart he had been in killing, hiding, and covering up what had happened to these two young women. That, and the fact that Scott wanted to get some fresh air and McDonald's.

On April 21, 2009, we checked Scott out of jail for the final time. By the time we drove him to Spring Canyon, our evidence teams were furiously digging in the only logical washes, based on our research and prior trips. All the work was being done under the supervision of Dr. Jim. Scott was extremely curious to speak with the geologist, as he was a new expert on scene, so he asked us to take him over there and introduce him. I was in earshot when they spoke.

> Scott: "So, I hear that you're our new expert and you're looking at soil erosion and plant life?"
>
> Dr. Jim: "Yes, I've considered the size of plants surrounding these washes, estimated their ages and growth rates and am quite comfortable with the maximum excavation depth I've recommended."

Scott: "You've accounted for the blizzards and heavy rains in this area? The arid summers?"

Dr. Jim: "Great question! Yes, I've also looked at the weather patterns back to 2003 and taken each season into account."

They continued going back and forth on matters involving excavations, cadaver dogs, and ground-penetrating radar as Scott tested Dr. Jim in each area. Then I picked up on this next part of the conversation:

Scott: "I think I saw you on a documentary about five years ago. Were you on a *Discovery* true crime show discussing why killers normally take their victims downhill because of the difficulty of lugging dead weight uphill? Was that you?"

Dr. Jim didn't respond for a few seconds. He later told me that all the blood rushed to his stomach and he felt ill.

Dr. Jim: "Umm, yes. I did make a comment to that effect."

Scott: "I thought that was you! It was because of that documentary that I took my victims uphill."

Dr. Jim did not respond as Scott thanked him for the visit, then turned toward me and announced, "While they're digging, there's something I need to see in Coal Canyon. I think it might be in everyone's best interest if we go there. And bring Dr. Jim, he'll be very helpful."

Dr. Jim became a friend to me over the next fifteen years as we worked together looking for adults and children who disappeared in the mountains of Colorado. Inevitably, that conversation in Spring Canyon crept into every future search as we rehashed how unnerving Scott could be.

We drove Scott and Dr. Jim through the neighboring canyons and Scott began to embrace the likelihood that Jennifer was in one of these, not Spring Canyon. He was examining an east-facing canyon wall with Dr. Jim when I walked up and asked, "What're you two talking about?"

Scott said, "Jon, I might've been turned around when I was talking to you guys earlier. Everything about this wash reminds me of that night in the Jeep—that over there (pointing to a vertical wash on the canyon wall) could've been the frame-twister, these are the size of rocks the driver used, and this canyon is more the size of the one I was in."

I had been able to remain patient and calm for months, but not this time. "Scott, there's no ranch gate here. No sheep pen. You've always indicated a west-facing wall because the sun was going down. Remember? We're already miles away from your non-negotiables!"

Scott shot back, "Jon, we've been over this. You've never killed anybody, have you? I'm doing the best I can! Maybe I was turned around that night. Maybe I saw the ranch gate, didn't like it and drove over here. I'm trying to find Jennifer. I have every reason to help you find her!"

I did not argue with him. It was not worth it. His attorneys were persuaded by the sincerity he could always muster when he needed it. Plus, our team had to show the court that we had exhausted every lead he gave us. I had a shovel on the four-wheeler and asked him to point to the spot in the wash where he thought Jennifer might be. Then I started digging. Furiously. I had to release some of the adrenaline unleashed during my argument with Scott, and my obvious frustration that all of this was a waste of time. Scott kept walking around with Dr. Jim as they discussed the terrain. Finding nothing, I joined them as they headed to the next canyon.

Now that Scott had shifted his non-negotiables, any canyon was possible. He pointed Dr. Jim to another similar wash—and this time, Gary and I started digging quickly and without comment. We were just knocking down Scott's claims and ruling out minute possibilities. As the sun was setting, we headed back to Spring Canyon knowing that our evidence team was not coming out of there with Jennifer.

The team's work in Spring Canyon was impressive. We found two trenches extending down the two washes, each about four feet deep and four feet wide. Scott had no retort; he couldn't say Jennifer could possibly be inside the now-gaping pits of either wash. We piled into the SUVs, drove around the curve through the dry creek bed, and gathered in the same pullout lot in front of the Hansmire Gate.

Scott's federal defense attorneys had not accompanied us into the adjacent canyons, so we briefed them on Scott's new claims that Jennifer might be in one of those other places. Megan's boss, Seth, was on the trip for the first time and also seemed to be drinking the Scott

Kimball Kool-Aid. I attempted to relay only factual information about our ventures into the side canyons, trying not to vent that Scott was a lying SOB. I repeated the agreement that we had reached with Scott and his defense investigator, Frank, regarding all of the certainties about Spring Canyon prior to that day's search.

A sheriff's deputy volunteered something none of us expected, "If you're looking for a canyon similar to Spring, there's one down the road at Green River."

Scott pounced, "Let's go check it out. I might've driven that far (with Jennifer)."

Green River was sixty miles from where he had buried LeAnn and over forty miles from where we were standing. It's an impossible drive on dirt roads because they do not exist west of Spring Canyon—you have to drive south to I-70, then west on the main highway for twenty miles, then back north on dirt roads. The drive would take hours. For the past five months, Scott had remained adamant that he did not get on I-70 when he drove by LeAnn's site on his way to bury Jennifer. He had stayed on dirt roads.

I responded quickly and a little too loudly, "That violates every other certainty we've been working under—that you 'drove directly from LeAnn's burial site to Jennifer.' You told us that you were concerned someone might've found LeAnn and put cameras up, remember?[126] So, you took that winding dirt road that we were on last trip, drove to that ranch gate (I pointed to the humongous wooden Hansmire Gate across from our pullout), and put her in the creek bed. Now that Green River's an option for you means *nothing* is factual from the past three months. I can't justify checking you out anymore."

Phil agreed, "We are done."

I do not remember if I rode in the SUV with Scott on the way back to check him into the jail or not. I don't know if I bought him one last Big Mac and fries. I was in a haze because we had failed in our mission and I had no good news for Jennifer's family.

---

[126] Scott said he (or "the driver") drove Jennifer's body up the road toward the canyon where he put LeAnn, then recalled that he got busted years ago by parks and wildlife for poaching in an illegal area. They knew he was doing it and investigators hid cameras in the rocks of Montana. He was seventeen.

## LEANN'S MEMORIAL

Prior to this last search day with Scott, Phil and I reluctantly agreed with the FBI victim witness advocates to fly the families of LeAnn and Jennifer to Utah because the parents wanted to see the area where their girls last existed. Unfortunately, we were confident that Scott was not going to show us Jennifer's location even though we had tried everything in our power to make it happen. In April 2009, the families met us at a hotel in Grand Junction the morning following that last futile, exhausting search with Scott.[127] We gave them the disappointing but not unexpected news: we had not found Jennifer. I escorted LeAnn's parents and sister to her recovery site, while Phil took Jennifer's parents and sister to Spring Canyon.

I drove the family down the dusty road leading from where LeAnn's car had been recovered to the horseshoe canyon with the drill pad. After driving approximately eleven miles to the entrance of Bryson Canyon, Howard told me, "LeAnn would've known she was going to die when Scott pulled into this canyon. There's no other reason to be here."

I had thought the same thing when I first parked in this spot, with Scott all excited in the back seat. And Rob McLeod had said those same words months earlier when we pulled up to the mountain where Kaysi was found.

We hiked up to the spot where LeAnn's remains were found and I told her parents the story of our search. Howard talked about her life and what might have become of her if she had been allowed to reach full adulthood. He said how sorry he was that she had to die in such a horrible manner. He urged us to do everything we could to make certain that Scott was not released from prison so he could never do such a thing to someone else's daughter. Howard gave a very heartfelt, moving speech, breaking down in sobs at times. Everyone there was in tears. He promised that he would come back later to place a memorial there to "turn these rocks into a place of remembrance instead of the scene of a homicide."[128] We walked to the vehicles in silence and drove back to the hotel in Grand Junction.

---

127 Personal journal
128 LeAnn's dad fulfilled that promise and placed a memorial at the recovery site months later.

# 19

# THREE BILLY GOATS GRUFF

I LEARNED weeks later that the search for Jennifer had not been a complete failure. Scott was so excited about the body hunts that he couldn't stop talking to fellow inmates as we were staging the trips. For months leading up to January 2009, he met regularly with his defense attorneys and with Cousin Ed inside the Park County jail. They were collaborating on the material for Ed's book while Scott and Attorney Lynn called me each week to plan things out. The Park County jail is located in the tiny, scenic town of Fairplay, Colorado, about two hours southwest of Denver. Immediately following the body hunts in Utah, Scott was shipped back to the Park County jail for a few months while the prison system figured out where to ultimately place him.

Scott was too smart to confess any hard and fast truths to those around him. None of us who know him think any truth resides in him. Instead, he plays games with the truth much like he did at the waterfall—walking people up close to it, dangling it like a carrot, then leading those around him away from it. He was like a street magician with a red ball in his palm that appears and vanishes at his will.

On May 4, 2009, Captain Dan called me from the Park County jail. He said that three inmates who were housed with Scott told him that Scott had talked to them about killing people. Scott also supposedly revealed some interesting details of his recent trips to Utah. For the sake of simplicity and anonymity, I'll refer to these inmates as Billy Goats 1, 2, and 3. Just as the three goats in the fairy tale grew in stature as they individually encountered the troll under the bridge, these inmates not only increased in size and maturity as I met them, but the details from their interactions with Scott grew in horrific detail.

On May 6, 2009, I drove through scenic mountains and across rivers to Fairplay and spoke with the smallest inmate, Billy Goat 1. He looked like he was fifteen, though he said he was eighteen and the captain confirmed it. He was nervous to speak to me because he was afraid of Scott—he rationally figured if he talked about this killer that he would be killed. I let the captain handle those concerns, explaining that Scott wasn't coming back to Park County, and if by some chance he did, the captain would keep them separate. Billy Goat 1 relaxed a little and said, "Scott told me about body digging in the Utah desert with the FBI."

I confirmed that was true, which helped calm this young man even more. He continued, "Scott said he'd killed a woman who was going to testify in a drug case and they (the FBI) needed to find her body. He told me, 'I killed her because a drug dealer hired me as a hit man. The girl knew too much.' Scott also told me that he would kill anyone if the price was right."

This youngest inmate told me a few more stories of Scott's supposed murders, but most of them sounded like fantasies to me. Scott was playing with this kid. I thanked him for his time.

I stayed in the room with the captain and we next spoke with Billy Goat 2. He was probably in his early twenties and had been in and out of jail for the past five years. He was not as afraid of Scott as Billy Goat 1 had been, and he was eager to talk to me since I was a "fed." Scott also told this young man that he had killed women and men while acting as a hit man. Scott described to Billy Goat 2 how he led the "FBI agents to a woman's skull in Utah," and when he picked up the skull he was slammed to the ground by the agents. Billy Goat 2 said Scott told him that he "tried to draw the trip in Utah out as long as he could." Scott bragged he was "making a show of trying to find one of the girls" and told the FBI, "It could have been there . . . or maybe she's over here."

Scott boasted that he was flim-flamming the FBI and teasing them with phrases like, "Maybe it's in this spot. Maybe the water changed the creek bed or the soil." He fooled the FBI with statements like, "She's in this spot right here. I guarantee it."[129]

This interview proved quite helpful during Scott's sentencing and bolstered our assertions that he violated the plea agreement. These inmates had no way of knowing these facts unless Scott told them. These particular details had never been released to the public.

Even though it was getting late in the afternoon, I asked the captain if I could speak with the third inmate. Billy Goat 3 was almost thirty years old and was in jail for serious charges. He had a glass eye (which was hard not to stare at) and seemed the least intimidated by Scott, or me.

Billy Goat 3 was experienced enough to ask, "What's in this for me if I talk?" By now, I had probably spoken to twenty inmates with whom Scott had played his twisted games, so I knew what to say. I couldn't give these guys a break on their jail sentences or any type of benefit because for twenty years that's exactly what the justice system had given Scott, a break on his sentences—and that didn't work out too well, did it? That being said, I promised to work with the captain however I could, to put in a good word for him. The captain confirmed my no-promises-but-interested spiel.

Scott told Billy Goat 3, "I brought the FBI to the right spot the first time but acted like it wasn't the right place." He added, "I led them around in circles and talked with a geologist about all the dirt that had been sliding down."

Billy Goat 3 added, "Scott believes this entire process is a game—he's just out to prove that he's smarter than you and your team."

Scott told this inmate that while he was out looking for bodies he learned that a flash flood had changed a lot of the land. He said, "I remembered where the grave of one of the girls was—I'd placed her in a little cave and masoned her up with rocks."[130]

After this last revelation, I looked at the captain and shook my head. Billy Goat 3 was describing events he should not know. The "little cave and masoned" statement regarding LeAnn was almost word-for-word what Scott had told me with Attorney Lynn on the

---

129 State of Colorado, County of Boulder v. Scott Lee Kimball. Warrant for Arrest Upon Affidavit. 2009-CR-0001626. Signed October 5, 2009. Received July 26, 2024, p.8
130 State of Colorado, County of Boulder v. Scott Lee Kimball. Warrant for Arrest Upon Affidavit. 2009-CR-0001626. Signed October 5, 2009. Received July 26, 2024, p.17

phone prior to our Utah searches. The flash flood referred to the erosion of soil and rocks that had changed the washes in Spring Canyon. There was no way Billy Goat 3 could know such things without Scott telling him directly. This inmate had precise details of our conversations and searches in Utah that no other human had outside of our team and Scott. This interview provided solid proof that Scott had violated our plea agreement.

Billy Goat 3 perceived his information was valuable and added, "Scott said that he saw that girl's skull and noticed the mandible was missing. He picked the skull up and told the FBI, 'I don't remember her being this tall,' before the agents tackled him. He'd fooled this girl—I think he called her LeAnn—by telling her that he was taking her on a hike as he marched her up the cliff. When they stopped hiking, LeAnn said, 'Scott, your face just changed. I know what this is about.' LeAnn mentioned her boyfriend's name, that I can't remember, and Scott replied, 'Yeah.' He ordered her to take her clothes off and to turn around and get on her knees. Scott said he shot her with a .40-cal in the neck."

Almost word-for-word, Billy Goat 3 echoed the same details I documented of LeAnn's murder and recovery. The part about picking up the skull and getting tackled was fantasy, of course, but the rest of the scene? Wow. Then came one last assertion. And again, Scott's comment would reflect our own thoughts about the events of the day.

"Scott smiled as he told me (Billy Goat 3) that he knows *exactly* where all of these people are buried. He bragged that he buried all of his victims uphill 'cause law enforcement always looks downhill for bodies."[131]

Billy Goat 3 was not done yet. Next he told me about Uncle Terry.

"Scott said his uncle was sexually assaulting one of his boys and he caught him in the act. They got into a huge fight in the house and Scott knocked out his uncle, then he tied him to a wall in the shed and cut off his penis and fed it to the pigs. He let his uncle bleed to death before dumping his body on Vail Pass."

---

[131] Scott would later try to refute these accounts to me, saying they just made stuff up from the news. It goes without saying that none of these conversations or details were public knowledge, much less in the news.

Billy Goat 3 asked me, "Is any of this stuff true? 'Cause I have a hard time believing this shit."

I told him that his interview was extremely helpful, but I could not let him know what was factual and what was not. I explained that he had to remain a witness to what Scott had told him, and if I said what was true or not, it would affect *his* recollection. He nodded his head and said there were a lot more stories, but they sometimes ran together.

Scott also told this inmate about Kaysi, saying, "I worked for a Sons of Silence guy I met in prison—he gave me a list of people and paid me $50,000 per head. Once I was out of jail, I began tracking them down one by one. Maybe the most difficult person to track down was Kaysi, the girl the feds found in the mountains near (Billy Goat 3 couldn't recall the town). Kaysi was going to testify in a drug case against the head of the Sons of Silence, so I figured how I'd get close to her—I targeted her mom (Lori).[132] We met at a casino and she trusted me right away. I eventually even married her just to get near Kaysi. I convinced Kaysi to use Ecstasy with me and I slept with her. You've got to know that very few killers would marry the mother of a target just to get to the target.[133] I killed that one by choking her with a dog collar."

Each of these inmates provided additional stories of Scott chopping up people and sticking them in suitcases, "pink misting" others by blowing their heads off with rifles, and torturing prostitutes with hot coat hangers. To Billy Goat 3, Scott said he "found a pretty prostitute on Colfax Avenue in Denver, took her, and killed her." Billy Goat 3 then accurately described Scott doing something sadistic to her postmortem that was a holdback, something that only the detective on the case would know. None of the Billy Goats knew which stories were true or fantasy, and each of them hesitated to talk about the lurid details because they thought I would dismiss them, laugh at them, or rebuke them for lying to the FBI. Instead, I was completely interested in any words from Scott's mouth and they could sense my curiosity.

---

132 State of Colorado, County of Boulder v. Scott Lee Kimball. Warrant for Arrest Upon Affidavit. 2009-CR-0001626. Signed October 5, 2009. Received July 26, 2024, p.13

133 I believe Kaysi's murder was sexually motivated. I am confident that she was not remotely interested in Scott. The choking reference correlates with not finding her hyoid bone and no other trauma to her remains.

On my drive back to Denver I called Bernard, the Westminster Police Department detective who had come to see me after the press releases about Scott being a serial killer hit the news in 2008. At that time, he told me about his case involving Cat, a victim involved in prostitution who had been severely beaten and tortured, her hands severed and then displayed publicly in a parking lot. I had told the detective back then, "I don't know if Scott did this, but if he ever blames a cellmate for her homicide, then it's him."

Scott did not blame Billy Goat 3 for Cat's homicide, but he told this inmate holdback things that happened to a woman matching Cat's occupation, age, and description with accurate detail. Billy Goat 3 had no reason to know these details because they had not been released to the media. Detective Bernard agreed it was very promising and asked if I was okay with him talking directly to this inmate. The detective was in Fairplay the next day.

Talking to these three inmates put me on a course to investigate other murders Scott may have committed—the ones like LeAnn we did not yet know about. There were specific consistencies in all three Billy Goat stories: Scott said he had killed at least seventeen people, and he had tortured some victims brutally before he killed them, blaming his behavior on his murder-for-hire contracts.

He told the two older goats, "The first time I killed someone I was on a raft. I was thirteen years old on a Boy Scout trip and I watched a fat kid fall out of the boat. I held his head underwater until he drowned. I just wanted to see what it was like."[134]

Two years down the road, Scott would give me a twenty-one piece puzzle that provided additional clarity to the themes I learned from the older goats.

---

134 Personal journal

## 20

# A SURPRISE TRIAL

U.S. District Court Judge Marcia had sternly mandated a June 1, 2009, deadline for us to wrap up our Felon in Possession of Firearms case against Scott. I did not fault her impatience for a second. She was the same judge who heard the arguments for Scott to be released to FBI supervision as an informant in late 2002. That did not work out so well for anyone besides Scott. Then, AUSA Dave filed the gun charges against Scott in June 2006. Because of the prisoner transports to Utah, and Scott's defense attorneys (correctly) wanting to take care of the body hunts first, the firearm matter kept getting pushed back. Judge Marcia was having no more of it.

By June 2009, Scott and his federal defender, Lynn, had agreed to plead guilty to the Felon in Possession of Firearm charge. Dave had disclosed our evidence, including recoveries of the guns and the list of witnesses we could call to support our claims. The hearing to accept Scott's guilty plea was taking place while I was waiting on the ballistics reports from the bullet that killed LeAnn.

During our last trip to Utah in April 2009, Scott had leaned over in the back seat to tell me, "AUSA Dave isn't going to like what's going to happen in the hearing about my guns."

Scott arrived in federal court clean-shaven; his gray hair was long in the back, but he had wetted it down. The whole look was extremely creepy, but he was brimming with confidence. Just before the judge entered the courtroom, the FBI Lab phone number appeared on my cell. I hurried out of the room to take the call. I learned that the DNA from the blood stain on the subfloor of Lori's house on Huron was Uncle Terry's (explained in the next chapter) and LeAnn's skeletal remains were positively identified. I whispered the news to Dave as I took my seat. The hearing began.

Scott's attorney indicated that, against her advice, Scott wanted to take the stand to testify about the handgun and the rifle. He was sworn in and confidently asserted he *never* had possession of the handgun and the rifle qualified under the "sporting exception." Thus, a felon such as himself could legally possess it.

At the prosecution table, Dave was seething because he wasn't given notice by the defense to prepare for any cross-examination. During Scott's testimony, Dave was furiously scribbling notes and when it was time, he took his best shot at Scott. However, Scott boldly asserted once again, under oath, that his brother, Brett, along with Denise, Gamblin, Bender, and Melissa were all liars. So, Dave did the only thing he knew to do—he asked the judge for an opportunity to allow these witnesses to rebut Scott's claims. The request was granted. We were going to trial in a few days on a gun charge that was supposed to be a no-brainer plea deal. Dave, normally in total command and control of the courtroom, was dejected. When the room emptied, he said, "Sorry, Jon-Jon, I let you down today." I told Dave, "Let's get these witnesses in front of the judge and challenge Scott's testimony. He can't get away with blatant lies on the stand." Within the hour, Dave had drafted the necessary subpoenas that would require the witnesses to appear in court. I sent the documents out by email before the day was over.

My weekend was spent apologizing, encouraging, coaching, and then telling the witnesses that each had to appear in federal court next week. The hearing lasted only one day, but the witnesses were phenomenal. Their candor and detail of recollection impressively matched what I had written down when I spoke with them during their initial interviews. Scott took the stand to rebut them, but this time, Dave was ready. He completely destroyed Scott on the witness stand. With spectacles low on his nose and his slightly irritating air of confidence, Dave ripped apart Scott's assertions when compared to the witnesses' testimonies. Judge Marcia had enough proof to rule that Scott was a friggin' liar. Here are a few of the findings from his subsequent appeal:

"The court stated Kimball testified falsely by claiming the applicability of the sporting purpose adjustment and denying relevant conduct concerning possession and use of other firearms, notably the handgun. Based on Kimball's false testimony, the district court applied a two-level enhancement for obstruction of justice and sentenced Kimball to seventy months imprisonment."[135]

Though six years of imprisonment does not seem like a tremendous amount of time to someone like Scott, Judge Marcia ordered it consecutive to any other sentence he might receive in Boulder. This mini-trial, though a total pain, would serve as a drainplug in the event Scott could somehow manage to slip out of the murder charges that were headed his way.

Following the hearing, the U.S. Attorney's Office allowed Dave to speak to the press about the victory and, specifically, what it was like to tangle with Scott. Boulder, Colorado's *Daily Camera* reported, "'He has a very sincere presentation,' said U.S. Attorney Dave Conner, who prosecuted Scott Kimball on federal firearms charges. 'Mr. Kimball always has something to tell you that you want to hear.'"[136]

---

[135] https://www.ca10.uscourts.gov/sites/ca10/files/opinions/01018349505.pdf. Appellate Case 09-1245. Date Filed 1/15/2010. Downloaded July 24, 2024.
[136] John Aguilar, "Chapter 1: On the Loose," *Daily Camera*, March 7, 2010 (Archived from the original on January 12, 2020. Retrieved June 29, 2024.)

## 21

# TRASHED TERRY

Uncle Terry disappeared in August of 2004, within two to three weeks after arriving at Scott's Broomfield house and while Justin was recovering in the Denver hospital from his grave injuries. Terry supposedly won the Ohio State Lottery and relocated to Mexico with a stripper. Now, we knew he was actually on Vail Pass, alone and discarded like garbage—wrapped in a gray tarp with rope around him. We just had to find him and prove that Scott killed him.

I could only prove the negative of anything involving the actions of Terry in his last few weeks on earth. Somebody was involved in a check-kiting operation using Terry's name and ID between July 19, 2004 (just days after Justin's injuries) and November 18, 2004. Terry's MasterCard was used in Alaska to pay for rental cars and hotel fees from September 25, 2004, through September 27, 2004, when it was just Lori and Scott on the trip. The Ohio State Lottery never issued any winnings to Uncle Terry, nor did officials in Mexico have any recorded contact with him.[137] The email that Terry supposedly sent in September 2004 to Scott's dad, Virge, asserting, "Ginger and I are in Mexico and doing great! She doesn't like visitors, so please don't think about coming down," came from a Yahoo! account that was created in August 2005, the day before it was sent.

---

137 State of Colorado, County of Boulder v. Scott Lee Kimball. Warrant for Arrest Upon Affidavit. 2009-CR-0001626. Signed October 5, 2009. Received July 26, 2024. p. 19

Approximately $15,000 cash in Uncle Terry's briefcase from his pending divorce settlement was deposited in two separate transactions—one to Scott's personal account and one to his sick and dying cattle business.

Much like the monster mosquito gorging itself on the sheriff's forehead in Walden, Scott sucked up his uncle's money, along with his identity and any credit associated with Terry's name. With Terry's nomadic and unemployed past, he was an easy fall guy for the check writing scams. Our serial killer started the stealing and sucking by emptying his uncle of his life, blood, and any possible future. It was now our job to find Terry's remains that had been hidden for five years on the side of a snow-covered mountain.

Detective Gary and I went up to Vail Pass once in March of 2009 after we retrieved LeAnn. We thought that we could build momentum and add Terry to our recovered list. Cale, the sheriff of the county for Vail, spent the day with us inside the Snowcats as we ventured back through the logging roads to an area close to the X on Scott's map. We could not get to the specific tree that day because the snow was eight feet deep. What Gary and I thought were full pine trees were merely the top halves showing above the deep snow. Sheriff Cale said he could come up with some snowshoes for cadaver dogs if we wanted to let them out of the vehicles to see if they hit on anything. Though it was an intriguing thought to see what such an endeavor might look like, we decided to wait until the snow melted.

By May 2009, we knew Terry's last verifiable location was at the Broomfield house where Lori had been living with Scott. Gary and I went to ask her where the couch that Terry slept on had been before she saw it covered with vomit on the front porch. She met us, along with our evidence team, at the old house. The property had been vacant for a few years and was run-down from squatters—we marveled at paint cans sticking out of the drywall in the living room. Lori said, "He (Terry) didn't stay in a bedroom, he just slept on the couch. And it was right there (pointing to the middle of the living room)."

We walked with her through the rest of the house to determine if there were any more clues that would reveal what happened to Terry. While standing in the laundry room, Lori commented, "Scott used to always come home late at night and throw his clothes in the laundry, then do his load by himself. I always thought that was weird. He also repainted the laundry room walls before he fled to California. That was weird, too."

Our Evidence Team Leader, Leslie, was eager to see if her squad could help us learn what happened to Terry. They started right away, while Lori took us outside to the barn and the pig pens. Scott had left behind tools, trash, some clothes, and a few boxes of documents. Gary and I were going through those dusty items when Agent Leslie came running up, "You're gonna want to see this!"

We pushed through the plastic draped over the entrance to the house and found Leslie's technicians kneeling around a section of the blue carpet in the living room that had been cut out. They were looking at an eight-inch wide bloodstain on the subfloor. Exactly where Lori said the couch had been on the day Terry disappeared.[138] Leslie told us that they had bagged the carpet and padding already. It was obvious to all of us standing there—Scott had scrubbed the blood through the carpet so it couldn't be seen. Leslie then said, "You've got to see the laundry room!"

The laundry room was darkened as Leslie directed us to look at the left wall next to the washer. She started spraying the wall with Luminol and a faint handprint slowly appeared under the blue light. Only blood would make such a print materialize. It was a man's left hand, with somewhat chubby fingers, and precisely at the position and height on the wall that someone would place his hand to steady himself as if he were taking off his clothes.

The print basically testified, "Scott must've thrown his bloody clothes into the wash one night while Lori was sleeping." They also found traces of blood around the baseboard leading back to the laundry room door.

We sent the results to our lab and received confirmation that the blood in the carpet, the pad, and the floorboard was Terry's. A crime analyst had located Terry's long-lost daughter in Boulder, Colorado, and she agreed to give me a saliva sample for familial comparison.

---

138 State of Colorado, County of Boulder v. Scott Lee Kimball. Warrant for Arrest Upon Affidavit. 2009-CR-0001626. Signed October 5, 2009. Received July 26, 2024, p. 19

Terry's daughter had not spoken to her dad in twenty years, describing him as a drifter and a deadbeat parent.

We did not get confirmation that the blood from the laundry room belonged to Terry because it was too degraded. I still don't know today whose blood that was.

On June 25, 2009, I flew as a passenger in the FBI Cessna plane over Shrine Mountain, the mountain where Terry was supposed to have been discarded. I used a video camera, filming through the plane's window the heavily treed area on the west-facing side of the mountain. I learned after flying in circles for about fifteen minutes that it's not a good idea to film while you are looking through the lens. My skin turned green from the nausea and dizziness—at least it felt green—and I closed my eyes for the rest of the flight. The pilots used the camera attached to the bottom of the plane to complete the video. Other than seeing incredible Colorado scenery and confirming the roads were dry, we didn't accomplish much that day.

## VAIL PASS

Sheriff Cale called to say the snow had mostly melted and that the end of June would work for him and his crew to take us to the spot where Terry should be. On June 29, 2009, Gary and I met ten sheriff's employees from Eagle and Summit counties who agreed to escort us up the mountain.[139] Sheriff Cale had noted that from Scott's map, "the tree" could be found on one of two possible small mountains, so he advised we divide into two groups to cover both. I went with the sheriff and Gary went with the other group. We drove together into the forested mountainside for about thirty minutes until we turned right and Gary's group turned left off the dirt road. Sheriff Cale and I, along with the other three deputies, fanned out and walked down the side of the hill, looking for a gray tarp and the skeletal remains of Terry. After about thirty minutes, Sheriff Cale got a call on the radio that the other group had found him. We hustled over to the

---

139 State of Colorado, County of Boulder v. Scott Lee Kimball. Warrant for Arrest Upon Affidavit. 2009-CR-0001626. Signed October 5, 2009. Received July 26, 2024, p.20

other trail where I found Gary about one hundred feet down from the road. He was pointing at a mass of something gray resting against a large pine tree.

I skidded down through the dirt and pine needles as Gary told me how he had seen the gray material that looked out of place and went to explore. I saw the exposed human spine jutting out from the weathered and gnawed edges of the tarp. The bones were yellowish-white and had no flesh on them. No head, neck, or arms. No blood, hair, or organs. The lower spine disappeared into the tarp and I could see the waistband of Uncle Terry's jeans. A braided rope tightly wrapped and knotted in multiple ties over the tarp kept his waist, legs, and feet intact—appearing to substantially fill in the 3-D form of a large human's lower body hidden under the wrapped material. The body rested against a large pine tree that had prevented it from rolling downhill. The deputies were already finding pieces of Uncle Terry further down the hill. I walked twenty or thirty yards down and helped sort through dead branches and fallen trees. We recovered as much of Terry as we could: pieces of his cranium, his arm bones, and his torn shirt and glasses. This was not a whodunnit, but we still photographed all of the items before we moved anything. Sheriff Cale called the coroner and informed us that it would take an hour or more for him to make his way up there.

I hiked back up to the logging road and discussed with Phil how Scott might have accomplished this. He used his Jeep or truck, or maybe even Terry's Tahoe, to get up these winding dirt roads, then apparently rolled his considerable-sized uncle onto the dirt road. He dragged Terry around until he was parallel to the road and pushed or kicked the wrapped body to start it rolling. Scott's uncle meant nothing to him on Shrine Mountain—simply three hundred pounds of damning trash that needed to be disposed of. This quiet time in the pine trees spent waiting for the coroner was our way of remembering this forgotten soul who had no family to mourn for him.

Sheriff Cale had asked us to go ahead and load Terry and all his parts into the blue body bag and carry him up the hill. Even with five of us, that was quite the workout. We positioned the large bag in the middle of the dirt road—Terry waiting for the coroner to collect him.

Phil and I were sitting about six feet above the dirt road in a grassy spot on the hillside eating sandwiches. With his huge left hand, he pointed across my face to a stump with a flat rock sitting on top of it and asked, "Hey Jon, what's that?"

I took the few steps over to the stump and observed a reddish triangular rock, about eight inches long on each side. Ironically, it had been positioned so it was pointing directly toward the blue mass in the road and the tree beyond it—the exact place where Terry now rested. Looking closely, I saw that an X had been etched into the rock. Phil examined it and said, "Holy shit. That's Scott's marker. He knew he might come back here someday." There was no other explanation. We later wondered what similar signs we had missed with Kaysi, LeAnn, and Jennifer.

## HOT POTATO

You would think the opportunity to examine the victim of a serial killer would be unique and intriguing enough that it would not have been a problem finding a coroner to autopsy Terry. But, like everything else in this case, nobody wanted to touch it. The coroner from the county where we recovered him said he had not been killed there, so he did not want it. The coroner from the county where Terry was shot in the back of the head on Lori's couch said, "We don't know for certain that he died there."

Really?

I could offer conjecture as to why both of these people answered like they did, but let's just move on and focus on the positive. Dr. France, my anthropologist friend, agreed to bail me out of yet another bind and met us at the Arapahoe County Coroner's Office—the only office in the Denver area that agreed to take Terry's remains. On July 6, 2009, Gary, members of my evidence team, and the Boulder prosecutors and I watched Dr. France unzip the blue body bag and go to work.[140] She took out the scattered bone and clothing pieces we

---

140 State of Colorado, County of Boulder v. Scott Lee Kimball. Warrant for Arrest Upon Affidavit. 2009-CR-0001626. Signed October 5, 2009. Received July 26, 2024, p. 21

had found on the hill and laid them out neatly, explaining what each bone fragment was before she placed it on the table. She noted the complex rope knots that held the tightly wrapped tarp around Terry's legs and grouped the loops of rope together to show us that the killer (Scott) had devised a somewhat ingenious pulley system. The knots and loops were intentionally spaced to allow the body to be dragged around efficiently, demonstrating that they could be grouped into a central grip to move the victim around like he was in a cocoon. Our anthropologist was impressed.

She cut the ropes and unwound the gray tarp and found two blood-soaked blankets wrapped around Terry. Once she unwrapped the blankets, tiny, white, wriggly, squirming maggots spilled out everywhere. His legs still had plenty of meat on them, protected by the tarp and cold weather during his almost five-year wait to be recovered. I didn't get sick, but I was certainly unnerved to see what type of almost alien life invades this type of death.

Dr. France was not affected in the least as she wrapped the blankets back around Terry's legs to control the maggots and focused on the puzzle pieces of bones from his head and torso. She picked out four flat, curved pieces of bone and explained to us like we were sitting in her anatomy class which lobes of the cranium she was finding. She held the jagged edges together to form the top and back of Terry's head. It was a complete cranium, except for one perfectly round hole in the top of his head. We all saw it at once—an assassination-style bullet had traveled straight into his brain.[141]

While we stood there gawking at the hole, Dr. France moved on to see where the bullet had lodged. She found Terry's lower left orbital bone and pointed to a rusted metal object lodged inside of it. The bullet slug. Our evidence team collected the slug, packaged it up, and sent it to our lab. Within three weeks, the lab called to confirm what we suspected—the bullet had been fired from the same Firestar handgun used to kill LeAnn.

---

141 The photo on the book cover.

## 22

# SENTENCING

By summer 2009, Team Kimball had recovered three of Scott's victims, two killed by gunshot wounds to the head and one likely by strangulation. We had driven back to Utah twice to search Spring Canyon and the surrounding canyons with cadaver dogs. Sheriff White and his deputies had returned to the canyons we had searched numerous times, hoping to find any clue of Jennifer as they walked miles of creek beds. They called me each time they left the canyons. "Sorry. We got nothing," was the answer each time.

The Boulder prosecutors, Katharina and Amy, asked me to write an affidavit for Scott's arrest for the homicides of our four victims: Terry would be one count of Complicitor for Second Degree Homicide, and Jennifer, LeAnn, and Kaysi would be a separate count. Katharina had spoken to the judge and explained how Scott tried to lead us away from LeAnn at what he called the waterfall, and the games he admitted to playing regarding Jennifer's location. The judge needed documentation, so that fell to me. The information in this affidavit became a pillar of my story to this point, because it provided a summary of how Scott came to know each of the victims, how he killed them and hid them, and his violation of our plea agreement by misdirecting us.

What's a Complicitor and why did we allow Scott to plead to that? Great question. I can see why the problematic DA didn't want to sign our agreement before we went on the body hunts. Complicitor is the same as aiding and abetting, meaning Scott was only *present* during the homicides. Even worse, it implied he was not the principal actor. Worse than worse, we all knew it was first degree (his planning and premeditation were off the charts), but he was pleading to second degree. To understand why, you have to go back to where we sat before we recovered LeAnn or Terry: Scott would not sign any agreement without the exact word "Complicitor" being central to it. If we did not agree, he was going to walk away and we would be left with no cause of death for Kaysi and no other victims coming home to their families. The Deal with the Devil was this deal. We were stuck with it, but we were going to make Scott eat it.

I presented the affidavit to Boulder County Judge Klein in September 2009. I inspected a stationary bike in his chambers to pass the time as he read through the twenty pages. Katharina and Amy had red-inked my draft multiple times until it was grammatically and factually solid. The judge asked me to stand and raise my right hand and swear that the information contained in the affidavit was true to the best of my knowledge. "I swear." He thanked me and signed it.

I spent the next few weeks preparing for the sentencing hearing by looping in the families of the victims, FBI upper management, and the law enforcement agencies that helped us develop probable cause to charge Scott with the murders. He was scheduled to plead guilty to the counts and be sentenced on the same day, October 9, 2009, in the Boulder County Courthouse. It would be another packed house, filled with families and media.

Here are some excerpts from a local news article about the sentencing events that day:[142]

> Tammy Marcum (Jennifer's sister) angrily confronted Scott in court Thursday. "He has yet to show me where my sister's body is. He promised me this and told me he wanted to give her a Christian burial, and that is not possible for my family because we do not have Jennifer's body, her remains," she said. "I ask he think a little harder about where he wants to be

---

[142] Felisa Cardona, "Serial killer Scott Kimball pleads guilty in Boulder, gets 70-year sentence." *The Denver Post*. October 8, 2009. https://www.denverpost.com/2009/10/08/serial-killer-scott-kimball-pleads-guilty-in-boulder-gets-70-year-sentence/ Downloaded on July 6, 2024.

because there is not going to be anyplace for him or his soul if he does not truly repent, until he tells me where my sister is."

Scott Kimball entered the courtroom in a wheelchair because he "hurt his leg," said nothing and showed no emotion.

Ed, a man who described himself as Scott's cousin and spokesman, is writing a book about the case. Ed outraged victims' family members outside the courtroom when he read a statement from the defendant: "I deserve to be held accountable and punished for my crimes," the statement says. "However, I did not act alone. I was part of a very intricate state, regional and international organized crime enterprise that involved millions of dollars."

The FBI spokeswoman declined to comment on the statement. No evidence has been presented that any of Scott's victims were involved in crimes.

The victim's relatives sobbed uncontrollably as they told Judge Klein about the impact from the loss of their family members and how much they loved them. LeAnn's father told the court he does not hate Scott.

"I had a right to hate Scott," he (Howard) said. "In the beginning I did hate him, but I choose not to hate him for two reasons: I know he does not care what I think of him; he only cares about himself. To hate him would only hurt myself."

Mr. Kimball is charged with two counts of murder, but the elected District Attorney said Scott had to agree to take responsibility for all four murders as part of the deal.

Scott began his killing spree in January 2003 while he was working as an FBI informant.

"My sincere condolences to the family," said (the Special Agent in Charge) of the Denver office. "I thank them for their perseverance in making sure they did not fall through the cracks."

LeAnn, 24, disappeared in January 2003. She had told her father she was planning a camping trip.

Jennifer, a dancer at a Glendale strip club, disappeared February 17, 2003. Her car was found abandoned at the Denver International Airport parking lot. Kaysi was reported missing in August 2003. She was never seen after Scott Kimball was supposed to pick her up from a hotel in Thornton. Scott married Kaysi's mother, (Lori), later that year.

Uncle Terry, 60, disappeared in late 2004, shortly after he began to stay with Scott. FBI Agent Jonathan Grusing got to know the serial killer over a three-year period and accompanied him on searches for the victims. He said Scott never showed remorse.

"When we found the remains of LeAnn, he walked up and there was totally no emotion whatsoever."

"Scott's lack of conscience," Grusing said, did not leave room for agents to appeal to his emotions to help them find Jennifer.

"We can't make him feel sorry for the victim's family," Grusing said.

## GUILTY

The jailers wheeled Scott into the courtroom and placed him at the defense table. I was once again in the jury box along with Gary, Phil, and other law enforcement officials. The families of the victims murmured their disapproval over Scott being in a wheelchair; they knew, like me, that he was only "injured" so he did not have to stand for the final sentencing. Judge Klein called for order and directed the prosecuting attorneys and the defense attorneys to enter their representatives into the court record. He explained the order of the proceedings to the attentive courtroom. The Boulder prosecutors and defense attorneys volleyed back and forth, working through the formalities of the wording and their understanding of the day's agenda.

The judge read the charges of second degree homicide and asked Scott how he wanted to plead to the first count. Everything we had worked for over the past three years hung on this manipulative, psychopathic, narcissistic man's next words.

"Guilty, your honor."

The entire courtroom breathed an audible sigh of relief. Shoulders relaxed, some heads bent forward in prayers of thankfulness, and Phil leaned toward me and whispered, "Nice work, Jon!" Scott was now a convicted murderer. A serial killer.

Judge Klein read the second charge and Scott's answer was the same. "Guilty."

Thank God.

Judge Klein spoke as to what these guilty pleas meant and moved on to the victim impact statements before he would hand out the prison sentence for the killings. The following victims spoke, not necessarily in the order I have recalled.

Lori's statement was the most surprising. "I forgive Scott." She said that to hold on to bitterness and anger would be too much to bear and, as a Christian, she was commanded to forgive. We were all expecting her to drop the hammer on the man who married her a week after killing her only daughter. Scott had demonstrated ultimate cruelty and sadism, taking Lori for their honeymoon to the mountainside where he had discarded Kaysi. Those of us who knew Lori were well aware of the grief, guilt, and horror that she bore daily, as she blamed herself for bringing this monster into Kaysi's life. Her gentle statement, however, angered Jennifer's sister, who possessed a fiery personality to begin with. She jumped out of her seat and went to the microphone.

As stated in the news article above, Tammy was plainspoken about what Scott did to their family. Her mother followed and voiced the evil and pain that embodied Scott and anyone he came into contact with. Jennifer's dad, Bob, spoke of his quest to find her killer and Scott's statement to him that he "would never tell where he put her."

LeAnn's parents could barely speak through their intense grief and tears. They provided a clear picture of LeAnn's childhood, promising teenage years, and the life she would never experience thanks to this man.

Kaysi's dad, Rob, said that he "was present when Kaysi took her first breath as she entered this world and Scott Kimball was present as she took her last breath." He painted a plausible picture for the courtroom of what might have been, describing the future children and grandchildren who would never exist—solely because of Scott.

## SEVENTY YEARS

Judge Klein paused for a few moments after the families were finished speaking to allow their grief to settle in for everyone present. He then moved on to the sentencing portion, explaining how all of us had sat in this courtroom months ago with the understanding that Scott would receive a forty-eight-year sentence for the two second-degree murder charges if he led us to the three missing victims. He acknowledged the facts set forth in my affidavit, saying it was clear that Scott did not intend to lead us to LeAnn as evidenced by his actions on March 11th and his statements to us that day. Furthermore, Scott had admitted to other inmates that he was playing games with us and leading us in circles in our quest to find Jennifer. Scott had breached his agreement, giving the judge the freedom for an upward departure in sentencing. He sentenced Scott to seventy years in prison.

There was no look of surprise on any face at the prosecution or defense tables—they had worked this out ahead of time. However, the families exhaled sobs mixed with relief and vindication. This killer was not getting out to terrorize society again.

If Cousin Ed was inside the courtroom, nobody noticed him until we walked out with celebration on our minds. He positioned himself on the stairs across from the foyer and loudly announced that he had something to say on behalf of Scott. I was standing near Lori and Rob as we listened to this socially awkward, middle-aged man dressed in a heavy leather bomber jacket and wearing a patriotic ball cap. Cousin Ed said that he was Scott's spokesperson (not an enviable job, I thought) and had a prepared statement that had been cited earlier in the media report.

Scott's claim, through Cousin Ed, was that "these murders involved an international crime ring." Outlandish but not surprising. But Ed's statement that Scott's being an FBI informant "drove him into the extremely dangerous underworld" outraged Lori. I watched her tense up as Cousin Ed continued talking about Scott being "a member of the Montana Freemen" and of his "heartfelt sympathies to the families."[143] Lori finally interrupted, "Ed, you have no idea what you're talking about! Scott killed my daughter all by himself. You should be ashamed for bringing this shit up today."

Cousin Ed shot back, "Lori, you should take some responsibility yourself for Kaysi's death!" Everyone gritted their teeth at that assertion. Deputies stepped in to remove Ed, hoping to prevent someone from beating this man senseless. Once the disturbance was silenced, our prosecution team quietly slipped away to a Mexican restaurant in Boulder and celebrated a rare victory over Scott with chips, queso, and margaritas.

My celebration did not last long, however. I was already working with Detective Bernard from Westminster on his investigation of Cat's murder. She was on our radar screen because of Scott's homicide boasts to Billy Goat 3. Cat must have been more than a murdered prostitute, so I began my venture into learning who she was.

I also learned a week later that Scott had been pulling strings behind the curtain of his jail cell to sprinkle his pixie-dust on Cousin Ed, local news reporters, and his defense attorneys. He continued to insist that this whole murder plea agreement was an FBI cover-up. Scott supposedly provided proof to Ed that I had framed him for the four homicides and made him the fall guy.

---

143  Ed Coet, *SLK Serial Killer* (Publishamerica, Inc., 2010), 462

## 23

# I FRAMED SCOTT KIMBALL

SCOTT HAD accused me a handful of times of lying—he said I had lied on the search warrant and arrest affidavits, on my agreements to check on why his TV was not working, his prison phone privileges being revoked, and on and on. I answered each time, "Scott, I have no reason to lie, especially on a court document. This is an important case, but you're not worth losing my job, possibly my family, and even my freedom to knowingly *lie* on anything. I wrote down what people told me or where the evidence led me." He never accepted that explanation, though, figuring that if he lied all the time, I must be doing the same.

On Wednesday, February 10, 2010, I woke up at 4:50 a.m. and went for a run in the cold morning air. A slight breeze brought tears to my eyes because of the chill. I ate a quick breakfast, said goodbye to April and the kids, and got to work at 6:45 a.m. I went through some leads before heading to the Sterling Correctional Facility (SCF) near the Colorado-Nebraska border to interview Scott about Cat's murder. Detective Bernard was with me.

For the last few months, I had been completely engaged in the homicide investigation of a local prosecutor, a case totally unrelated to Scott. I had been able to forget about Scott for that brief period of time, but my knowledge of his hidden life came rushing back as I talked with Detective Bernard about interview strategies during the drive. I explained we must be prepared to walk away and end the interview, otherwise

Scott would bleed us dry of all the case details, while we would walk away with nothing. We needed to show him that we were serious about investigating every detail of Cat's death and his involvement. I talked to Bernard about the respect Scott would demand from us, and how he would shut down if he thought we were treating him any differently than we would treat a fellow cop. I knew Bernard was easygoing and would not offend Scott by being an in-your-face interviewer.

Once we were in the prison conference room Scott was brought in by the guard. He greeted me warmly, smiling and shaking my hand. Is that a good thing? I introduced Detective Bernard and explained that he had some questions. Scott said, "That's fine, and I'm more than willing to clear up any investigation on anything else. I've already pleaded guilty to any and all deaths that I was involved in. It won't take us long to clear up any other misunderstandings."[144]

Scott quickly knocked Bernard off balance, alleging that the detective was "insulting his intelligence by beating around the bush." He told Bernard, "Detective, maybe you should let Agent Grusing ask the questions."

Bernard was patient, though, and worked through the firestorm while I put Scott at ease, again telling him we both knew how intelligent he was and that he would never confess to something he did not do. We went back and forth with Scott, dueling with him while he continued to assert his innocence. It was déjà vu. I was back in Montana in 2007, interviewing Scott for the first time when he swore, "Kaysi and Uncle Terry are still alive and I only *heard* about Jennifer's death." I smiled as I recalled the very same phrases and professions of innocence he was using now. Scott caught the smile and asked, "Is something funny, Jon?" probing to see if I had made the cardinal mistake of mocking him about something. I passed it off, "No, Scott, sorry. My mind was wandering somewhere else. Nothing to do with you." We ended the interview when I said I had to get going. Bernard and I left thinking that Scott was certainly interested in Cat and our evidence but unwilling to take any responsibility for her death.

As we rode back to Denver I bounced something off Bernard that didn't sit right with me. Near the end of the interview, I told Scott it

---

144 Personal journal

was plausible that other victims like Cat were out there. I used my interview with Steve 2 as proof—Scott did not volunteer anything about LeAnn until Jennifer's Steve told me about her in late 2007. Then she was added as part of the plea deal.

Scott had countered with, "So you say."[145] He gave me a mischievous grin and I knew he was referring to the rumor being spread through Cousin Ed that Detective Gary and I knew about the deaths of LeAnn, Kaysi, and Jennifer much sooner than I had cited in my affidavit. I didn't see what Scott gained from this narrative, but I acknowledged his Cheshire Cat grin and told him that I had heard of the conspiracy gossip.

I did not know at the time that Scott had doctored three of my official FD-302 investigative report documents into a seven-page ramble that fit his government conspiracy, clearly casting me as a liar and him as the fall guy.

## HE'S NOT GUILTY!

By March 2010, Lourdes, the *48 Hours* producer assigned to the Kimball story, had spent significant time with me and "KW," our Denver FBI media coordinator. Following Scott's sentencing, we were given the green light from FBI Headquarters to talk to *48 Hours* for their documentary. Lourdes, Harold, Cindy, and their crew had interviewed Scott in the Sterling prison the previous day. They were fascinated by his magnetism and repulsed by his arrogance and lies. Lourdes called while I was in Phil's office and I put her on speaker. I wanted to be sure either KW or my boss heard any conversations I had with the media.[146]

With uncharacteristic hesitancy, Lourdes said, "So, uh, I don't know if I should be telling you guys this at all, but Cousin Ed sent your local news reporter, Jay, some FBI documents I think you should see. The station is going to air the contents of these reports at six."

Phil and I looked at each other. I said, "Well, thanks for the heads up, Lourdes, we're happy to look at them if you'll send them to us."

---

145  Personal journal
146  Personal journal

A few seconds later, I showed Phil printed copies of the three "FBI scanned reports" as we called Lourdes back. She said, "Scott told our *48 Hours* interviewers that he had six hundred more documents like this FD-302, which prove a government conspiracy."

I was reading the first document while Lourdes was talking. I was initially impressed by the format, layout, and verbiage, until I read it more closely. Scott had spelled my name "Jonathon," and in bold type at the top of the page, "Federal Bureau of Investigations." For those not grossly familiar with the FBI, there is no "s" on the end. I told Lourdes of my two initial finds as we continued to read through Scott's grandiose tale. In his version, Gary and I had interviewed Steve, Jennifer's boyfriend, before I was even assigned the case. My forged FD-302 asserted that I spoke with Steve in February 2006, not October 2007, and that the "whole picture" had been laid out to us by Steve.

In this work of fiction, I immunized Steve and falsely charged Scott with the murders, though Scott was only a small part of a big drug ring. Scott got carried away near the end of his prose when he described in salacious detail a dream home he and Steve had purchased. In the fantasy house, college girls would take their clothes off for cameras all day long and thus live rent free. I knew it was Scott's writing because of the sexual deviancy reflected in this fantasy that accelerated as the paragraphs continued. The snuff film images on his laptop and his conversations with Gamblin came to mind as sex fantasies gave way to darker passions. Scott wove Jennifer and LeAnn into my supposed interview, saying they were at the "nude party house," as he fantasized about LeAnn performing repulsive acts.

*48 Hours* interviewed me the next day about the false documents. They asked me about two other fake interviews Scott had dreamed up and typed out involving Dr. Alderman and Billy Goat 2, both former cellmates. He portrayed me as interviewing Dr. Alderman in October 2005, over a year before I was assigned to the Kimball case. The doctor was discussing his ventures involving strippers and Ecstasy in Las Vegas. (Uncle Terry winning the lottery and moving to Mexico with a stripper was more believable, I thought.) The fake document written about Billy Goat 2 alleged disgusting things about Kaysi that were not even remotely true. The fake documents read like a diary, detailing my schemes and plans to frame innocent Scott, even though one report did say he "bragged that he'd killed seventeen people."

Lourdes asked me, "Why would Mr. Kimball include such horrific details about these dead girls?"

I replied, "If he could dirty the memory and reputation of these victims, his brutal crimes of murder would not appear to be so heinous."

That same day, Cousin Ed found out the documents were fake and called Phil while I was still in Phil's office. Ed said, "I feel like a total fool." He explained that he had paid Scott $300 for copies of the thousand-plus pages of Scott's discovery, which included all of my FBI reports Ed was using to write his book. Inside my reports were seven pages of the alleged FBI conspiracies to frame Scott. The "facts" contained in my so-called interview where Steve confessed to the cover-up in February 2006, had prompted Ed to read Scott's statements out loud after the Boulder sentencing to stir up the victim's families. Phil decided to have a little fun with Ed for being fooled by Scott's trick, asking, "Ed, how do we know that *you* didn't forge those documents?"[147]

With a tremor in his voice, Ed said, "Lynn (Scott's federal defender) got the thousand pages directly from Scott, and he got them straight from Megan (Scott's state defender). When Lynn saw the 'Steve document' that outlined how Scott had been framed for the murders, she called me and I got copies. I then called the news stations. I felt sorry for Scott at his sentencing, knowing that he was taking the fall for the FBI. I never thought he'd be able to forge FBI documents in prison!"

Ed said I should call Lynn right away because she was taking this harder than he was. He agreed to turn all of his documents over to the FBI office closest to him. We sent an agent to retrieve them that week.

Lynn told me, "Scott gave me the discovery that came from Megan. He only had it in the Sterling prison for a few days before I got what he had to make my copies. It didn't even enter my mind that *anyone* could type up forged documents in prison, much less FBI ones! I've been holding on to these for months, thinking that you were sending an innocent person to prison. On the day of sentencing, I drove around the Boulder courthouse for hours, crying in my car, trying to figure out any way to keep Scott from taking the deal. He was resolute,

---

147  Ed Coet, *SLK Serial Killer* (Publishamerica, Inc., 2010), 476

though, telling me, 'I'm going through with it.' I can't believe he pulled this off. I can't believe he did this to me. I feel so stupid!"

I told Lynn, "Everyone who spends time around Scott feels stupid. The closer you are to him, the more you're going to lose to him. You've done as well as anyone could've done to shepherd him through the plea deal."

I called Randy, the lead investigator at the Sterling prison, and told him what had happened. I had to explain it twice because he couldn't believe it. "We're the most secure prison in Colorado besides the penitentiary. That stuff just doesn't happen here. But I'll look into it."

One week later, I drove to Sterling to meet with Randy. He had already pulled Scott's belongings from his cell and had them waiting in a conference room for me to examine. I spent about two hours searching through Scott's porn, hidden in his prison box, to find the original false documents he had manufactured. The typed pages were an interesting read, as they provided a further glimpse into how Scott saw himself. He believed he was the victim of a federal government conspiracy, but he was highly confident that he was smarter than the government. He took responsibility for *talking* a lot about death and being a hit man, even the killing of Uncle Terry. He wrote about the house he supposedly rented out to college girls in 2003. The girls agreed to pay no rent as long as Scott could "install cameras in their showers and they agreed to walk naked through the house." Some of his other fantasies were included, the details of which I have purposely forgotten. The warden heard about my visit and my collection of the fake documents. He learned through an internal investigation that his librarian had allowed Scott access to her computer for an unknown period of time, shortly before he received the discovery from Megan. The warden was livid. Scott was going to have to find a different prison to spend his time in.

Scott's stunt was simple but effective. The Boulder DA's office had numbered the documents in the bottom right corner from one to a thousand-some. The numbers were handwritten, so all Scott had to do was make certain that his forged FD-302s were the same page length as my documents and that his handwritten numbers resembled the others. He slid his three fakes in and guided Lynn to review the "Steve" report. Scott's con caused his cousin Ed and his defense attorney, as well as those around them, to panic—we were the ones who had to extinguish Scott's wildfires of conspiracy and cover-up.

## THE LAST SKELETONS

On February 12, 2010, I drove Uncle Terry's remains to a funeral home to be cremated. Nobody was waiting there to watch the cremation. I had spoken with Terry's brother and Scott's dad, Virge, to make the arrangements. I also let Terry's ex-wife and daughter know—they were appreciative but did not ask any questions or show much interest. I thought about the long and difficult road we had traveled to find this poor soul in the wilderness. I wondered if we would, by some miracle, ever find Jennifer, as I watched the box containing Terry's skeletal pieces disappear in the flames.

On February 23, 2010, I checked out a large box containing the remains of LeAnn from the FBI evidence room. After I signed the evidence log and took custody of the box I walked to the elevator. The fire alarm suddenly went off and the elevators were shut down. The funeral home manager was waiting for me and I didn't want to reschedule, so I carried the sealed cardboard evidence box down the eighteen flights of stairs of the federal building. With the alarm echoing in the concrete stairwell, it felt like an odd sort of processional to honor LeAnn. In the basement of the parking garage, I placed the box in the back seat and began driving to the crematory. I turned off the radio out of respect for LeAnn and her family during the trip. I thought about her tragic ending in the Book Cliffs of Utah and her unrealized potential as a nurse, a bride, and a mother. I thought of her sister's statements at Scott's sentencing, that LeAnn had no chance at being an adult because Scott had stolen that portion of her life from her. The mortuary director signed the release of property for the box, inspected it, and placed it in the incinerator. I called Howard as I was leaving and tears sprang to my eyes because he was crying. He told me he wished he had stopped her from leaving the house that day she set out to go caving in Mexico.

On March 3, 2010, I took Kaysi's remains from the FBI evidence room to a mortuary in Wheat Ridge, Colorado. On March 10, 2010, a memorial service was held for Kaysi at Bethlehem Lutheran Church with two hundred people in attendance, including Kaysi's family members and friends, Detective Gary, the Boulder prosecutors, and me.[148] LeAnn's parents and Jennifer's parents flew in to attend as well. I attempted to suppress images about the awfulness of what had happened to Kaysi as I watched her casket descend into the earth at the gravesite. I was grateful that Kaysi's parents were able to remember her in this way and that Scott would never have the freedom to do this to another family.

---

148  https://kaysi2.rssing.com/chan-16454715/latest.php. Downloaded on July 7, 2024.

## 24

# LARISSA REVISITED

IF THERE is a central figure to Scott's frustration, misdirection, and murderous thoughts and regret, it's Larissa, the mother of his boys. She had the courage to divorce him. Like the rest of us, she was deceived and manipulated by him, but she walked away from him many times when no one else would. Chapter 25 will summarize the two years of my life spent looking into a fifth homicide possibly committed by Scott, which I believe was a rage-kill because he kept losing to Larissa.[149] He misspoke to me and his cellmates a few times, saying that he killed Larissa when he left her by a dumpster. He tried to have Steve 2 kill Larissa if Steve 2 could escape from prison, but that plan did not work out. In these instances, Scott was talking to me and several cellmates about *someone* he actually killed, most likely a proxy for this brave woman who continually thwarted him. I kept speaking with Larissa throughout this investigation because Scott kept bringing her up in monitored phone calls and during our interviews in jail cells. As Scott's frustration with Larissa mounted, I kept looking into what happened in Spokane from 1997 through 2001, those terrible years that had scarred her mind and soul. This time period also provides a glimpse into why Scott was able to manipulate the FBI in Alaska and

---

149 My definition of "losing" regarding Scott entails Larissa's perseverance through the atrocities that I'm about to describe and willingness to look candidly at herself and Scott, admit her errors in judgment, and move forward in an attempt to live a better life apart from him.

Denver so effectively—he had four years of watching how Spokane PD, better yet law enforcement in general, reacts to violent crimes in their reporting, investigation, interviews, and treatment of information as it funnels into them. It was a tutorial on how informants are treated. Scott was being treated as an informant and so was Larissa, simultaneously. Scott learned more every time, getting a little better and bolder with his abductions as he was preparing for the big stage in Denver and the national spotlight.

From Spokane Police Department (SPD) Report 99-343834, dated December 18, 1999,[150] Larissa called at 10:40 a.m. to say, "I was raped by my ex-husband, Scott Kimball." She brought a friend with her to the department for support. The detective asked if she would submit to a rape kit and she replied, "It wouldn't do any good. He always makes me take a bath and he did that again." Larissa continued, "Scott had the boys, Justin and Cody, at his house for the weekend, and he came to my house at 11:30 p.m. last night. He said, 'I want to have sex with you,' and I asked him to leave. After he left I fell asleep. I awoke at 2 a.m. with Scott on top of me as I was lying on my stomach. I could feel a gun pressed against the back of my head."

(I'll skip through the forced sex paragraphs, as Scott used handcuffs and threats with the revolver, and made her bathe for twenty minutes to remove evidence, then handcuffed her to a door while he showered.) Larissa showed the detective the red marks on her wrists, from the times she intentionally pulled the cuffs against the wrist bone to prove this was not a nightmare or an attempt to malign her ex-husband. The detective noted "such marks," but embedded a tone into the report that suggested she probably did this to herself. Larissa stated that Scott forced her to send four voicemails to his phone. She kept having to redo them because they were not to his liking, but she could not tell the detective what the messages entailed. Scott wiped his fingerprints from whatever he touched in her bedroom and bathroom, ordered her to put her hand on the gun, and flushed his condoms down the toilet. During one of the assaults in the bedroom, Larissa had a few seconds to try to call 911, and Scott said, "Go ahead, it won't work."

---

150 Damon Antal, "Kimball Files." Alternative Reality Television. Received by Jonny Grusing, August 5, 2024. (Attachment p.114)

Scott reconnected the phone line and warned her, "If you tell the police, I'll just do this to you again."

The detective asked her for a written statement and she wrote in all capital letters, "I HAVE CODY NOW, HE HAS JUSTIN NOW!!" She went on to describe the assault, the abduction, and her visit to the hospital on December 6, 1999. She wrote that the same course of events occurred *again* on December 18, 1999. When Larissa filed the next report, she explained, "If I press charges or get a restraining order, he'll just do it again."[151] There is no need to expound upon handwriting and statement analysis to explore the desperation of her statement.

The detective asked Larissa if they could go to the house to collect the bedsheets, but she said that she was too scared to return. He said he would be with her, so together they went to the house and collected the sheets. He noted in his report, "There were no signs of a physical struggle."

Larissa said to him in what had to be exasperation, "This is the fourth time I've been raped by him. The last one was on December 6th (1999)." When the detective asked why she did not have a protective order against Scott, he noted, "She just looked at me with a somewhat dumbfounded look." No charges were filed.

Larissa *had* filed for a protection order on September 12, 1998, but Scott had steamrolled over it on the day it was served to him while in jail. No wonder a dumbfounded look appeared on her face a year later, when asked about it by the detective.

A six-page declaration by Scott, filed through a Spokane attorney on September 17, 1998, delineated dates and times of intimate periods with Larissa and of his time spent with Justin and Cody, in an effort to quash the order of protection that was filed on September 12, 1998.[152] (Scott was served the protection order while in jail on September 16, 1998.) Attached to Scott's declaration was a letter from Larissa, in which she asserted, "Since October 1997, Scott has shown great enthusiasm toward the boys and been an active part of their lives.

---

151 Damon Antal, "Kimball Files." Alternative Reality Television. Received by Jonny Grusing, August 5, 2024. (Attachment p.309)
152 Damon Antal, "Kimball Files." Alternative Reality Television. Received by Jonny Grusing, August 5, 2024. (Attachment p.292)

He has been prompt in paying child support and often stops by with groceries. The boys thoroughly enjoy having their father around."

In response to Scott's request that the protection order be quashed, the judge ruled, "This court should immediately proceed to hear the respondent's motion to modify the order for protection and allow the status quo as it relates to parenting arrangements to resume." The protection order Larissa asked for was thus dismissed.

In one of my many calls to Larissa during 2008 as I was receiving the reports, she told me that in December 1999, while she was sitting in the passenger seat of Scott's Jeep, he began stabbing himself in the arm with a small pocketknife. I learned from these reports that the stabbing happened on the afternoon of December 18, 1999, after she filed the report with the Spokane PD and the detective visited the house. Scott filed a request for a protection order against Larissa with Spokane PD on December 21, 1999[153] with his own written statement, "On Dec 18th, my ex-wife Larissa Kimball punched me in the face and stabbed me eight times in the arm with a small pocketknife. She told me she is going to kill me, kill our children, then kill herself. I fear for the lives of my children and my own life. She said she would kill Justin and Cody our sons before she will let me see them."

And that is why no charges were filed.

These abductions happened sporadically over the next three years. Larissa told me that she and Scott had periods of peace, even romance, and a semblance of marriage during 1999 and 2000, while he was in and out of jail. However, those détentes abruptly ended with violence, assaults, and mind games. Larissa had blocked many of the incidents from her memory entirely. Per my suggestion, she submitted to a session with a forensic hypnotist that I observed in 2015. During that session, she was able to recall additional attacks clearly, one of which was the final kidnapping in August 2001. It was this attack that finally resulted in criminal charges against Scott.

---

153  Damon Antal, "Kimball Files." Alternative Reality Television. Received by Jonny Grusing, August 5, 2024. (Attachment p.178)

## THE FINAL KIDNAP AND ASSAULT

On August 1, 2001, Larissa called Spokane Police and reported that she had been kidnapped.[154] Officers arrived and found her sitting on the couch looking "very tired but calm." She reported that Scott had been in prison in Montana but had skipped out on parole. She received a call that he was "in the wind" a day earlier, so she locked her doors, and called the police and requested extra patrols. Scott called her from a blocked number and said, "My P.O. falsified my UA (urinalysis test) and I'm never gonna see my kids again." When Larissa told him he should turn himself in, he hung up.

At 3 a.m. the next morning, Larissa "heard the sound of knees popping and cracking and knew that Scott was in the house." He came into the bedroom, threatened her, and said, "We're going to Denver to see my boys."[155] He handcuffed her right wrist to the shoulder strap of the seatbelt and drove the Jeep to the gas station. As he was filling the Jeep with gas, Larissa raised her handcuff to show the attendant, but he either did not see it or ignored it. They stopped in Lewiston, Idaho, and Scott paid cash for a motel room. He made Larissa call friends and co-workers to inform them she did not feel well. As Scott drove her south the next day she began to cry. He told her, "You've pushed me over the limit." He stopped in a desolate area, then duct taped her legs together at the ankles and handcuffed her wrists together in front. He laid her in the back seat, and while holding a knife taken from her butcher block to her throat said, "If you lift your head, I'll stab you with the knife. One stab to the heart will kill you."

Scott eventually changed his mind about driving to Denver and took her back to Spokane, arriving at her house at 11 p.m.

Larissa told the detective that Scott had bragged about using a credit card to get past the door lock in the garage and that he had hidden in the crawl space until she came home. Larissa's neighbor, Denise, told the detective that the day before Larissa disappeared she was very worried about Scott being on the run and had stayed that night at Denise's house.

---

154 Damon Antal, "Kimball Files." Alternative Reality Television. Received by Jonny Grusing, August 5, 2024. (Attachment p. 277)

155 Larissa sent Justin and Cody to stay with Scott's mom, Barb, for weeks at a time while these periods of violence with Scott continued to happen.

The next day after Larissa returned home, Denise noticed that Larissa did not put her trash cans out front like she normally did. She knocked on Larissa's door and found it open and unlocked. Denise called the police and told them that she could not reach Larissa by phone. When the police officers arrived, she showed them how the phone lines around Larissa's house had been cut. Officers searched the house and found a makeshift bed up in the crawl space along with soda cans.

The detective wrote, "Larissa said that Scott told her that police would believe him over her because he was so convincing. She stated that she has reported numerous rapes and kidnaps to the police and Scott has never been charged. Larissa said that she's putting her house on the market and moving to Denver where Scott's mom, Barb, can help raise her children. I asked what Scott will do and she stated, 'Spend more time in prison, I hope. He will probably follow me wherever I go.'"

In September 2001, Spokane PD finally filed kidnapping and assault charges against Scott Kimball for this last incident. Scott had to form a powerful ally to get out of his first serious charges, so he changed his name, and sailed to Alaska where he first became an informant for the FBI.

# 25

# CAT

WHILE WE were in the middle of searching for Uncle Terry back in June 2009, I took an afternoon to drive to the west Denver home of Cat's sister. Detective Bernard told me this woman, Dachelle, was the only known relative of Cat, and was the person who identified Cat from the news stories. No one else was seeking justice for Cat, as had been the case with Uncle Terry, because of her vulnerable lifestyle and terrible childhood. Dachelle stepped out onto the front porch of an older duplex to greet me. She was not what I expected, rather, she was beautiful, intelligent, quiet, and emotionally tired, with long brown hair and discerning eyes. She told me that Detective Bernard had recently informed her that Scott was possibly the person responsible for her sister's murder, adding that she had seen the news stories about this serial killer. I explained that, yes, it was entirely possible, but we had a long way to go before we could determine if that was true.

Dachelle said, "I'm not really Cat's sister. I'm her sister-in-law. I married Cat's brother who's in jail down south and is gonna be there for quite a while. He was abusive to both of us, and even though I love him he should probably stay in prison.

"Cat and my husband were raised in an extremely dysfunctional foster home and neither of them knew who their bio parents were. For a year before she was killed she got involved in heavy drug use, then turned briefly to prostitution to pay for her drugs. She disappeared for days at a time."

When Dachelle saw the news coverage she didn't even know Cat was missing.

Here's an excerpt from a subsequent news story, months after my first interview with Dachelle:

> FBI informant-turned-serial-killer, Scott Kimball, is under investigation in the unsolved 2004 murder of a woman whose mutilated body was dumped behind a strip mall in Westminster, according to a family member.
>
> Dachelle told *The Denver Post* on Tuesday that a detective involved in the case has told her that Scott is being investigated as a potential suspect. The woman also said she has been interviewed by the FBI agent heading the investigation of Scott, who has pleaded guilty to four murders committed after he was freed from prison to act as an informant in a drug case.
>
> Cat, a 26-year-old who had struggled with drugs, was bludgeoned late the night of Oct. 24, 2004, or early the next morning. Her killer severed her hands—perhaps to conceal her identity. She had 'Lil Cat' tattooed on her left hand, her sister-in-law said. Her nude body was dumped behind a strip mall in the 7500 block of Sheridan Boulevard.
>
> If Scott is ultimately linked to the murder, it would be the fifth killing tied to him following his release from federal prison in December 2002—a move that was made after he convinced an FBI agent that his cellmate had asked him to kill a witness in a drug case.
>
> Cat had a difficult life—she and her brother were abandoned by their parents, and she had problems with drugs and scrapes with the law. Dachelle, who noted that the three women Scott has been convicted of killing all had difficult lives, said that that vulnerability could have made her a target.
>
> "She didn't do drugs all the time," Dachelle said. "The way that they basically present her to the public was that she was

this hooker and she was this druggie. Not true. Every time I saw her, she was sober and she was hungry and she was clean and she loved to play with my daughter, and she was happy."

After Cat was killed, her sister-in-law began a drive to raise money to buy her a headstone but has received about a third of what she needs. In the meantime, she regularly visits the unmarked grave, leaving flowers in the grass. "Nobody knows there was a real person there," she said. [156]

Dachelle's statement is exactly what Scott attempted to narrate with each of his victims. "There's not a real person there, no one we should be looking for, a drug dealer, child molester, or runaway." However, I saw Scott's victims through the lens of the family members—a daughter with promise who was beginning to figure life out, their baby girl who was loved even through pain and heartache, and the potential mother of children and grandchildren whose next fifty or seventy years was taken without consent or warning.

I spent the next two years investigating Cat's homicide with Bernard at my side. Cat supposedly worked at Taco Bell in Aurora, Colorado for three months *after* she was murdered. At least, that's what her social security number told us. I was interested in this particular lead because her purse and backpack were never recovered. I wondered if the thief, or someone who knew the thief, was the Taco Bell employee working under Cat's name. It took me a couple of months to track down former Taco Bell managers and to persuade one to take me to their records warehouse. He watched as I pulled down boxes filled with employee records, standing on the top rung of an eight-foot ladder, hoping to find her application. (Just before I grabbed the top box, off-balance, ladder swaying, I thought about calling my wife, April, to tell her and the kids I loved them.) The Taco Bell manager, unsuccessfully suppressing a small grin, watched with interest as I made my way down the ladder. After checking the records in that particular box, I found that someone had stolen Cat's identity. The former employee was not Cat.

---

156 Kevin Vaughan, "Serial killer Kimball investigated in 2004 unsolved murder." September 14, 2010. https://www.denverpost.com/2010/09/14/serial-killer-kimball-investigated-in-2004-unsolved-murder Updated September 21, 2018, Downloaded July 23, 2024

I tracked down the not-Cat former employee and she admitted to writing down Cat's name, social security number, and birthday. She took Cat's paperwork when it was lying on the clerk's desk as she (not-Cat) was being booked into the Aurora jail for a misdemeanor. (Cat's homicide was circulated through law enforcement circles back in 2004, which is why the paperwork was in Aurora.) Not-Cat did not know Cat or anything about her backpack. Not-Cat was not here legally, so I turned her over to immigration. Another dead end.

## FINALLY, A FAILED POLY!

In August 2010, I took Bernard back to Sterling Correctional Facility for the second round of questioning Scott about Cat. The detective had done his research. Using Scott's gas receipts, he found a secret trip to the Denver area on the day Cat was killed, when Scott alleged he was in California. I had a subpoena from Boulder DA Katharina to collect all of Scott's discovery he had received from her office and the FBI, prompted by his fake FBI reports scam. Scott and Bernard dueled over the legitimacy of the gas receipts for a while. I finally chimed in and explained that Billy Goat 3 had shared details of Cat's homicide, which he learned directly from Scott. Of note, these were details that only the killer would know.

Instead of dismissing the claim or showing curiosity, Scott said, "Maybe, Jon, you should stop wasting time on me and start looking at him (Billy Goat 3) as your suspect."

Bernard and I glanced at each other and almost winked, but that definitely would have sent Scott through the roof. He had finally pointed at his cellmate as being involved in Cat's death. That opened a bigger can of worms, however. Scott knew he should not have let that accusation escape from his mouth, especially in front of me. So, as a diversion, he demanded that I review the details of all his suspected homicides. As I did so, he disputed established facts on the four known victims of the already solved Boulder cases. He blamed the three females for pestering him for sex, then he began boasting about the fifty women he'd slept with. We discussed a long list of other items that day, ending with Scott's assertion that he would take a polygraph test about Cat's murder.

A month later, Richard, our FBI polygrapher, found himself sitting with me in front of Scott, looking at the list of 124 questions that Scott had prepared for us to ask him. Richard thanked Scott for the suggestions, then announced that he would start with his own five questions about Cat. That was my cue to leave the room. The polygraph did *not* go well for Scott. Two hours later, Richard asked Bernard and me to come back into the room. Once we were seated, he informed us, in front of Scott, that his answers about "not being involved in Cat's death" were "deceptive." It was one of the few times I saw Scott lose control of his emotions. He started mad-crying, screaming he did not know why he failed the test. More importantly, Scott said, "If I told you what my cellmate told me about Cat, you'd think I did it."

There it was, again.

Bernard thought we had enough to file the case, especially if we could get Terry's Tahoe from Mexico and could prove Cat's blood was inside. Terry had been killed three months before Cat, yet his Tahoe was parked and abandoned in Westminster only blocks from Cat's recovery site. It was parked in the exact area where the cadaver dog had tracked the killer's scent after picking it up from where the killer had touched Cat's right calf. I knew the Tahoe had been in that area, based upon the evidence of a parking ticket from early October 2004, just weeks before Cat was murdered. Scott played a few shell games with the title for the Tahoe before it wound up in Mexico after November 2004. An FBI agent named Marco, whom I used to work with in Denver, was assigned to an office in Mexico. He tracked the Tahoe to a tiny town far south of the border, paid the owner the cost of the truck, and prepared to ship it to Denver. Marco and his FBI evidence team processed the interior and found significant amounts of dried blood around the edges of the side panels in the rear compartment. The blood had no DNA remaining in it, however, and the FBI Lab guessed it had been "baked out in the Mexican sun."

Detective Bernard filed charges against Scott for Cat's homicide, but the district attorney said there was not enough evidence to be certain it was him. I cannot say that I argue with either position. Just like Scott's reporting to the FBI and local law enforcement, he cannot help but lie and manipulate people. So, it is possible he was just toying with Bernard and me. However, the pieces of the investigation not pointing *away* from Scott included: His alibi of being out of town did not hold water; the dog tracked the scent of Cat's killer to the same block where Terry's Tahoe was at the time; Billy Goat 3 described the holdback facts of injuries to Cat; and Scott was known to have been in and around her abduction area (the 7-11 on Colfax) and body disposal area in Westminster. Finally, in October 2004, Larissa won another custody battle in Arapahoe County Court against Scott, just days before Cat disappeared. Could this be a proxy kill? Maybe. Scott knew he could not kill his mother or his ex-wife—he had tried and failed to hire Steve 2 to kill Larissa and Gamblin to kill his mom.

As it turned out, there were also more murders like Cat's.

## 26

# OTHER MURDERS

I FOUND it challenging enough to compile and compress a logical account of investigating the murders of Jennifer, Kaysi, LeAnn, and Uncle Terry. To also discuss *who else* Scott had likely killed was an even greater challenge because he was innocent until proven guilty. By the time Scott was sentenced, I was investigating between fifteen and twenty unsolved missing person and homicide cases that "sounded like Scott." With each recovery of the three victims in 2008 and 2009, ViCAP, the FBI's crime comparison unit, ran a new search that cross-referenced Scott's whereabouts with unsolved cases with murders consistent with our three. By 2014, I had a twenty-page printout of a timeline containing every law enforcement query, and every social security number use, credit card use, or name check of Scott starting with his eighteenth birthday. The timeline helped me research unsolved murders and keep straight who went missing at the same time and in the same place Scott had existed.

From the FBI website "The Violent Crime Apprehension Program," ViCAP facilitates communication and coordination between law enforcement agencies that investigate, track, and apprehend violent serial offenders. ViCAP maintains a nationwide data information center that collects, collates, and analyzes crimes of violence (homicide, attempted homicide, missing persons, child abductions, sexual assaults, and unidentified deceased persons). ViCAP analysts examine crime data and patterns to identify potential similarities among crimes, create investigative matrices, develop timelines, and identify homicide and sexual assault trends and patterns."[157]

ViCAP Analyst Stacy and I spoke weekly between 2007 and 2010. Over the years of her research, she compiled three different notebooks of murders possibly committed by Scott. I then called the jurisdictions who had unsolved cases and spoke with them about my investigation of Scott. From hitchhikers shot in the mountains of Montana in the mid-1980s to couples killed in Utah and Idaho, prostitutes in Spokane, and John Does and Jane Does in California, Scott's suspected homicides numbered in the low twenties. Based upon the research Stacy and I had done this number was our best guess. From those victims who were recovered, some of the women were strangled, others were shot or stabbed, while most men were stabbed or shot. No DNA was recovered, nor were there any witnesses to any of these murders. During my prison visits to Scott from 2011 to 2020, he continued to play with my suspected homicide list like a cat with a ball of yarn.

## THE FIRST TIME, I WAS ON A RAFT

The earliest suspicious death that we could find involving Scott occurred in the Bitterroot River outside of Missoula, Montana in 1985. I requested the police report and learned the incident stemmed from an investigation into Scott as an eighteen-year-old when he worked for Caras Nursery. Over a six-month period, trees continually disappeared from the nursery lot. Unbeknownst to the manager, the trees were showing up in various front yards around nearby Hamilton, Montana. The thief had raked over the soil to cover the holes where the trees had been. The nursery manager, Wendy, told the local sheriff's deputy that her register was losing money as well. She only had one employee—Scott Kimball. But she did not suspect him because he was "so likable."

Wendy did not call the cops about the thefts. She called because someone had driven through the nursery grounds in a truck, running

---

[157] https://www.fbi.gov/how-we-can-help-you/more-fbi-services-and-information/freedom-of-information-privacy-act/department-of-justice-fbi-privacy-impact-assessments/vicap Downloaded July 25, 2024

over hundreds of plants and destroying them completely. The vandal had then cut flowers off plants not damaged by the drive-through and cut the water hoses in half. Deputy Chin responded to the call and asked Wendy, "Do you think the stolen trees and vandalism could be connected?"

Wendy replied, "I think they probably are, but I have no idea who'd do such awful things."

Deputy Chin asked, "Did you have any confrontations with your employee, Scott, over the past few days?"

"Well, yesterday I told him that he hadn't been fertilizing the plants like he should, but that's it."

Deputy Chin compared the tire tracks and shoe prints at the scene to Scott's and found intriguing similarities. Days later, Chin caught him stealing from the nursery during a sting operation. The deputy obtained a warrant for Scott's arrest and interviewed him at midnight. They released him on a $5,000 bond.

Deputy Chin had become a senior investigator by the time I called him twenty years later. He remembered Scott's thefts, vandalism, and arrest, saying, "What stood out to me was what happened the next day. Scott took his grandmother and five of her friends rafting down the Bitterroot (River). Apparently, while he was able to skirt around a waterfall, his grandma and her friends went over it and one of them died."

This resonated with what more than one of Scott's Colorado cellmates had said after our body hunts in Utah: "He said the first time he killed someone he was on a raft."

I read through the report Investigator Chin sent to me and learned the following:

Grandma Ruth and her five friends agreed to go on a rafting trip with Scott that took place on a June morning in 1985. None of the occupants of Ruth's raft were wearing a life vest. Scott and his girlfriend, Connie, were in the lead, in a smaller raft that maneuvered around the waterfall. Ruth and her friends, however, could not avoid the fall and went directly over the edge. Ruth suffered a broken sternum from smashing into a tree that lay across the river, and her friend, Frankie, age sixty-five, died by drowning. When deputies arrived, Scott was giving CPR to Frankie on the shore. The death was ruled an accident.

I tracked down a phone number for Connie and called her. She vividly recalled the day Frankie died on the river. She had been dating Scott for a few months when she rode with him to the rafting site. Grandma Ruth arrived with her friends and said, "Scott, thanks for bringing us out here, but a few of us can't swim. Don't we need life vests?"

Connie recalled Scott saying, "The current's very low and everything'll be fine."

Connie confirmed that Scott tried to save Frankie with CPR on the other side of the waterfall. She did not know about Scott's arrest the night before, the events at the nursery, or that he needed bond money. She described her dating relationship with him as normal.

According to Barb, Scott's mom, by the time Scott was eighteen, Grandma Ruth was his only option for a living arrangement. Also, he had stolen some checks from her prior to the river ride. When I asked Barb about Frankie's death and the timing of the nursery arrest, she said, "My guess is that Scott asked Ruth to bond him out and she refused, like the rest of us did. This sounds like he talked them into taking the rafting trip the next morning. It kinda reminds me of what happened to Justin."

## THE RABBIT HOLE

I remained the lead investigator for all things Scott-related over the next twelve years, as we continued to search for Jennifer, battled with him on other homicides, and interacted with law enforcement agencies across the western states who wanted to find out if he could be their serial killer. However, Scott was not my full-time job anymore following his 2009 sentencing. Phil started assigning me to other no-body or missing person cases that also took a lot of time and effort. Here are some examples:

- An assistant district attorney who was murdered in his backyard (one year of focused attention)
- A serial rapist who was stalking and assaulting older women (one year)

- A spree murderer just released from prison who was possibly hired by a prison gang to kill a top state official (six months)
- A ten-year-old girl who disappeared and was later recovered, deceased (six months)
- A thirteen-year-old boy who disappeared and was recovered five years later, deceased (I interacted extensively with his father, the killer, after his disappearance.)
- A fourteen-year-old girl who went for a jog in the mountains and never came home (ten years, on and off)
- A woman who had disappeared twenty years before I was assigned to the case, then a second person (child) in her husband's care died under unusual circumstances (two months, on and off)
- A husband whose first wife died when a Jeep fell on her, and his second wife who died when she fell off a cliff (two years)
- A seventeen-year-old girl who went home to get cookies for a school fundraiser, brutally murdered in her home (three years)
- A young mother who disappeared thanks to the help of a registered nurse who helped her secret boyfriend clean up the blood from a crime scene and pretend to be the victim. The nurse made and received calls on the victim's phone days after the murder to deceive the police (six months on and off)
- A twelve-year-old boy who disappeared while last with his stepmom (two months, then extensive trial prep)
- A woman who disappeared but was obviously dead, no crime scene, no body (three years)

Each of these cases required my full attention and engagement for bursts of days, weeks, and sometimes months. I worked closely with local agency detectives, people like Gary, who were investigating the cases. We all became grossly familiar with both the victims and the suspects. I spent a lot of time away from the Safe Streets Office and in the smaller police departments and sheriff's offices around the state while we spoke with possible killers. I formed relationships with most of the suspects, as well as the victims' families, but few turned into lasting friendships like those I developed with some of the victim families surrounding Scott Kimball—primarily due to the duration of the investigation and its intensity. We were able to bring resolutions (arrests) to all but three of the cases, and each of those is still being investigated. Scott sent me a letter in 2012 while I was investigating the ten-year-old girl who had disappeared, telling me Hannibal Lecter-style how I could find the victim and identify the killer (further explained in Chapter 28).

# 27

# PROFILING SCOTT

I WENT to a handful of Behavioral Analysis Unit conferences over the next few years, learning more about profiling, case studies, and violence prevention. Inevitably, I would meet up with Art and his co-worker Don, along with my fellow BAU field coordinators out of New York and Los Angeles for lunch or drinks. They were fully aware of Scott, our search for Jennifer, and the other unsolved murders possibly connected to him around the western states.

In May 2011, I asked Art and Don if they would be willing to come to Colorado and profile Scott. Art looked at me like I had lost my mind. "You know I don't really profile people and give them some label, like they expect me to."

"But Art, Scott doesn't know that. I think he'd be so eager to impress true profilers that he'd talk all day. And you might get him to say something he won't say to me about Jennifer or our other unknown victims."

Art and Don accepted the challenge. The next week, Detective Bernard and I went to see Scott, and I asked if he was willing to talk with Art and Don. As I guessed, Scott was all over it. I explained to him that he and his mom and her partner, Kay, would all need to fill out a General Assessment Questionnaire (GAQ) ahead of time to help determine his temperament, affinities, tendencies, and other personality characteristics. He practically begged me to return soon so he could fill out the form.

By now, Scott had been moved to the Colorado State Penitentiary in Canon City, Colorado, as punishment by the Sterling warden for the fake FBI document stunt he had pulled off in prison. Detective Bernard accompanied me, and Scott answered the hundred-plus questions with what I knew at times were completely bogus answers:

Q: Most influential person you your life?

A: "Uncle Terry because he's a lawbreaker and a rebel. And because he sexually abused me."

Q: Have you been sexually abused?

A: (Besides listing Neighbor Ted and Barb 2) "My babysitter, Mike, when I was about nine years old, got me drunk and sexually assaulted me. He died of a drug overdose in the early '80s but I didn't have anything to do with that."

Q: What are your driving habits?

A: "I drive fast and furiously, as fast as I can without getting pulled over. I only need about four hours of sleep a night so I can get to places faster than most people."

He also claimed to have PTSD, Borderline Personality Disorder, Bipolar Disorder, Dissociative Disorder, and Multiple Personality Disorder. I told him the profilers would review everything and we would be back to visit him. He was as animated on that day as he was the first day we went on body hunts in Utah. Detective Bernard tried to question him about new facts regarding gas receipts that showed Scott in the same place at the same time as when Cat's body had been disposed of. He informed Scott of the cadaver dogs scenting from Cat to Uncle Terry's Tahoe (two months after Scott killed Terry). The detective also asserted that Scott's alibi of being at Brett's house in California when Cat was murdered was bogus. Scott sidestepped all the questions and accusations, just saying he would be ready when the profilers got there.

## PRE-PROFILER WORK

In July 2011, I spoke with Neighbor Ted one last time. He said after his attorney convinced him to plead guilty to molesting Scott, his insurance company, USAA, paid out $1 million to Scott and other victims. Scott received most of the proceeds. Ted's attorney agreed that the only substantial evidence was Scott's testimony, and it was compelling. Ted again told me the reason behind Scott's allegations was that Scott knew Ted had money and knew he could win in court. Considering what Scott was willing to do to other family members years later for money, I found Ted's arguments intriguing.

In August 2011, the Colorado State Penitentiary investigator sent me a drawing by Scott depicting thirty tombstones. Four of the tombstones bore the names of the victims in our case. Other names were victims of Wayne Nance, a serial killer active in western Montana when Scott was growing up in the 1980s. When I made that connection, I wondered if Scott was pointing me to the origins of his own murderous path. Another tombstone recorded a woman named Karen Nelson who was brutally murdered in 1988 in eastern Colorado. Scott had written a poem months prior to this meeting about "Karen being set ablaze but no one knew who did it" and sent it to local news stations. He was taunting the news (and me, since he knew I was reading his mail) to ask him if he had murdered Karen Nelson. The pending profiler visit was obviously stirring him up.

During that same month, I interviewed a handful of inmates from prisons in Sterling and Canon City because Scott had confessed homicides to these men. In all of the stories, he was a hit man for hire who killed people for money and for fun. His victims ranged from U.S. Attorneys to hitchhikers to news reporters. Every one of these inmates was hopeful that the information was going to be valuable enough to be their ticket out of jail. On the contrary, they each left the interview room with shoulders slumped and feet shuffling after I told them Scott's stories were simply him having fun with them.

## SCOTT MEETS THE PROFILERS

Just before Halloween 2011, FBI profilers Art and Don accompanied me down to Canon City where we spent fourteen very long hours with Scott in a small interview room. Art began the session with, "Hi Scott, we've heard a lot about you from Agent Grusing. We're not here to question you about homicides. We're here to understand you. We reviewed the GAQ and you are a highly intelligent man who can offer our unit insight into homicide investigations and behavior."

For three straight hours, Scott launched into the sexual abuse he suffered at the hands of Neighbor Ted, Uncle Terry, Barb 2, and a variety of babysitters. The torture and sexual acts involved ants, knives, and blood. The details were more grotesque than he had explained in court, to me, or to his family. Scott had an audience and he was compelled to impress. The more he talked, however, the more I began to believe Ted's version over Scott's. Scott boasted to Art about his hunting prowess and his ability to track and kill any type of large game. He also talked about how he swindled hunters out of their money while acting as their guide.

Scott asked me if we ran cadaver dogs over his cattle property in Broomfield, hinting that he had used an excavator on that land in 2004. He suggested I check that area for one of the "missing people" he might have buried there. He asked to see a map of his property and wanted me to turn the recorder off, so I did.[158] But when I asked him to pinpoint where he used the excavator he refused to be specific so I turned the recorder back on.

Scott told us how he tricked LeAnn into parking her car past the state line, and how he drove her into the horseshoe canyon and told her they were there to call her boyfriend, Steve 2. He parked his Jeep and walked with her up the canyon wall to the eventual spot of her recovery. Scott said that LeAnn looked at him and said, "Hannibal, your face just changed."

Scott told us, "I smiled, pulled out my gun and told her, 'Strip.' She obeyed and I told her, 'Get on your knees.' She cried as she got down

---

158  The purpose of Scott's request was clear to all of us present. He was about to confess to a homicide.

and I shot her in the neck, not the head, like you've been saying, Jon (looking at me). I gathered her clothes and walked back to the Jeep, then I took off my clothes and put them in two separate garbage bags. I cut slits into the bag with my clothes and placed some large rocks inside. I used wet wipes on my skin to remove any potential DNA or gun residue and then drove straight to Green River (Utah). Once I found a bridge over deep water, I tossed the weighted garbage bag with my clothes into the river."

Scott then drove to Las Vegas and threw the bag containing LeAnn's clothes into a dumpster. He met his brother, Brett, at a hotel in San Bernardino the next day and took a photo of a stripper wearing Brett's shirt in case he needed it for leverage someday. He gave LeAnn's credit cards to the stripper as payment and told her to wait until she got back to Los Angeles before using them. The stripper's use of the credit cards would confuse both law enforcement and LeAnn's family as to when and where she actually disappeared.

Most of Scott's story matched our known facts for LeAnn's murder, but there was no way for me to confirm what actually transpired between him and LeAnn on that day in Bryson Canyon. If I had to bet my paycheck, I would say half, or more than half, of what he told me was BS, but he knew I could not factually contradict him.

Scott told us he injected Jennifer with ketamine and kept her sedated for three days before driving her to Utah. He said he attempted to choke her, but that didn't kill her so he shot her in the head. I challenged that story for multiple reasons, but I stopped when he got super-defensive. I could see he wanted to look good for the profilers. We supplied him with food and drink throughout the long day but he barely touched either. He was too focused on filling the profiler's brains with his own display of intelligence and how much of a victim he was. He did not hesitate to tell them my shortcomings, primarily that I would not believe him when I should. Around 6 p.m., he asked us to come back the next day. Art and Don agreed.

We grabbed a fast-food burger that night in Colorado Springs in heavy snow because not much else was open. We crashed in hotel rooms that night and drove back to the prison in the morning and spent another four hours interviewing Scott. Unfortunately, that interview session was spent with Scott making himself the hero in Terry's death. In gruesome detail that I found unconvincing and repulsive, Terry was portrayed as a sexual predator who abused one of Scott's sons. Scott claimed he started a huge fight with Terry that took place throughout the Broomfield house before Scott finally killed him.[159]

Scott was also supposedly a victim and target of Kaysi's alleged lust for him. Since she could not have a "prize" like Scott all to herself, she blackmailed him.[160] So he *had* to murder her. He told the profilers he killed Kaysi by injecting a lethal amount of heroin into her arm. She then fell into their campfire and died.[161] I waited before challenging each of Scott's homicide stories because this was about him and the profilers talking, not me. Once he paused, though, I scolded him for wasting the profilers' time—he was asserting he was *only* responsible for the murders of the four known victims. "All the research, and even your own statements, Scott, point to many more victims," I asserted.

In response, Scott offered a "red Jeep and blue Jeep" scenario for the total number of murders he had committed. He suggested we focus on the states of Colorado, Alaska, Wyoming, Montana, and Washington where these Jeeps/victims were located. He refused to tell us who he killed in which states, though.

Exhausted mentally, physically, and spiritually, we said goodbye to him and walked to our cars. Art, who had consulted for ten years on the worst-of-the-worst murders in the nation said, "Jonny, that is the most narcissistic person I've ever met."

Scott went into such detail during those two days about his stepmom, Barb 2, forcing him as a teenager to have sex with her, that I asked an FBI agent named Monte to question her about the claims. Agent Monte submitted a fifteen-page report about his interview with Barb 2 and her very logical refutations of each claim made by Scott. The bottom line of that interview was that Scott's dad and Barb

---

159 This was not close to matching the couch crime scene or Terry being shot execution-style in the back of the head.
160 "Prize" was my term. Scott's narrative was that Kaysi was in love with him—which I find completely repulsive. She can't refute it, though.
161 I had already run this story by Dr. France because Scott was trying to sell it in the prison. She did not see any fire damage to Kaysi's skeletal remains, which she would have seen if it was the fire that killed her. His most consistent story to other inmates about Kaysi involved strangulation, which Dr. France agreed would be more realistic.

2 were united in their decision to kick Scott out of their house at age sixteen, and Scott hated Barb 2 for it. The decision to put Scott out on his own had nothing to do with sex—it did, however, follow an unending series of thefts, forgeries, lies, manipulation, contacts with law enforcement, and arrests that made life with Scott unbearable. Scott lived in Canada for a year but got booted out of there for more fraud. With no other option, he went to live with Grandma Ruth, where the thefts, lies, and arrests continued.

## 28

# 21 HOMICIDES

ALTHOUGH FIVE months of preparation and two days of painstaking interviews with the profilers did not provide any immediate results, like what occurred with the Billy Goats after the body hunts, Scott became so stirred up he had to talk about murder with someone. Since arriving in Canon City, he had been in solitary confinement and was going slightly bananas. He had no one to manipulate, steal from, lie to, or listen to his complaints about me. So, with nothing else to do, Scott wrote a letter to me with these instructions, "Jon, I need you to come down here with *Gazetteer* map books of Alaska, Washington, Idaho, Montana, Wyoming, Colorado, Utah, Oregon, Nevada, California, and Arizona. Trust me, this will be worth your while." He ended the letter with, "P.S. It's rude not to tell me when you're coming, so please let me know a day in advance."

I showed the letter to Phil. He laughed and agreed to sign off on buying the map books if I would take him with me to the interview. I gladly accepted his offer, saying, "I doubt anyone else would want to come."

In November 2011, Phil and I drove to Canon City, checked in at the prison, then sat down in the interview room with Scott and showed him the map books he had requested. He said, "That's good. Now, tell me I can't have an attorney."

In each of the dozens of interviews I had conducted with Scott, I always advised him of his Miranda Rights. Most of the time he signed the required form without even glancing at the paper. Every once in a while he would play a game with the form. Once, with Detective Gary and me, he leaned forward and scribbled something on the form, covering his scribble with his left hand to shield it from us, and then turned the form upside down. Even though we asked several times what he had written he would not let us see it until the interview was done. At the end, he slid the Miranda form over to us with a wide grin. On the signature line where he was supposed to confirm he was waiving his right to an attorney, he had written, "They refused to get me an attorney."

On this particular day with Phil, I hesitated to agree to Scott's no attorney request, but Phil was game. "Okay, you can't have an attorney. Whatcha got, Scott?"

Scott then claimed he killed a man for fun in western Montana in the late 1980s. He told us about a particular mountain pass, and we, like eager students, dutifully located the site in the Montana map book. He said, "That's number one." He said number two had been a hitchhiker in Utah, also in the late 1980s, and told us which exit off I-70 near where he had disposed of yet another body. I marked it in the map book. This continued for another five or six victims, mainly hitchhikers in various states, until Scott again asked Phil, "I still can't have an attorney, right?"

"No, Scott, you can't have an attorney," Phil said with a grin since all three of us knew this was Scott's game to play.

Scott described killings in the early 1990s by bow and arrow and gunshots, including a female in Spokane, Washington, and a couple in Idaho who wanted him to guide them through the forest. He said he shot a man in Hite, Utah, while on a bridge. He put that victim in a large bag, weighed it down with rocks, and threw it into the lake. His last victim, number twenty-one, was a man in Wyoming whom Terry had shot in the 1980s while Scott was present. I counted this as a homicide for Scott since he had placed Terry in the "driver" role and cast himself as the "complicitor," just as he had for those months in the Utah desert.

When Scott appeared to be finished, I asked, "Scott, I don't really know why you're doing this, but you know I'm going to have to check on each one of these, right? And if you're making this up, and none of this is true, you know I get paid the same whether we find any of these people or not?"

Scott looked directly at me and said, "Agent Grusing, I promise you this will be worth your time."

That evening, I started calling the various jurisdictions across the western states. I began with Sheriff White in Utah because there were supposedly three more victims in the same Grand County where we had recovered LeAnn and searched for Jennifer. The sheriff did have one unsolved hitchhiker homicide with a bullet to the head, but not in the spot where Scott reported. Many investigators from the other states had to call me back once they had checked the area of the supposed burial sites, so I did not have a complete answer for two or three weeks.

Guess how many of the twenty-one victims we recovered from this confession?

If you guessed twenty-one you're not following this story very well. I did not drive back to Canon City to see Scott because I had my fill of him over the past few months. Instead, I called the investigator down there and asked him to grab my favorite serial killer and put him on the phone.

I asked, "Scott, I ran down the twenty-one leads you gave and guess how many recoveries we have? Zero. I told you I get paid the same anyway, so I don't really know why you put me through this exercise."

I will never forget Scott's response: "This isn't a waste of time, Jon. It's a puzzle. There's a truth to everything I said. You've got to figure it out."

When I tell this story in lectures today, I assert with a totally straight face that I was with Scott in the prison when he said that to me—in response, I drew my gun and shot him. The audience inevitably responds with a gasp and, "You did?" My dry sense of humor, and the aggregation of years of frustration in dealing with this man make it easy to believe. Instead of killing him, I committed to remembering word-for-word his puzzle quote. This bogus homework assignment gave me the answer I cite most often when asked, "How many people do you think Scott's killed?" I can answer directly, "He told me twenty-one."

## 2012 AND 2013

In April 2012, AUSA Dave and I visited Scott because Scott had indicated he was ready to strike a federal deal and accept a life sentence. Dave knew it was likely an exercise in futility, but he also knew I was still hoping to recover Jennifer, so off we went. Scott toyed with Cat's homicide, asking for a Memo of Understanding up front, guaranteeing he would not be charged with first degree murder. Dave said, "No deal." Scott looked at my new list of suspected homicides and gave me a "maybe" beside some of them and a "no" beside others. Dave quickly grew tired of the games so we drove back to Denver.

In October 2012, I was working on the case of Jessica Ridgeway, a ten-year-old girl who had disappeared during her walk from home to school in Westminster, Colorado. I was on the news during the first few days of that investigation because I was walking in and out of the victim's family home and talking to her mom. Scott wrote me a letter, informing me where to look for Jessica's body and pointing to a lake southwest of the search area. He theorized that her backpack being so overtly placed in Superior, Colorado was "just a diversion." Nice, right? He was living up to his Hannibal nickname, providing me with a consult on where the killer might have hidden his victim.

Scott was correct, though. Jessica's killer had in fact staged the backpack as a diversion because police were searching in his immediate neighborhood. Days later, the suspect placed her remains in a location south and west of his neighborhood in the same area Scott had correctly guessed.

I worked on another unpleasant missing child case in 2012 that extended into 2013, so I did not have time to respond to Scott's letters or calls. In the summer of 2013, he wrote me the funniest line I could remember from our pen pal relationship. The letter stated that he was "ready to find Jennifer and bring her home to her family." At the end, he added a P.S. like he always did, and then "P.S.S. It's rude to not write back to someone when they write to you."

And Scott did speak truth—it *is* rude not to write back, unless that person is a serial killer. I did not write any letters to Scott. There was no way anyone could anticipate how he might twist, reword, or otherwise manipulate such responses and then send a different version to someone else. I am confident he would have tried, and he would have succeeded.

In December 2013, I took Gary with me on another trip and we talked to Scott about where Jennifer might be. We had a serious allegation of a sexual assault we knew would really scare Scott, even if it was false. He was rocked by the allegation, and denied it, of course. We asked how we could trust anything he said about, well, anything. To bargain, Scott wanted to see my list of his possible murders again because he wanted to adjust some of his answers. He put question marks beside five victims and added a female named April who had disappeared from San Bernardino ten years before. The detective from that case flew out months later and was interested in Scott as a suspect for almost a year, until Scott gave us a detail about her disappearance that could not possibly have been true. He made an educated guess from what was publicly available, but the detective had already disproved the claim. The details Scott provided about April's supposed abduction and homicide caused us to search Barb's house to disprove April had been killed there. We looked for the hidden hypodermic needle, tranquilizer, and cadaver scent because of what Scott alleged had occurred in Barb's attic. I apologized to Barb before the search for the inconvenience and somewhat public spectacle in front of her neighbors and she said, "Don't worry, Jon. I get it."

# 29

# THE OPPORTUNITY KILLER

The year 2014 was my next-to-last heavy year of investigation into Scott Kimball. Through his former state public defender, Megan, and her investigator, Frank, Scott was ready to make a global deal that wrapped up all of his unsolved homicides. The Boulder County DA Office's second in charge, Assistant DA Brackley, volunteered to be the lead prosecutor for this agreement. I agreed to serve as errand boy along with Gary to ferry Scott back and forth from the prison to the FBI Safe Streets Office, so he could meet with his attorneys. Scott had demanded appropriate living conditions, improved prisoner classifications, and meals, of course, for these "tell-all" days. I made calls during January and February of 2014 to acquire all the approvals from the prison and the FBI to make these things happen. For each request, I included something along the lines of, "Please don't do anything that you wouldn't do for any other prisoner in these circumstances. Scott has already received special treatment from the judicial system and law enforcement, and he used that to kill people. I don't want to commit the same error by giving him extra latitude that he shouldn't have and enable him to do something illegal with it." By April, we were ready to go. Again. Gary and I showed up at the Denver County Jail bright and early and received Scott, all bright-eyed and bushy-tailed. I handcuffed him, then placed him in the back seat of my Bureau car and drove him to our Safe Streets building.

Because our task force office was not as secure as the main FBI building, a SWAT operator sat outside of the space in case all of this was just a ruse for Scott to take a shot at freedom for a short period of time.

After Scott carefully inspected the room for listening devices, thinking we would be interested in his every word to his attorneys, they shut the door and started working on his list. Each hour or so, Frank would emerge and ask something like, "Jonny, where was Scott in September 1987?"

I would consult my timeline and reply, "He was arrested by Ravalli County Sheriff's Office in Hamilton, Montana on August 13, 1987, then a warrant was issued for his arrest in Ft. Collins, Colorado on September 15, 1987, for failure to appear."

I would then check to see who, from my missing person and homicide list, matched Scott's request. I discussed results with Gary and Phil while Scott continued to talk privately with his attorneys. We went back and forth like this for most of the day. Occasionally, Scott would request my presence in the room so he could ask me additional questions about the timeline of his activities. Yes, this routine was designed to signal to us that he could toy around with me, manipulate me, and make himself feel important, but I played his game and took from him what I could get. As we approached 5 p.m., everyone agreed that we would resume the meeting the following week. Gary and I loaded Scott into the back seat again and took off for the jail.

I began this story by quoting the following dialogue that took place during this particular ride back to the jail. But, after reviewing eight years of interactions with Scott, I want to retell it with a little more detail. It is important to understand why it was so appropriate and impactful.

As we headed east on Denver's I-70, approaching the Quebec Street turnoff to the jail, Scott asked, "Why didn't you guys ever name me?"

Always slow to adjust to a question I am not expecting, I asked, "What do you mean, name you?"

"You know, Jon. Name me. Like Green River Killer or BTK? Why didn't you name me?"

My first thought was to say, "We did think of a name, Scott. How about The Defenseless Girl Killer? Or The Unsuspecting Family Member Murderer?" But I knew such a response would only provide me with a sense of satisfaction, and Scott's inevitable extreme response was not worth it. So, I asked, "I don't know, Scott. What should we name you?"

"The Opportunity Killer. Because I killed someone when I had the opportunity."

Gary and I sat there in silence as his claim settled like a weight, as the deeper meaning slowly clicked other gears into place. What we had suspected all along was true. Scott had killed a lot of people. That unguarded, nonchalant statement was one of the few true statements Scott made over the many years I dealt with him.

We continued these full circle transports between the jail and Safe Streets through April. After the second meeting, Defense Attorney Megan sent Boulder Assistant DA Brackley an email that indicated their team had a list of thirty of Scott's victims to date, with 50 percent still being classified as missing persons. I thought about the extremely remote areas where we had recovered Kaysi, Terry, and LeAnn. Fifteen more victims like that? We never found Jennifer. How in Hades would we ever find all these other people, knowing the mind games Scott played?

During the third meeting at Safe Streets, Scott asked, "When was my first marriage date to Larissa? We had a formal marriage on June 26, 1993, but when was our informal wedding?" I knew that Scott knew the answer, but it was his way of making me work a little harder. He wanted me to feel like a student appearing in front of his professor, waiting to have his project graded. I was already looking into an unsolved case involving a woman who went missing from Spokane on the same day of Scott's first wedding. She had been discovered beaten to death in Idaho. I asked Scott about that in front of his attorneys and everyone just looked at each other. I was tossed out of the room and they went back to work.

## DONE, AGAIN

By June 2014, Scott and his defense attorneys had compiled a list of between forty-five and fifty people he had murdered. Scott's attorney requested that I use what we were learning from Scott's requests for information and contact the appropriate district attorney's office for the county of each of his suspected victims. We had to get each county prosecutor's commitment *not* to seek the death penalty if we told them about a victim in their county. I kept a spreadsheet of whom I had spoken with and their responses. On Scott's next visit to the Safe Streets interview room, I asked, "Scott, would you like to review my homework assignment?" I handed over my list of counties and he rolled his eyes.

Scott had a distaste for sarcasm and was clearly irritated that I called it my homework. However, I knew he thoroughly enjoyed assigning tasks to an FBI agent and then telling me what I had guessed wrongly.

When we began the 2014 meetings, the agreement from the very start was that Scott, with the help of his attorneys, would provide a complete list of his victims. In return, he would not be charged with a death penalty case. After this particular meeting, Scott and Frank called the Public Defender, Megan, and set up a final meeting to finish the highly sought-after full list of Scott's victims.

Two days later, Assistant DA Brackley and I met Megan at the Denver jail that housed Scott. After locking up my weapon, signing in, passing through the metal detectors, and making small talk, we waited, anxiously. The prize I had chased for almost eight years—Scott's complete list of homicides—was finally within reach. We met the Department of Corrections investigator who walked us to the interview room. As we were walking, Megan handed me a piece of notebook paper with Scott's neat handwriting on it, a double-spaced list of thirty-three. Thirty-three counties. Not homicide victims. It was a list of the names of thirty-three *counties*. I was walking in the prison yard staring at the list and wondering, "What am I supposed to do with this?" I turned to Megan. "Counties? Not victims?" I handed the list to Brackley. I explained that we needed a list of *victims'* names. For example, Clark County, which includes Las Vegas, is a county containing hundreds of unsolved murders. Scott's list did us absolutely no good. How were we supposed to know which unsolved murder was his handiwork? I do not remember Megan answering me. I told her, and Brackley agreed: "No proffer would be made with just a list of counties."

Scott pulled Brackley, Gary, and me back to the jail a few weeks later and tried a completely different approach to confessing to his homicides, giving us four names of supposed victims in Arizona, Montana, and Nevada. We all quickly sniffed it out as bogus and walked away without looking back or apologizing.

# 30

# AN UNEXPECTED DEATH

On Tuesday, December 2, 2014, at about 7 p.m., I was coaching my son's eighth-grade basketball practice in a middle school across the street from my home. I gave the kids a water break and walked to the bleachers. I checked my phone and saw that a few U.S. attorneys had tried to call me, so I called one of them back. "Dave died," AUSA Greg told me. I stood by the bleachers with my phone in my hand as the team waited for me. Blood rushed to my head and the gym dissolved from my vision as I absorbed the awful news.

Dave had been battling cancer and death for many years, so it shouldn't have been a surprise. Suddenly, my best ally, my solid bridge between the FBI and the U.S. Attorney's Office, was gone. I felt like a balloon with the air escaping. I stood there, wondering if my success with the FBI was only because I had Dave's favor—I was fearing what my work life would be without him. I know it sounds corny, but I have since carried Dave's voice inside my head. It serves as my armor and legal wisdom when I run into difficult new cases or roadblocks in old ones. His F-bombs are included, naturally. I wake up some mornings thinking I need to run a theory or new fact past him before I fully awaken and realize he is not around. Dave was my larger-than-life prosecutor, mentor, friend, and hero. I miss him greatly.

The US Attorney's Office released the following statement on December 3, 2014:

DENVER—It is with profound sadness that U.S. Attorney John Walsh announces that Assistant U.S. Attorney Dave Conner passed away yesterday following a prolonged illness. Dave passed away peacefully at his home yesterday afternoon, after battling cancer for over fifteen years. Dave worked up until the day of his death.

"Dave Conner was no ordinary prosecutor. Over thirty-two years of service in the state and federal courts, he dedicated his heart and soul to the pursuit of justice," said U.S. Attorney John Walsh. "Dave's skill, integrity and fierce commitment to fairness made him a legend among prosecutors, law enforcement and defense attorneys alike. He was a living, breathing model that prosecutors should aspire to, and a teacher of generations of young prosecutors, in both word and deed. We will miss Dave terribly, but the chords sounded by his memory will forever link our hearts to him and to what he stood for."[162]

I couldn't have said it better myself. Rest in peace, Dave.

## DIFFERENT JANE DOE

When Dave died, I was in the middle of another all-consuming serial killer case that lasted through the next year. I went to Canon City to visit Scott rarely, only when his letters indicated it might be worth the drive. He was released from solitary confinement after one year of almost completely losing his mind. Scott's behavior was exemplary at the Canon City prison, so they reassigned him back to Sterling Correctional Facility.[163]

In June of 2016, I took a newer FBI agent with me to speak with yet another Sterling inmate who had information about a significant number of Scott's murders. Prisoner "Zee" had obviously lived a

---

[162] "Dave Conner, Assistant U.S. Attorney And Career Prosecutor, Dies Peacefully At Home After 15-Year Fight With Cancer." U.S. Attorney's Office, District of Colorado. December 3, 2014. https://www.justice.gov/usao-co/pr/dave-conner-assistant-us-attorney-and-career-prosecutor-dies-peacefully-home-after-15. Downloaded July 10, 2024.

[163] When a shark is not around other fish, it doesn't have the opportunity to tear things apart.

rough life because, while he was my age, he looked at least thirty years older. He had been in the same cell block as Scott for the past year. Zee told us, "Scott bragged to me that he killed between fifty and fifty-four people." Zee correctly related what happened to our four known Boulder victims, except Scott had said the driver had been the killer, and Scott had to kill this driver after Jennifer was murdered. Scott told Zee about a woman on horseback in the late 1980s who was reportedly his first victim. Zee had the same hopeful look as the other inmates who ratted on Scott until I explained that giving inmates a break on their jail sentence had not worked out so well for law enforcement in the past.

On two occasions in 2015, I chaperoned an investigator from Utah to the Sterling prison to meet Scott. I had contacted the detective several years back when ViCAP listed his victim as a "possible" on Scott's homicide list. I called him again when Scott told me in 2011 about the twenty-one people he killed, including one in Hite, Utah. This alleged homicide was within a few miles of the investigator's Jane Doe, who was discovered "wrapped up in a carpet with a bullet to her head." The complex series of knots the Utah killer used to tie up this victim were almost identical to the knots around the tarp wrapped around Uncle Terry. During the visits with the Utah investigator, Scott danced around the Jane Doe homicide, wondering aloud if he did it or not. The investigator wrote a search warrant for Scott's DNA, which I served on Scott, only to learn months later the DNA on the ropes did not match him. In 2018, the Utah Jane Doe's sister saw a news story about her recovery and connected it to her sister's husband.[164] In a roundabout way, Scott's false confession brought renewed scrutiny and a national spotlight to the case which allowed the victim, Lina Geddes, to be identified. Investigating these cases was a time suck for me, though, and was taking me away from other cases and not getting me any closer to finding Jennifer. I needed an excuse to break up with Scott for a few years, and he was about to give me quite a substantial reason.

---

164  https://www.newsnationnow.com/us-news/midwest/dna-from-rope-helps-put-1998-murder-case-to-rest/ Downloaded March 22, 2025.

# 31

# THE HELICOPTER ESCAPE PLAN

I PARKED in front of the Drug Enforcement Agency office in Englewood, Colorado, in April 2017. DEA Special Agent "Chris" had called a few days earlier and said he had information about Scott Kimball. He asked me to meet him, along with a recent parolee (the source of the information) at his office. There was no doubt in my mind that Scott had, once again, completely conned yet another former cellmate from Sterling prison. I knew it would be a waste of my time. But it had been a while since I had seen Detective Gary, so I asked him if he wanted to waste his time with me. "Sure, I'll be there. Why not?" Gary responded.

Once we were all seated, Jimmy, the parolee, reached into his back pocket and pulled out small, folded wads of handwritten notes and maps of the prison. His sister, Tam, sat in on the interview and made it crystal clear she was not a fan of law enforcement. She was certain that we were going to "screw Jimmy over" for helping us. I explained to everyone present what I had learned about Scott over the past eleven years: (1) he twists the truth as masterfully as an artist uses paint; (2) the FBI is still looking for homicides he has committed but will not confess to; and (3) he enjoys confessing to homicides he has not committed because of the chaos it creates.

Jimmy was absolutely convinced he was the sole possessor of the one and only instance of a truth escaping Scott's lips. He told us how Scott had promised to pay him to kill Bryon Dathe, the friend of Lori (whom he correctly named as Scott's third wife) and "Fifty," the father of Scott's current cellmate, Marc. Scott was going to pay Jimmy $1 million to kill Fifty, steal his guns, then torture Bryon to get Bryon's credit card PIN and use Bryon's identity to rent a helicopter. Once in the air, Jimmy would use a weapon, likely a knife, and threaten to kill the pilot if the pilot refused to land in the yard of the Sterling Correctional Facility. When the helicopter landed, Scott and Marc would jump aboard, and the pilot would take them to a getaway vehicle that Jimmy would have staged near the prison. Scott would then drive Jimmy to the money and they would part ways.

Detective Gary and I were not surprised Jimmy was totally convinced this plan would work and he would be one million dollars richer. Jimmy was not naïve; he had spent forty years in prison and seemed fairly savvy in the ways of prison speak, cons, and pitfalls. So, I patiently wiped the pixie dust from Jimmy's eyes by telling him how Scott had tricked us. Then, I convinced Jimmy to work with us to get Scott on recorded phone calls, confirming the plan to have people killed and escape from prison by helicopter. After a few phone calls with me, the local district attorney and Sterling prison investigators were totally on board with the plan. With their assistance, Jimmy made eleven phone calls over the next few months, and the calls were recorded to prove Scott's intent.

It turned out to be a messy ordeal. Smack in the middle of this sting operation, Jimmy was arrested for doing foolish things unrelated to the case. I knew better than to help an informant with legal troubles, so we waited for him to be released. Marc mailed Jimmy letters from Sterling prison, complete with new plans and instructions. However, Marc could not get Jimmy's street address correct, so the letters never arrived. Some of the recorded calls were pure comedy, as neither Jimmy, Scott, nor Marc could remember all the code language they were using for these grand plans. The escape plan was often referred to as "the cattle auction" and Fifty was so-named for the .50 caliber guns Jimmy was supposed to steal after he killed him. Even with all of the hiccups, the three of them continued to talk about the planned murders and helicopter ride with such sincerity that I felt compelled to remind Jimmy fairly often that this was all just a ruse.

## SCOTT, YOUR MOM DIED

On August 5, 2017, I got a call from Kay, Barb's partner. Barb had passed away. She had lived on borrowed time for the past ten years as she carried around the enormous weight and guilt of being the mother of a serial killer. Kay and Barb had grown to trust me, and they consulted me in delicate family matters, such as: "What should we do about Scott's boys asking questions about him? Scott's asking for money again—should we give it to him? Do you think Scott's lying to us about Jennifer? Is Scott really getting out of jail soon?"

I told Kay how sorry I was for her loss, and how much I respected and appreciated Barb. Kay asked, "Could you please call Scott and tell him about Barb's death? I don't want to do it. Scott's brother said he won't do it either and of course Virge wants no part of it."

"I'll get the message to him, Kay."

When I hung up, I knew immediately it was a bad idea for me to be the one to break the news to the same guy I was investigating for the helicopter escape and murder-for-hire endeavors. I called Randy, my friend in the Sterling prison investigations unit, and relayed Kay's request.[165] He said the chaplain would do it. Randy then voiced what I was thinking, "This is what happens when you lie, steal, and cheat your family members over the past thirty years of your life. They don't even call you when your mom dies."

## NO HELICOPTER, SCOTT

The FBI flew in an undercover (UC) agent from out of state who pretended to be a paralegal for Jimmy's attorney. The UC agent met with Marc (Fifty's son) at the Sterling prison and recorded the conversation. The purpose of the meeting was to verify that Scott, whose code name for this escape and murder plan was "Montana," was orchestrating this and had the money to pay Jimmy for a ride that would most definitely put his life at risk. Marc told our UC agent that he had verified "the

---

[165] Randy and I had talked so often we had become friends. He told me the disturbing news that for a few months, Scott had a photo of me above his television in his cell. He took it down after he got upset with me, which I wasn't disappointed to hear.

money was good" to pay Jimmy. We concluded the investigation in September 2017 by convincing Scott and his cellmate that Jimmy had killed Bryon and Fifty, and Jimmy was headed their way in the rented helicopter.[166] I sent Jimmy photos of the houses where Fifty and Bryon lived, as well as photos of each of them. I knew Scott would test him to make sure the hits were legit. Jimmy was so excited that he had "fake killed" these two that he was *too believable* when Scott and Marc questioned him about what had happened. Jimmy's voice, tone, and excitement during the calls were right in line with someone who had psychopathic tendencies and had just done something awful.

Just before the final recorded call to the prison, when Jimmy was supposed to be renting the helicopter for his suicide mission to rescue Scott and Marc, I asked Jimmy, "Where are you now?"

He replied, "I'm in Broomfield, about to rent the copter."

"No, Jimmy, where are you really?"

"Oh, I'm sitting beside a lake, drinking a beer."

Marc called Jimmy a few minutes later and asked him if he was coming to the cattle auction. Jimmy replied, "I, uh, I've already got a flight ready to go and uh, 12:30."

Marc said, "Alright, well, I'll have fun at the cattle auction. I'll see ya after a while."

Jimmy replied, "Yep, you will."

This operation may have been the one and only time I was able to truly fool Scott—and it was all caught on camera at the Sterling prison. Scott and Marc went out to the prison yard dressed in multiple layers of clothing. They sat at a table watching the northern horizon for hours, waiting for the helicopter to rescue them. I really wanted to be inside the helicopter when it approached the prison fence. I imagined filming the looks on the prisoners' faces when Scott saw it was me, and not Jimmy, inside the helicopter. However, my bosses wisely advised that using an actual helicopter might cause Scott and Marc to injure or kill a prison guard if they believed this to be a real escape opportunity and someone got in their way. They were right, of course.

---

166 Kevin Vaughan, "Serial killer planned to hijack helicopter to escape." *9News Colorado*. December 19, 2017.
https://www.khou.com/article/news/serial-killer-planned-to-hijack-helicopter-to-escape/285-500672038. Downloaded on July 8, 2024.

We did, however, form enough probable cause for the district attorney to file charges against Marc and Scott for the escape attempt. Marc went to trial against us and lost (Jimmy was spectacular as a witness on the stand), while Scott and his attorneys tried to form a deal that he would, once again, trade other homicides and Jennifer's burial site in return for not getting hit with the charges.

News of this helicopter escape attempt spread around the country, as illustrated by this piece from KHOU 11 in Houston, Texas:

> "A notorious Colorado serial killer stands accused of hatching a multi-pronged plot of revenge, murder and escape from behind the bars of a state prison in Sterling, according to KUSA, our sister station in Denver."

A section of the article included an interview of Bryon:

> Today, (Bryon) Dathe looks back on his dealings with Scott—the fake checks that looked so real banks eagerly cashed them—somewhat ruefully.
>
> "Sometimes," Dathe told 9NEWS, "I felt almost guilty or gullible that I did fall for it, and then when you hear from authorities about all the people that he, that he pulled the wool over their eyes—like, I was just one of many people."
>
> Dathe returned from a road trip to a message that FBI agents wanted to talk to him.
>
> "They told me that Scott tried to put a hit on me from the prison," Dathe said.
>
> He said he found himself in disbelief.
>
> "I mean, how do you come home from a road trip by saying that somebody tried to put a hit on you?" Dathe asked. [167]

---

167  Kevin Vaughan, "Serial killer planned to hijack helicopter to escape." *9News Colorado*. December 19, 2017.
https://www.khou.com/article/news/serial-killer-planned-to-hijack-helicopter-to-escape/285-500672038. Downloaded on July 8, 2024.

The article included a few quotes from me, such as: "I don't think Scott minded sacrificing other people in case it would work," Grusing said. "I don't know the probability he would put on this plan that it would work, but he certainly wouldn't mind other people getting hurt, arrested, or killed trying to carry out this scheme."

I have used Bryon's true name throughout this story because I had permission to do so, and because he was such an innocent, likable human being who was deceived and used by Scott so many times over a seven-year period. Bryon represents all of us who lost so much time, money, and dignity to this man. "Us" includes law enforcement, the families of our four-plus homicide victims, Scott's family, his neighbors, cellmates, and even his own mom, dad, brother, wives, and children.

## A TRADE FOR JENNIFER

By August 2018, Investigator Randy and I, and the Sterling prison district attorney, had agreed with Scott's defense attorney, Rachel, that for *this* case, if Scott guided us to Jennifer's remains he would receive leniency on the attempted helicopter escape scheme and murder-for-hire charges targeting Bryon. In our initial conversation about how to approach this interview, the Sterling DA said she was going to tell Scott that it was *her* decision whether Scott would get to go on a trip to Utah to find Jennifer. She also boasted how she "was going to get in Scott's face" to get his cooperation.

After running a draft email past my new boss, Mike (Phil had moved on by 2018), to the Sterling DA, I sent it, hoping to stop the train wreck from becoming a reality with the following suggestions:

1. Don't tell Scott what "he knows." He will trap you and you won't get out. You can express levels of confidence in things you think are true, but it's never worked for me to tell him, "I know you." We can't really ever know what he knows.

2. If the trip to Utah is really going to happen, limit him to one day. Blame it on me. The longer you give him, the more he'll draw it out.

3. Insist that he gives you the location first. Nothing he's given us has been accurate so far. The less you say the better. He's already decided whether he's going to do this or not. I've never talked him *into* anything, only out of things by getting him riled up.

I also called Rachel, Scott's attorney, to help me manage this delicate conversation. She did not want to waste her time on this agreement either if it had no chance of succeeding.

The Sterling DA called me hours later, excited from her first face-to-face interrogation of a serial killer. Unfortunately, that is all it was—an attempted interrogation. She told me (and Rachel confirmed such when she called afterwards), "I told Scott that he *knows* exactly where Jennifer's body is and he got really pissed off at me. So, I told him that I'm the one, no one else, who decides if he goes on this trip or not. He got upset again and asked me how much authority I have over DOC (Department of Corrections) and the FBI to be calling the shots."

So far, it had gone exactly the opposite of how I hoped it would go. I asked, "What happened next?"

"He told me that he needed proof I had power over DOC and the FBI. He said Jennifer's body is in an area that's about twenty miles wide, but he required a deal in writing up front before he gave any specifics. So, obviously I couldn't give him something like that."

Bottom line? No trip. No deal. No closer to finding Jennifer.

## MORE JENNIFER SEARCHES

In September 2018, twelve years after I started working this case, I again met Sheriff White in Spring Canyon. He had found what was supposed to be the best set of cadaver dogs to run through the canyon. We had no other leads to where Jennifer might be. I had kept Jennifer's mom, and Bob, her dad, in the loop during the entire helicopter escape and murder-for-hire escapade with the hope of trading information with Scott. I told them we were taking yet one more stab at finding her. Neither of them held out much hope, but both were appreciative of the effort. We ran the dogs all through the canyon. In the process of hiking up and down the canyon washes I lost my Bureau cell phone in a crevasse when I slid down a gravelly slope and knocked it out of its belt clip. The cost to me included two days of paperwork, promises I had not given it to a Russian spy (or the like), and multiple apologies to my superiors and FBIHQ.

I returned to the Denver FBI office to meet with Scott's defender, Rachel. She had a large envelope from Scott addressed to me. After our mail room scanned it to make sure the envelope was not filled with something that would kill me and those around me, I unfolded a drawing of a 4 x 11-foot map. Sheets of 8.5 x 11-inch printer paper were held together by the sticky strip edges around stamps. It depicted the western border of Colorado and the northern and southern borders of I-70 as it ran westbound fifteen miles into Utah. It contained a scale and a legend and was highly detailed. I hung it on the wall in our squad area so we could study it and so new agents could marvel at it. A large X marked the spot of Jennifer's hidden remains. It looked like we could follow Scott's directions and drive there once we consulted Google Earth, but Sheriff White and his crew said there was no actual road like the one Scott had drawn. Sheriff White and his team actually drove there to make sure and sent me photos.

Sheriff White teamed up with FBI agents in Utah and they drove through all of the same canyons we had explored in 2009. Still, nothing made sense except Spring Canyon.

Scott was whispering loudly in Rachel's ear that the map she gave us would definitively lead us to the exact spot where Jennifer could be found. Rachel told me about their conversations, indicating that she was beginning to believe Scott was really trying and, this time, it might be true. I told her that she was welcome to work with Sheriff White directly and he could drive her to the exact road leading to Jennifer, per Scott's map. Rachel and her co-counsel drove to Utah, met with Sheriff White, and he accompanied them down a dirt road ten miles west of Spring Canyon that dead-ended into a Bureau of Land Management gate which had been closed and locked with no access beyond it for twenty years.

She called and apologized for not believing me that Scott's claims about the map and Jennifer were bogus. I replied, "Rachel, you did exactly what you were supposed to do and what any good investigator should do—you took the time to investigate what he said and proved to yourself and your team the truth. If you hadn't done that, you would've always wondered if Jennifer might be buried there."

## 32

# MAKING SCOTT CRY

Throughout October 2018, Rachel and her team met with Scott about Jennifer's possible burial site. He volunteered information about the 2001 murder of a red-haired female in Dutch Harbor, Alaska. He described the sweatshirt she was wearing from the state of Washington and knew she was an exotic dancer there before she came to Alaska. He also told them about a hitchhiker he killed in Colorado in 2005, the motive being he wanted the cash from the man's wallet. He said he shot the guy with the same gun he used to kill Terry and LeAnn. Scott told them about a third victim who told him his name was Tex and was hitchhiking from Colorado to Texas. Scott told Rachel that he killed the man and put him in a creek bed before placing rocks on top of him.

Rachel and I had spent enough time together by now that we enjoyed each other's sarcasm and candor. I told her that I was from Texas and I had never known a Texan to call himself "Tex." I knew that Scott was aware of my Texas roots and figured he was trying to appeal to something familiar to me, to draw me in to talk again. The Alaskan redhead was one of my suspected cases from the ViCAP research, and Scott knew I had been investigating that case for years. She was the person suspected of having a threesome in Fiancée-Catherine's bed just before Scott talked Catherine into throwing the sheets away. I asked Rachel to keep me in the loop if she heard any more details, but for now I was staying put and working on other cases.

On October 25, 2018, I was talking to the brother of a high school girl who had been brutally murdered in a small mountain town when Scott called.[168] When I told him I was in the middle of something and I would have to call him back, he said, "We must talk now, we need to work this deal out. You won't believe me if I tell the truth; you'll hate me."[169]

"I don't hate you, Scott. I answered your call just now, even though I'm in the middle of a very important conversation. I also took time out of my weekend to treat your boys, Justin and Cody, to lunch. They watched the recent *Dateline* show and have a lot of questions about you. Another reason I met them was actually for you. I told your boys, 'I sincerely hope someday you can have a relationship with your dad. But before that can happen, your dad must deal with whatever trauma or dysfunction he went through to make him into the killer he became.'"

I said directly to Scott, "Once you deal with that, you might give them a chance to talk to you."

Scott started crying loudly and said, "Jon, I want to come clean! I want to be a dad and put all this behind me!" I highly doubted him, of course, but did not say so. I told him we would talk soon and said goodbye. Although I had stepped away to take the call and Scott wasn't on the speakerphone any longer, the teenage brother and ATF agent were waiting for an explanation of the wailing sound coming from my phone. I told them, "The person you heard 'boohooing' is a serial killer who's trying to figure out how to be a dad."

## LAST PERSONAL VISIT

On December 4, 2019, I met with Scott for the first time in over eighteen months. Although I had seen him in court, he could not talk to me during the murder-for-hire and escape-by-helicopter trial. Rachel had asked me to see him because he did not want to go to trial and

---

168  Yes, the serial killer had my Bureau cell phone number. He had it for the past nine years at least, going back to trying to hammer out the gun charges and what he did with Kaysi, Jennifer, and LeAnn.

169  Sounds like a comment made to an intimate partner, right? I'd been working this case for too long for Scott to feel the need to say something like that.

lose like his cellmate, Fifty's son Marc, had lost. Scott wanted to trade a homicide or two in exchange for us dropping the escape charges. Rachel knew about it from a briefing I had given her about his twenty-one hitchhikers confession and puzzle, and she knew about his claims to Boulder defense attorneys about killing forty-five to fifty people. She believed this trip would be worth my time. I also wanted to avoid another circus trial on the helicopter stuff, so I agreed to the four-hour round trip even though the week was one of the busiest in recent years for me. I was hosting an FBI Defensive Tactics Instructor school for local law enforcement in our office on Monday. On Tuesday, I was showing a photo spread to a witness on the high school murder victim case and prepping with the U.S. Attorney to indict Robert Dear, the Planned Parenthood shooter from 2015. The road trip to visit Scott on that Wednesday would give me phone time for planning sessions to extract Dear from the Pueblo State Mental Hospital on Thursday and get him in front of a judge. That week I was taking critical calls from Russia on how to get a Denver murder suspect back to the USA, even though we did not have an extradition agreement with the country. So, my mind was buzzing at night with solutions and rearrangements for that busy week. But I wanted to be done with Scott, so I agreed to the day-visit.

    I got to the Sterling prison at just after noon, checked in with my DOC buddy, Randy, and we met Scott and his attorneys in a conference room. He was all smiles to see me again. His long, white beard hung past his chest, and he acknowledged his extra weight from eating too much. Scott tore into Randy about the unfairness of his prison living conditions during the first seven minutes we were there. I wrote on the top of my notepad, "Eight more mins," and slid it over to Scott's attorney. The attorney wrote back a question mark and I mouthed, "I'll explain later." The puzzled look remained on the attorney's face, as if I were warning him that something dangerous or monumental was about to happen—like perhaps he should run for cover. Later, I explained that Scott always spent at least the first fifteen minutes complaining, bargaining, berating, and asserting that he was owed innumerable benefits just for showing up to any meeting with me. We had not seen each other in a long time so Randy took the beatdown this time. I might have been off by a minute or two, but once Scott was done whining we got down to business.

Scott told us, "I killed a homeless wino in July 1997 in Hamilton, Montana, because the wino stole money from me." He gave details of injuries that matched the coroner's report and were part of the police investigation, but by now I was already bored and fairly certain this was another time suck. He was edging right up to the line of taking responsibility but was not going to cross it until I promised him a deal. I put down my pen and asked, "Is this another puzzle? Can you add something I can take to the DA up there? They're already aware of you as a suspect, but there's no family member looking for resolution on this one."

When he said that he would be better off back in the incentive pod for telling me about a legitimate murder, I told him, "Well, you're lucky you're dealing with me, Scott. Because I have complete control over the Colorado prison system. If I just snap my fingers, they do exactly what I say."

I wish I had a snapshot of Scott's face. I saw the flat, expressionless look I had seen before whenever I used sarcasm. One of his attorneys snickered nervously, wondering if I was joking or serious, because my facial expression doesn't change when I'm joking around. I continued, "See? Your attorney gets it! I have zero control over DOC, which you know by now after thirteen years of dealing with me. I'm happy to make you promises I can't deliver on if that makes you feel better."

No change in the flat, dead look. Rachel understood I was playing with him because I had no other answer for him. And she told him so. I am fairly certain he wanted to kill me that day—for no other reason than because he thought I was making fun of him. And I guess in a way I was.

After attempting to give me a detailed explanation of how he killed the Montana wino, Scott moved on to tell us that he had killed red-haired "Nicole" in Alaska in 2001. His attorneys were grinning anxiously while he described weighting a crab pot with ten-pound rocks after killing her in Dutch Harbor. His motive was to grab the thousands of dollars in cash she made from prostituting herself to the deep-sea sailors who were loaded with cash and in need of some pleasure. I had heard Scott's crab pot story through a handful of his former cellmates, but it was unverifiable because, if true, Nicole was at the bottom of Dutch Harbor. Exploring the harbor was logistically a no-go. I motioned to Scott's attorneys and to Investigator Randy that I was ready to head back to Denver. Of course, Scott was offended that I didn't have more time for him. They asked if I would please wait, assuring me that this story was legit, so I reluctantly spent another hour looking at Google Earth and listening to him pinpointing where he "dropped Nicole overboard." When the next pause presented itself I announced I had to leave, and before long I was in my Bucar for the two-hour trip back to the office.

That was the last time I saw Scott Lee Kimball. And my wife April could not have been happier!

## 33

# MOD PIZZA

ON JANUARY 31, 2020, I was waiting for Agent Peeples outside of Mod Pizza in north Denver. I had known Agent Peeples well for more than twenty years. Our kids were the same age, we attended the same church, and we bounced parenting advice off of each other during numerous boring surveillance shifts in Denver. I had just finished jumping through all the Bureau hoops necessary to secure the informant payment for the former inmate, Jimmy. We had been able to keep Scott in prison because of Jimmy's fine performance as the informant on the helicopter escape/murder plan. Jimmy helped the judge see clearly that it *could* have happened.

Agent Peeples drove up and was on his phone when my Bureau cell rang. The caller ID showed a call from the Colorado prison system. I took the call, thinking it was Jimmy. The voice on the other end asked, "Hey, Agent Grusing, you know who this is?" Scott's higher-pitched voice was unmistakable—beginning with the word "Hey."

With feigned uncertainty I replied, "I have an idea who it is but don't know for sure."

"Ha-ha, Agent Grusing. I always enjoy your sarcasm."

I whispered to Agent Peeples, "It's Scott, you mind if I talk for a second?" By this time, Scott needed no introduction to any agent in the Denver FBI office. Thanks to the numerous documentaries and presentations over the past five years, everyone knew about Mr. Kimball. Agent Peeples smiled and said, "This should be good."

Scott and I had sat across from each other at a table in the Sterling prison just a few weeks earlier, along with his attorneys, as he tried to trade two homicide victims for the pending helicopter escape and attempted murder charges. After more than thirteen years of living and breathing this man, of course I knew it was him.

Scott had not called me for over a year because his attorneys clamped down on him to stop—not that he could be deterred if he really wanted to talk to me or anyone else. He had avoided trial a few weeks prior by pleading guilty to a reduced escape charge and his recent case was now finished. Pushing aside his annoyance at me, Scott asked, "So, Jon, are we gonna be adversaries forever? Do you really want to get to the bottom of everything? Can we work together?" Agent Peeples was looking at me with the unspoken question of, "Are we going to eat or what?" Scott was talking a hundred miles per hour and I didn't want to be rude to my lunch friend, so I put the murderer on speaker. I told Scott that I had learned a lot from him and made a lot of mistakes along the way in doing so. But I was working on other cases that demanded my full attention and didn't have time for just the Montana wino or Alaskan crab pot stories. If Scott was willing to candidly talk about what we both knew to be true, I would listen. That meant telling about *all* of his homicides. Apologies and ownership go a long way if they are sincere, even if I am with the FBI and he is a convicted murderer. I was also letting Scott know I had more important cases than his and didn't have time for him to jerk my chain again.

Scott gobbled up my apology with gusto, saying, "Not many FBI agents will admit when they're wrong." He pressed on by asking why I listened to other inmates when I knew they were telling lies about him. Scott's incentive pod privileges were stripped because of his recent escape attempt, but he was much more agitated about the fact that I was looking at his mail again. You see, this was a problem for him, and my timing could not have been better. He was working on securing Wife #4, a naïve woman named Elizabeth who had already taken Scott's last name, even though she had not met him and likely never would.

## MARRY A SERIAL KILLER?

The first letter Elizabeth sent to me arrived at the FBI office in late 2019—her head was spinning. A deputy in her jail (yes, she was an inmate in another state) showed her the latest *Dateline* episode about my sparring partner, Scott, who was also her new lover. Her note read, "Can you please call me??" The deputy had given Elizabeth a crash course about Scott, including the following insights about her future husband: The man was responsible for at least twenty-one homicides; he tried to kill his own boys for money; he had been an FBI informant who snitched on other inmates before killing their girlfriends; and the deputy quoted from the show that Scott "is the greatest manipulator the FBI will hopefully ever learn from."

I had avoided Scott's calls while taking some calls from Elizabeth after she saw the documentary. I simply confirmed to her what she already knew from the deputy—that Scott was the most dangerous person she would likely ever run across, much less marry. I never told her what to think, nor gave her any advice on what she should do. I answered her questions with the same information that was already out in the public domain, knowing full well that Scott would squeeze out every word I said to her and use it against me the next time we spoke. She already had pixie dust in her eyes, and that stuff does not come out easily.

I told Agent Peeples about Scott's girlfriend and my desire to extricate myself from whatever was happening between her and Scott. I knew after the twenty-one person puzzle, and the forty-five-or-fifty-homicide exercise, and the final two murder confessions, that any further discussions with him were a waste of time. We enjoyed our pizza and caught up on our families after what would be my last call with Scott.

## TOO MUCH FOR COLORADO

One morning in June 2021, Barb's partner, Kay, called. Her tone was frantic as she demanded to know, "How did Scott escape from prison?? Do you think he's coming to get me??" My desk phone was also now ringing with a call from a local news reporter who wanted an answer to the very same question: Why wasn't Scott listed in the Colorado DOC inmate records anymore? Did he escape for real this time? Next, Jennifer's mom called, wondering why she had not been notified (as she should have been if Scott escaped, was transferred, or was dead). And finally, Larissa called to say that she had heard Scott was deathly ill; she was wondering if she could finally breathe a sigh of relief because he was finally dead. All of my DOC connections in the main office had retired. I had no one on speed dial that would have given me a heads up, nor anyone to call to find out what was going on. I hit up Randy, the Sterling investigator. Scott was not dead. He had been transferred to Florida.

After some digging, I learned that Scott had been transferred to USP Coleman in Florida under an interstate compact agreement. It simply means that, "We get rid of someone who's causing us too much trouble, and you can give us (Colorado) your worst pain in the ass prisoner." The helicopter escape plan had been the last straw for inmate Kimball, who had previously worked to get a guard fired, used the librarian's computer to type fake FBI documents, embarrassed a warden or two, and kept getting out of jail on writs for special treatment and body hunts. Colorado DOC did not care who they got—the unknown Florida inmate could *not* be any worse than Scott. I had traveled to Scott's new home at USP Coleman a few years before when I accompanied a female U.S. Attorney for an interview with an inmate on our "stomping" homicide case at the Supermax. I can assure you USP Coleman is not a vacation resort.

As I told the parents of Scott's victims when I made my round of calls to settle everyone down, USP Coleman was not a place *any* inmate would ever want to be. I thought I was going to get shanked, or worse, when I visited the prison. My prison escort left me unguarded and unarmed, sitting inside an unclean medical treatment room with blood on the floor. Next to me was an attractive female prosecutor, the likes of whom these predators had not seen in years. Unrestrained inmates freely roamed through the area, eyeballing us like packs of hyenas salivating over small prey. The U.S. Attorney and I were grateful to get out of there with all our limbs intact.

When I got the news that Scott had been transferred to USP Coleman, I called the investigations lieutenant and warned him about some of the bad things that were going to happen with his new tenant, Mr. Kimball. The lieutenant shrugged it off, thanked me for the call, and implied that he knew a lot of inmates like Scott. Within a year, Scott was "transferred for unknown reasons" to a prison in Kentucky, then again to the U.S. Penitentiary in Florence, Colorado. The most secure section of the Florence federal prison is more commonly known as The Supermax, as it is designed for the most dangerous inmates in the country. I don't know what Scott did to necessitate these transfers, but I'm sure the stories would be quite interesting. His first projected release date is 2082, making him a ripe 116 years old before he will face the consecutive federal gun charges.

## GOODBYE

On July 30, 2021, I retired from the FBI. It is a day I will not forget, for many reasons. Lori and Rob (Kaysi's parents) and Bryon Dathe came to my office for my retirement celebration. They told my family and my FBI co-workers how much my dedication and friendship meant to them. Gary and Katharina attended, along with other investigators and U.S. attorneys who had carried me through this and other intense investigations. My wife, April, described the feeling in the room: "It was magic." My mom and my grown kids, Bethany and Ben, were there too. Nobody said I was the smartest guy they ever met, but they did mention "persistent" a time or two. I hated walking away from an agency that had become a deep-seated part of who I was, but after twenty-three years of working on unique violent crime cases like Scott Kimball's, the FBI was assigning me to work on civil rights matters. April and I thought about moving, but our kids were staying put in Colorado. It was time to try something new.

## 34

# LORI & KAYSI REVISITED

In August 2024, while reviewing some timelines, journals, and reports, I came across a Westminster Police Department (WPD) report documenting a call made by Bryon Dathe on March 25, 2003.[170] Someone had made charges to his credit card while he was out of town. Detective Gary had mentioned this to me early on—Kaysi supposedly stole Bryon's credit card and made a variety of purchases while he was out of town. She had confessed to it. While fifty or so similar incidents existed in Scott's scams of family and friends, this one nagged at me for a couple of reasons. The facts of this simple credit card case will help explain some "whys" behind Neighbor Ted, Alaska, and Denver FBI manipulation, what Scott learned with the Spokane PD and Larissa stunts, and what Machiavellian looks like when it takes the form of a person.

For ten days in March 2003, Kaysi had been in charge of feeding Bryon's dog during his trip. She had the keys to his house. The WPD officer, Scott, Kaysi, and Bryon went to Lori's house where Scott was already living (Scott and Lori had started dating in February of 2003), hoping to figure out what had happened. After hearing that almost $2,500 had been charged to Bryon's card over a ten-day period, Scott took Kaysi "into the bedroom where they spoke for about forty-five

---

170  Damon Antal, "Kimball Files." Alternative Reality Television. Received by Jonny Grusing, August 5, 2024. (Attachment pp. 602–606)

minutes." Kaysi came out and admitted to using the credit card. She apologized but said she never signed his (Bryon's) name. She did not provide details on the expensive camera equipment that was purchased from Soundtrack or the numerous other purchases, except that she gave it to Dachelle. Nor did she know where the credit card was, other than "thrown away."[171]

Kaysi later told WPD in April 2003 that she had given all the stolen items to a woman named Angel (not Dachelle) who lived in a trailer, but Kaysi did not know where the trailer was. Kaysi could not tell the detective what happened to the money she made when she sold the items. The Soundtrack receipt, by far the largest amount spent, listed the purchaser as Dachelle Bovill in Englewood, Colorado.[172] Twenty transactions occurred on the card during a two-week period, with six at Walmart stores in three different suburbs, single meals at McDonald's and Burger King, and an Office Depot purchase.

I called Lori on August 9, 2024, because while I had some theories regarding this report, I was more interested in her thoughts. I asked, "What do you think about the time Kaysi was arrested for using Bryon's credit card when he was out of town and she charged up his account?"

"Jonny, I've never heard of this. I can tell you this before you tell me anything else. It wasn't her. It was Scott. He had signed up for another card under his name on Bryon's account and charged that card to the max without telling Bryon about it. I didn't even know about this incident involving Kaysi."

I told her it happened in March of 2003 and involved $2,500 of charges for cameras, printers, Walmart and Target purchases, and McDonald's and Burger King meals in Thornton, Aurora, Westminster, Englewood, Arvada, and Denver.

---

171  Three things assert to me that this was Scott's handiwork: (1) If you're alone with Scott you'll say or do things you never would otherwise; (2) the "never signed his name" assertion was how Scott responded to numerous check fraud allegations, even getting Gamblin to sign Dr. Cleve's name in 2005 to eleven checks; and (3) Kaysi didn't know the details but had a "fall guy" that law enforcement couldn't verify, not unlike the "driver" in the Utah desert.

172  Bovill is the last name of Kaysi's boyfriend, CB. If she was trying to get away with these twenty fraud charges, she was foolish to list that last name which would come right back to her.

Lori responded, "Kaysi didn't own any cameras. Scott certainly did. His mom lived in Arvada and he had an apartment in Englewood at that time. Kaysi also didn't have a car in March 2003. How could she get to all those places? For Kaysi, it would've been a misdemeanor, for Scott it meant going back to prison. He told me that many times—he puts things in people's heads, like 'I'll get in so much more trouble than you will. You've got to do this for me.' Somehow he made it well worth her while when he talked to her in that bedroom. Kaysi knew everything about Bryon; if she was gonna steal from him, it wouldn't have been a credit card. He left money and expensive things all around his house. I left money laying around all the time and Kaysi never stole from me. Stealing a credit card or using someone else's is Scott's deal."

Lori continued, "Bryon's old roommate, Jeff, was accused of stealing cash and silver dollars, collector's coins. Scott told us he saw Jeff going into stores using the silver and paying for things. Bryon and Jeff were roommates and best friends. Scott convinced us all that Jeff stole from Bryon and that caused a break-up of their relationship. Jeff swore on God's name he didn't do it, but Bryon said Scott's statements contained such detail . . . Jeff couldn't overcome the lies.

"When Scott got an American Express card under Bryon's name with Scott as an account holder, he sent me to the ATM to use the card to get cash, always giving me a different reason why it needed to be me. I know now that it's because he didn't want to be on the ATM camera. I don't know if Bryon had to pay back all the debt, but I'm guessing he did. Scott also stole a $10,000 engagement ring that Bryon bought for his fiancée, Christine, though we didn't figure out that until much later."

Recall that Lori met Scott around Valentine's Day 2003 and they started dating within days. Lori's jewelry went missing in March 2003, which she estimated was worth maybe $10,000 to $15,000. Weeks earlier, Scott had borrowed her car keys to "clean her car." She kept the jewelry in a blanket, folded up inside of another blanket in a space-bag in her closet. Scott had seen her put the jewelry there, but she never considered it might be *him*, because he worked for the FBI and he did not need the money. Scott always carried around a huge stack of hundred dollar bills, so why would he steal from his new live-in girlfriend?

After Lori told him that her jewelry was missing Scott said, "It must've been Kaysi or one of her drug friends. Let's do something about these drug addicts together!" Lori told me, "He got me all worked up about them being responsible, and I never thought about *him*."

I asked her, "What caused you to finally realize the jewelry thief was Scott?"

"It was when you showed me that bank robbery picture, Jonny. At least, I think it was you. I forget when that was, but for some reason, my brain had finally relaxed and I knew that he took my jewelry."

"It was me, Lori. In 2008, I showed you a surveillance photo from a 2005 bank robbery in Clifton, Colorado. The robber talked about his sick kids at home as he held up the teller at gunpoint. The camera footage was poor, but as you told me, 'The robber has the same build, stance, and facial features as Scott.' The robber *did* look like Scott, but we couldn't prove it was him. Circling back to Kaysi and Bryon, Kay (Barb's partner) talked to me about how effective Scott was at dividing family members against one another. How do you think he got Kaysi to take responsibility for stealing Bryon's card and never tell you about it?"[173]

"He separated us and set me against his mother, Barb, when we first started dating," Lori replied. "Scott said, 'I hate to tell you this, but my mother really doesn't like you. She thinks you're an alcoholic.' That was ironic, because Scott was the one putting a drink in my hand at every opportunity. After Scott's arrest in 2006, Barb flew me to Arizona and told me that he told her the same thing—that Scott convinced her I hated her, probably for the Neighbor Ted stuff and leaving Scott alone with Ted. Barb and I made up on that trip and realized Scott had built the wall between us over the past three years.

"The morning that Scott had me arrested for the vacuum cleaner incident, I not only found his girlfriend's hairbrush, I told him that I was going to call Barb about the $1,000 that I had been paying her over a few months that she never got. Barb bought a lemonade tent, tables, and citrus press for the farmer's markets for Scott's beef business. He

---

[173] I told an FBI Agent named Ken with whom I worked closely on this story and he said, "Once Lori saw Scott in the photo and effectively placed him inside that circle of people who steal things, her brain connected and unlocked the possibility that he was the thief of her jewelry."

asked me to pay her back through him, so he could wire the money to her. Barb, Brett, Gamblin, and I were all learning in late 2005 that Scott's beef business was simply a scam on all of us to pay *him* for expenses that he never paid. He was stealing from all four of us at once.

"I tell you those stories to say, 'Who knows what Scott said to Kaysi in that bedroom?' I can tell you he promised her something and made it worth her while to lie for him."

## 35

# KAY REVISITED

I CALLED Kay on August 5, 2024, hoping to acquire some additional understanding on a few things I had heard while sitting with her and Barb at their dinner table in their Arvada home. But, I had not ever put those things in the case file, for reasons you will see.

I started with, "Kay, I know you and Barb told me that when Scott first got out of jail in Denver in December 2002, Agent Carle and the FBI agent from Alaska brought him to your doorstep and said something like, 'He has to stay here.' Can you tell me more about that scene? What exactly happened? Were you there with Barb?"

"I was there, alright. I remember that well, Jonny. When they came to our door, Agent Carle was wearing a suit coat and he swept it back so we could see his gun and badge when he told us that Scott was helping the FBI and he needed a place to live because of the type of character he was. Agent Carle said, 'It has to be here,' while he was showing his gun."

I asked, "Was it an intimidation sort of thing?"

"Exactly. Exactly. That's how I felt—really intimidated by him."[174]

"Thanks, Kay. I'm sorry that happened. I know that Scott stayed there for a while because of that. Switching over to Scott's allegations of Ted, did you ever see any signs of abuse on the boys?"

---

[174] I asked Carle about this in a June 4, 2025, call. He said he remembered meeting Kay and Barb when Scott was released, but if they saw his gun and badge it was not from any action he took to intimidate them. It was incidental.

"Not at all. Not at all. Whenever Ted wanted to take the kids—he was at grandma's house a lot, being her companion—when the boys got a chance to go up there, they were excited to go spend time with him. I don't recall a time when they said, 'Nah, we'd really rather not go.'"

I asked, "What were Barb's thoughts on how Scott talked his brother and cousin into testifying?"

"She thought that Brett said that he was in the other room most of the time and not the victim of much abuse and that their cousin was probably coerced by Scott to say that he was assaulted. It was the same with Blaine, my son, who won't even talk today about some of the things that Scott got him and his wife in trouble for, even though I'm confident Blaine had nothing to do with it."

I asked, "What do you think about Scott's allegations that Ted was still assaulting him in 1984? When Scott would've been about eighteen?"[175]

"I don't see that either, Jonny. Scott was a good-sized kid, playing football and wrestling and all. He wasn't popular at all, though, in school. He felt like he had to have a lot of money for people to like him."

What I didn't mention to Kay was Ted's journal notes, documenting that Scott visited him in June 1987 and brought someone named John with him. From the notes, it was a normal, friendly visit. When Scott was almost twenty-one years old in March 1988, he called Ted from California and said he was in trouble and not to tell anyone where he was. It would be over a year later on October 31, 1989, when Scott ran out of a Montana hotel room, crying and drunk because his girlfriend broke up with him, then pointed the gun at the roof of the pickup cab and pulled the trigger. Then, at age twenty-three, Scott blamed Ted for the suicide attempt and won a lot of money in the court settlement. Could Ted possibly have molested Scott? I wondered as Kay and I spoke. This was not for me to answer, even in 2024, but nothing in Scott's adult life of reporting to the courts or law enforcement had been true that I could verify. Ted was dead and Scott was in prison for life, so it didn't really matter, right? Except for the wreckage that became Ted's life. I consider his quiet, sensible denial: "Scott was only after my money," and it aligns with everything else I learned about Scott.

---

175 Damon Antal, "Kimball Files." Alternative Reality Television. Received by Jonny Grusing, August 5, 2024. (Attachment p. 45)

Kay continued, "Scott was so good at separating his parents, Virge and Barb. We learned later that when Scott was a teenager and he went up to Montana, he told his dad, 'All Barb and Kay give me to eat is hot dogs. Cold ones. They don't even cook them.' When in reality, we cooked a hot meal almost every night. But it *worked*; stories like that worked against Virge and Barb and set them at odds.

"The first time I met Scott he was playing in the carport and he jumped down on the hood of my car and dented it. I get in the car and the roof's almost touching my head. I was able to push it back up some. I asked Scott and Brett about it and they both denied doing it. Then Brett admitted they did, but Scott kept saying, 'No, we didn't,' even after Brett admitted it. You know, he was really young, then.[176] It just started early."

I told Kay, "You're very helpful in talking toward the central piece of what I'm trying to write about. I believe that Scott had a chance to be a decent human even though he was bent toward manipulating and fabricating stories. I think Scott kept making daily choices to lie, steal, and twist things and got increasing gratification from doing such things to people. I think he was so desensitized to people, to us as human beings, by the time he was released in 2002, that every emotion was an 'act.' He was very good, though, at pretending to be concerned for someone else."

"I agree with everything you just said, Jonny."

---

176  Scott would have been nine or ten years old.

## 36

# PERSPECTIVES

ON AUGUST 24, 2021, I was driving home from investigating a missing person case in the mountains when Lori called me, crying. I can tell you where I was when the phone rang—on a mountain pass near Buena Vista, Colorado. She said, "I just came home and found Bryon dead in the house. It was a sudden heart attack." We cried together at the shock, remembering this genuinely nice human being who positively affected all of our lives.

On July 8, 2024, while writing this piece of the manuscript I called Lori to tell her what I was writing about her, Kaysi, and Bryon. That's when I gained her permission to use their true names. Lori and I had been speaking every six months or so for the past ten years—I kept up with her health after she beat cancer twice and continued to connect with her even after she moved away from Colorado. She is still working in a nail salon and still answers the phone with an upbeat and welcoming tone in her voice; she maintains a skeptical yet positive outlook on life. Lori is consistently selfless during our calls, more concerned with how I'm doing than talking about herself. I told her that from my viewpoint, Bryon's trusting nature and perceived friendship with Scott embodied the process of target selection by predatory people like Scott. Lori said this:

"Bryon died on August 23, 2021, on the same month and day that Kaysi died. I came home the morning following his death and found him where he'd fallen off the bed. I'd never seen someone dead before but felt both extremely sad and honored to be a part of his life."

When I told Lori what I was writing about, including her two arrests surrounding the vacuum cleaner incident, she said, "When I saw that hairbrush, I didn't just think about Scott having an affair. I thought about him stealing from me and his mom. Sometimes those people who are calm in the moment are calm for a reason. They're manipulating you. I hope people can learn some things about dangerous people from what you're writing."

## LARISSA & JUSTIN

On July 11, 2024, I had coffee with Larissa and Justin at a trendy shop named Convict Coffee in Parker, Colorado. Larissa and I communicate a few times each year, and she has gradually grown physically and emotionally stronger as a result of being separated from Scott. Justin was the best I have seen in years. He still battles some physical challenges from the 2004 attempts on his life by his father, but he seems emotionally healthy. He was smiling, laughing some, and was very attentive while Larissa and I were discussing my efforts to write a book that would describe how we all wrestled with the devastation Scott left in his wake. I asked Justin, "So, what are your thoughts on all this stuff today?"

"I talked about my dad trying to kill me when other kids asked me about it in high school, when they saw my scars; but things were very fresh back then. Now, when people ask, I'll answer what I can, but eventually, when the conversation becomes awkward, I'll just say, 'You can look it up online. It's all there.' Today, I feel like it all happened to someone else when I talk about what happened to me."

After we left the coffee shop, I called Larissa, "Sorry I forgot to ask you . . . what stood out most over your years with Scott?"

"Wow. I'm gonna have to call you back on that," she said. Then she ventured, "Don't trust anyone, is my first thought. That's a little harsh, but that's where I've been since him. I have major trust issues. You'd think that being married to someone and having their children would cause them to trust you, but Scott never trusted me at all. He always had to know where I was and what I was doing and didn't believe my answers."

I interrupted, "Yet Scott was coming in late at night after seeing prostitutes, giving you terrible answers and demanding your trust."[177]

"Exactly. I guess I've come to the point that if someone says, 'X, Y, Z,' then I'm going to check out X and Y and Z until I'm sure that what they're saying is true. I've got to do my homework."

"Larissa, you've basically hit a central theme of my story about this investigation: you can't just take some things at face value. You have to do your homework."

# HOWARD

I called Howard, LeAnn's dad, that same evening. We hadn't spoken for almost five years. He was surprised and seemed pleased to hear my voice. For about forty-five minutes, Howard processed through LeAnn's story as he often did when we would speak years ago, and I learned some new facts about LeAnn.

"When LeAnn was married for three years to her drug addict husband, it was because she thought she could rescue him—she was very naïve and trusting. She had an undiagnosed bipolar emotional disorder with a lot of highs and lows. When she started dating Steve 2, the bank robber in prison with Scott, I wasn't happy with it, but I thought, 'Well, at least this guy's in prison and she can't get hurt.'

"I didn't know until much later that Steve 2 had convinced her that he was wrongly accused and that's why she wanted to help break him out of jail and meet him in Mexico. She colored her hair for the passport that she thought she was getting. I know that because I saw the email she sent to her cousin.

"I should have protected her more. I should've told her, 'You've got to understand that there are bad people out there who will use you.' Her ex-husband used her, Steve 2 used her. Scott used her and killed her."

---

177 I thought, "Scott hit the Dark Triad trifecta of narcissism, Machiavellianism, and psychopathy in his control, manipulation, and lack of compassion," with Larissa's brief observation.

Howard's intertwined grief and self-blame, still fresh after twenty years, was escalating quickly. I interrupted, "Howard, you're doing what good people do—blaming yourself for LeAnn's murder when the blame is not yours to take. You play the 'if only' scenarios to second guess what you could've done to stop it. Many people lost someone to Scott, and he is one hundred percent to blame."

Howard agreed and said he'd been told that many times, but it's hard for him to accept. He is now focused on raising his grandkids and deepening his faith in God and being a better Christian. He asked, "Could you please send me a copy of the book when it's done?"

I said, "Of course, I'll send you a copy."

# ROB

I speak to Rob, Kaysi's dad, more often than the other parents. We've had coffee together, been out to eat and at each other's homes, we keep up with what our children are doing and talk about how Scott affected our lives and our faith. In March 2024, Rob and his wife, Michelle, attended a presentation I gave on this investigation at the Cold Case and Cocktails event in Highlands Ranch, Colorado. I introduced him as Kaysi's dad and he spoke with a handful of people. Rob, like the others I mentioned, faced the devastation head-on, and through years of talking about it and searching his own soul and seeking wise counsel, he has arrived at a place where he can counsel others who have experienced tremendous loss to still thoroughly enjoy their present families and their lives.

When I called Rob on July 12, 2024, he answered while en route to southern Colorado and caught me up on what his daughters were doing. I told him about my struggles to write a book and how others had tried unsuccessfully—and that my first effort was an attempt to not stray from what the facts were and to pack in as many facts as possible. That manuscript read like an affidavit and was just too much of everything. So, I started over, writing as if simply telling a story.

Rob said, "I consider this a redeeming story. That's just me, and I know others wanted to assign blame like, 'It's forty percent Scott's fault, twenty percent Lori's fault, twenty percent the FBI's fault,' and so on. But for me, I have to put it at one hundred percent Scott's fault. Anybody can point blame at someone else, but it's just a waste of time. Jennifer, Kaysi, and LeAnn each had their struggles, but also had chances to be redeemed and to grow. Scott took away any chance they had at growth or redemption."

## SHERIFF WHITE

On July 23, 2024, I called former Utah Sheriff White and asked how retirement was treating him. "My blood pressure's down and I'm loving working on the farm all day, Jonny," was his response. I asked what stood out most to him about our time in the desert with Scott. Without hesitation he said, "He was just so damn evil." When I asked what caused him to say that the former sheriff said, "He was always looking at people, really *watching* them. He'd kill you if he could. But you'd just think he's the funny little fat guy who's not dangerous."

## BOSS PHIL

On July 30, 2024, I called Phil and we reminisced about working on Safe Streets and the things we missed about the FBI. Within minutes Phil brought up Scott Kimball and I told him that I was attempting to write a book about our investigation into Kimball. He reminded me, "Jon, I told you to take notes early on because you'd never have another case like this one. I wish I'd taken some." I told him that I did keep a journal and was keeping this story simple, without feeling pressured to include every detail because things can spin out of control quickly. I asked Phil, "What stands out most to you about the whole Kimball thing?"

"Those two dads coming in and then me going to the file. I was like, 'You gotta be shittin' me. We've got a big problem.'" Phil continued, "Then I came to you and we started looking at it together. Scott manipulated Agent Carle to the point where we would've never investigated the murders if those dads didn't come in. Scott rode him like a new bike. Agent Carle was even manipulated by Scott after he was off the case. Scott manipulates everyone he runs into and would've manipulated the whole FBI if he could've. He's a classic sociopath. I'll never forget those days in the desert looking for those girls."

## AGENT CARLE

In a statement to *The Atavist*, Agent Carle said he has been judged from the convenient vantage of hindsight. "Everything is always clearer on Monday morning," he said. "All the families lost loved ones. If they feel better to blame me for it, that's fine."

The journalist asked Agent Carle, "What about the moment you realized that Kimball might be a serial killer? Did it shake you to learn your informant was so violent?" Agent Carle said no. "I am not that shocked about what people do to each other anymore. People kill for a whole lot less."[178]

On June 4, 2025, I called Carle for perspective and he said, "We couldn't discount Kimball as a suspect in Jennifer's disappearance and death, so finding out he killed her wasn't a huge surprise. When Gary called about Kaysi, though, that was a shock. And, of course, I knew nothing about LeAnn's disappearance."

## MY THOUGHTS

Finding LeAnn's hair clip and Scott's response, "That's not her. Let's keep moving," probably ranks as my clearest memory during this investigation. A close second is Scott's National Forest comment, "What if one of these girls in on national forest land?" Also, the trash bag receipt proving Scott was in Walden on that day and my call to the forest service to find Kaysi. Justin's description of his dad trying to kill him while the boy was drawing awful pictures with crayons of people dying, the bright red sprays of blood very gory and expressive—those

---

[178] Jordan Michael Smith, "The Snitch," *The Atavist*. No. 115. (2021): 44 (Retrieved June 29, 2024)

images will not leave me either. Lori's dreams about Kaysi being dead and talking to her, carrying the remains of my three victims from the evidence room to crematoriums or the cemetery, and Steve's comment, "There's another guy named Steve who lost his girlfriend," hang around my mind and soul as well.

Like Phil, I'll never forget our trips to Utah and the body hunts to find Jennifer and LeAnn. When I drive west on I-70 near Vail, the image of Uncle Terry wrapped in the tarp fills my windshield. As I pass Rifle, I wonder if we should have circled back to Scott's first assertion of Jennifer's burial site while we had him with us on the searches. The road signs to Collbran bring back the bloody shed, and Grand Junction releases the smell of sitting with Scott in the back of the suburban, the heat of the rocks in the horseshoe canyons, and the late nights with our search teams, laughing about the insanity of what we had ignorantly signed up for with the court order.

I believe that people like Scott exist in law enforcement, government, businesses, dating sites, and churches. At his core, he is a manipulator who's focused on what brings him immediate satisfaction. When he was young, that consisted of money and sex. He learned that we as humans are trusting, especially of family and friends, and that we give those people who are close to us a break when something disappears from our wallet.

I think when Scott's manager at the nursery caught him stealing the trees and didn't buy his excuses, lies, and manipulations, he was angry-crying, like he was after failing the polygraph given by FBI Agent Richard—unmoored because his superpower was not working. At age eighteen, he cut the flowers, plowed through and destroyed the nursery, then sent his grandmother and her friends over a waterfall because she would not bail him out. He got away with the attempted murder of Grandma Ruth and the murder of her friend, Frankie. That tasted good to him as he felt the power of taking a life and fooling everyone who saw it. Then he figured he would do it again. Scott killed because he could. He restrained himself from killing family members and spouses over the next twenty years, focusing instead on hitchhikers and prostitutes. I am confident Scott committed several homicides when he lost major court battles with Larissa in 1997 and 2004. He knew that he would be arrested for killing her so he brutally murdered surrogates instead. He had no relationship with the surrogates so he did not have to hide the bodies.

Scott had relationships with Uncle Terry, Jennifer, Kaysi, and LeAnn, so he had to create an alibi for himself during their disappearances while pre-loading someone else to blame—Stripper Ginger, the lottery (Terry), Jason (Jennifer), CB (Kaysi), Athena and Steve 2 (LeAnn). He was able to effectively isolate each of the victims from their loved ones, gain their trust or favor, and misdirect their loved ones and any law enforcement who searched for them.

Why was Scott so effective at deceiving and manipulating so many people? I believe he appealed to a defective epistemic default that most of us carry around.[179] Those are fancy words a friend of mine taught me that basically mean that we're starting our logic, but we are trying to know something or someone by asking the wrong basic questions, hence getting the wrong answers. For me, it's the danger of being certain when we should not be, and our hasty reduction of people and things to small bits of information rather than seeing a larger, integrated picture.

When Agent Carle showed up to talk to Scott in 2002 at the federal prison in Englewood, Colorado, Scott in essence told him, "I'm a fraud guy. I've written a lot of bad checks, but I'm not a violent guy. I've never been convicted of any crimes of violence. Ever." He then went on to tell Carle about the murder-for-hire plot that only he, Scott, could stop.

However, I learned from Bryon Dathe and from subsequent investigations of killer-con men like Scott, that when they steal from people who trust them, and even care about them, they are killing a part of that person—the friend-victim. Like Larissa said, the trust part no longer exists. Stealing from a trusting person draws upon the dark triad components—the thief has to deaden himself to emotion and compassion while relying upon misdirection and manipulation to get away with the crime. These are the same components necessary to commit predatory murder. When I saw how Scott stole from Bryon multiple times from 2004 to 2006, then put Bryon's life at risk in 2017 by sending Jimmy to kill him and use his identity in the helicopter escape plan—that was when the two worlds of murder and fraud collided.

---

179 Esther L. Meek, *Longing to Know: The Philosophy of Knowledge for Ordinary People* (Baker Publishing Group, 2003)

C.S. Lewis explained from Plato's assertion, "Virtue is one," that we cannot allow some vice inside of us to go unchecked, or it will take over all of our good qualities. If we are selfish at our core, that "bent" will eventually triumph over our compassion, kindness, and patience. It's like a weed left unchecked in your garden; it gives birth to more and more weeds until, after years of not unrooting the ugly, thorny growths, there is no garden remaining.

Scott, through years of compromising and deadening his own soul, not unlike the villain Voldemort in J.K. Rowling's *Harry Potter* series,[180] became further and further removed from his own humanness as he snatched vital pieces of existence from those who attempted to care for him. He could still express emotion, like when he carried injured Justin into the emergency room. But it was only because he was on center stage and the spotlight encouraged him to perform well. He had killed the childhood Scott inside of himself by then—the side that wanted to explore life and form relationships.

From working with the families of Kaysi, LeAnn, and Jennifer over the past twenty years, we have all concluded that the worthwhile messages to be proclaimed following the horrors inflicted by this killer are: (1) evil people exist and if they are identified early enough the wreckage that follows them can be avoided; (2) beware of "it can't happen to me" or "I know him, he's a good guy" assertions, because we all have some weeds to pull; (3) learn something each day, and become a little wiser and more honest in your relationships without becoming cynical; and, (4) always do your homework diligently, especially in matters of importance.

We are all investigators. And, like the dads—Bob, Rob, and Howard—we try to figure out what is going on with our loved ones when they are not responding to us. We cannot always avoid evil in our lives, but we can be vigilant in watching for it, searching it out, and dealing with it.

---

180 J.K Rowling, *Harry Potter and the Half Blood Prince* (Bloomsbury Publishing, 2005)

# EPILOGUE

Early Saturday morning on August 10, 2024, I rolled my Home Depot flatbed cart filled with seven small trees, some miscellaneous items, and five or six metal tree stakes to the cash register. The checker scanned the items on my cart and I paid and got my receipt, but I forgot about the twine I was holding in my hand. The checker did not see it either. I took about three steps toward the exit, then turned around and asked her to ring it up.

When I got to my car, I loaded the trees into the back and separated the tree stakes; two were stuck together and the cashier had not rung them up separately. Two inner voices spoke to me in that moment. The first was closer to Scott's voice, "These are only five bucks each and you've already gone back for the twine. Nobody's gonna know and Home Depot doesn't care—you spent plenty of money there today already. It's a waste of your time and theirs."

The second voice came from my daughter, Bethany. From the time she was three years old, she was always concerned that someone at the register at Target, the grocery store, or Chick-Fil-A might not have charged us for an item. She consistently asked, "Did we pay for that? Did they give us too much money back?" Bethany's voice on that August 2024 day said, "C'mon, Dad. It'll take you three minutes and you'll be glad you did it. Don't listen to Scott."

The decision was not that difficult after all. I went back in. I believe we can each guard against the subtle seep and seduction of the poisonous voices in our heads and constantly weed out the selfish thoughts that might lead us away from acts of compassion, morality, and service to our friends and neighbors.

# APPENDIX A

# TIMELINE

| | |
|---|---|
| Dec 18, 2002 | Scott released from FCI Englewood prison. (Steve, Jennifer's boyfriend, stayed put.) |
| Jan 1–31, 2003 | Scott working on making a different female victim (LeAnn) disappear. |
| Feb 16, 2003 | Scott moved Jennifer's belongings into his apartment. |
| Feb 17, 2003 | Jennifer's phone shut off. Scott's phone shut off until February 20th. |
| Feb 18, 2003 | Just after 12 a.m., Jennifer's Saturn was parked at Denver International Airport. |
| Feb 20, 2003 | Jennifer's phone made ten random, one-second calls then shut off permanently. Scott's phone used a cell tower in Vernal, Utah. |
| Feb 21, 2003 | Scott reported to Agent Carle that Jennifer flew to New York City. |

| | |
|---|---|
| Mar 2003 | Scott told Agent Carle, "I haven't heard from Jennifer in quite some time."[181] |
| Apr 19, 2003 | Scott told Agent Carle that Steve's dad told him, "Jennifer's dead." |
| Jun 17, 2003 | Scott was arrested and closed as an informant. He told the Denver FBI that Jennifer had been murdered by Jason, a close friend of her boyfriend Steve. |
| Jun 20, 2003 | Scott passed a polygraph, attesting that Jason killed Jennifer and told Scott about her dead body being located near Rifle, Colorado. Agent Carle called Jennifer's dad to let him know she was missing. |
| Jun 30, 2003 | Scott reopened as informant for the FBI. |
| Jul 10, 2003 | Agent Carle wrote a search warrant for Jennifer's car. |
| Aug 23, 2003 | A third female victim (Kaysi) disappeared, last seen with Scott. |
| May 7, 2004. | Agent Carle listed Jennifer as a Missing and Endangered Person in the National Crime Information Center database. |
| July–August 2004 | Scott's uncle disappears, last seen with Scott. |

---

[181] Another breadcrumb in the search warrant affidavit.

# APPENDIX B

# PERSONS INVOLVED

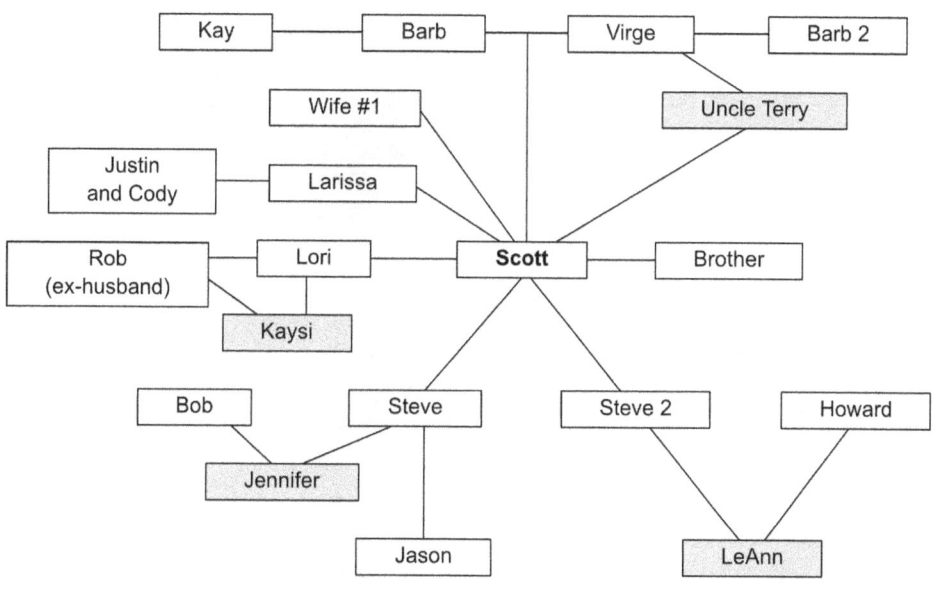

# REFERENCES

Aguilar, John (March 7, 2010). "Chapter 1: On the Loose." *Daily Camera*. Boulder, Colorado.

https://web.archive.org/web/20171021122521/http://scottleekimball.com/2010/03/07/chapter-1-on-the-loose/ (Retrieved, June 29, 2024)

Aguilar, John (March 8, 2010). "Chapter 2: Dead End." *Daily Camera*. Boulder, Colorado.

https://web.archive.org/web/20171021122717/http://scottleekimball.com/2010/03/08/chapter-2-dead-end/ (Retrieved, June 29, 2024)

Aguilar, John (March 7, 2010). "Chapter 3: The Informant." *Daily Camera*. Boulder, Colorado.

https://web.archive.org/web/20171021122611/http://scottleekimball.com/2010/03/09/chapter-3-the-informant/ (Retrieved, June 29, 2024)

Aguilar, John (March 10, 2010). "Chapter 4: Catch and Release." *Daily Camera*. Boulder, Colorado.

https://web.archive.org/web/20171021122347/http://scottleekimball.com/2010/03/10/chapter-4-catch-and-release/ (Retrieved, June 29, 2024)

Aguilar, John (March 11, 2010). "Chapter 5: Misplaced Trust." *Daily Camera*. Boulder, Colorado (Archived from the original, January

11, 2020) https://web.archive.org/web/20200111002548/http://scottleekimball.com:80/2010/03/1 (Retrieved, June 29, 2024)

Aguilar, John (March 12, 2010). "Chapter 6: Hurt." *Daily Camera*. Boulder, Colorado. (Archived from the original, November 3, 2018)

https://web.archive.org/web/20171021122430/http://scottleekimball.com:80/2010/03/ (Retrieved, June 29, 2024)

Aguilar, John (March 13, 2010). "Chapter 7: Uncle Terry." *Daily Camera*. Boulder, Colorado. (Archived from the original, November 3, 2018) https://web.archive.org/web/20171021122436/http://scottleekimball.com/2010/03/13/chapter-7-uncle-terry/ (Retrieved, June 29, 2024)

Aguilar, John (March 14, 2010). "Chapter 8: Meeting Scott Snitch." *Daily Camera*. Boulder, Colorado. (Archived from the original, November 3, 2018) https://web.archive.org/web/20171021122156/http://scottleekimball.com/2010/03/14/chapter-8-meeting-Scott-snitch/ (Retrieved, June 29, 2024)

Aguilar, John (March 15, 2010). "Chapter 9: Damaged." *Daily Camera*. Boulder, Colorado. (Archived from the original, November 3, 2018)

https://web.archive.org/web/20171021122324/http://scottleekimball.com/2010/03/15/chapter-9-damaged/ (Retrieved, June 29, 2024)

Aguilar, John (March 16, 2010). "Chapter 10: Unraveling." *Daily Camera*. Boulder, Colorado. (Archived from the original, November 3, 2018) https://web.archive.org/web/20171021122406/http://scottleekimball.com/2010/03/16/chapter-10-unraveling/ (Retrieved, June 29, 2024)

Aguilar, John (March 16, 2010). "Chapter 11: Rockstar." *Daily Camera*, Boulder, Colorado. (Archived from the original, November 3, 2018) https://web.archive.org/web/20171021122414/http://scottleekimball.com/2010/03/17/chapter-11-rockstar/ (Retrieved, June 29, 2024)

Aguilar, John (March 18, 2010). "Chapter 12: Connecting the Dots." *Daily Camera*, Boulder, Colorado. (Archived from the original, November 3, 2018. Retrieved, June 29, 2024.)

https://web.archive.org/web/20171021122341/http://scottleekimball.com:80/2010/03/

Aguilar, John (March 19, 2010). "Chapter 13: Mounting Evidence." *Daily Camera*, Boulder, Colorado. (Archived from the original, November 3, 2018. Retrieved, June 29, 2024.)

https://web.archive.org/web/20171021122604/http://scottleekimball.com/2010/03/19/chapter-13-mounting-evidence/ (Retrieved, June 29, 2024)

Antal, Damon. "Kimball Files." *Alternative Reality Television*. (Email received by Jonny Grusing, August 5, 2024. (Attachments))

CBS News, "Scott Kimball's Chilling Offer." https://www.youtube.com/watch?v=0AfsIVcmans. (Downloaded, June 30, 2024)

Cardona, Felisa, "Serial killer Scott Kimball pleads guilty in Boulder, gets 70-year sentence." *The Denver Post*, October 8, 2009. https://www.denverpost.com/2009/10/08/serial-killer-scott-kimball-pleads-guilty-in-boulder-gets-70-year-sentence/ (Downloaded, July 6, 2024)

Coet, Ed (2010). *SLK Serial Killer*. Publish America.

https://www.fbi.gov/how-we-can-help-you/more-fbi-services-and-information/freedom-of-information-privacy-act/department-of-justice-fbi-privacy-impact-assessments/vicap (Downloaded, July 25, 2024)

https://kaysi2.rssing.com/chan-16454715/latest.php (Downloaded, July 7, 2024)

https://www.newsnationnow.com/us-news/midwest/dna-from-rope-helps-put-1998-murder-case-to-rest/ (Downloaded, March 22, 2025)

https://www.cbsnews.com/news/serial-killers-life-of-crime/ Updated on: June 16, 2024/1:07 AM EDT/CBS News (Downloaded, July 19, 2024)

https://web.archive.org/web/20160908184559/http://scottleekimball.com/the-series/the-cleanup-man/ (Downloaded, June 29, 2024) https://web.archive.org/web/20171021122424/http://scottleekimball.com/2010/03/20/chapter-14-deal-with-a-killer/ (Downloaded, June 29, 2024) https://web.archive.org/web/20171021122711/http://scottleekimball.com/2010/03/21/chapter-15-still-waiting/ (Downloaded, June 29, 2024)

https://web.archive.org/web/20160601032548/http://scottleekimball.com/the-series/still-conning-from-behind-bars/ (Downloaded, June 29, 2024)

https://web.archive.org/web/20151009192738/http://scottleekimball.com/wp-content/uploads/2003/07/affy2.pdf (Search Warrant for 1996 Saturn, Signed July 10, 2003. Downloaded, June 29, 2024.)

https://web.archive.org/web/20190118041634/http://scottleekimball.com/2007/09/29/hunter-finds-human-bones-in-routt-national-forest/ (Downloaded, July 20, 2024)

https://www.ca10.uscourts.gov/sites/ca10/files/opinions/01018349505.pdf. Appellate Case 09-1245. (Date Filed, January 15, 2010. Downloaded, July 24, 2024.)

https://www.dailycamera.com/2010/04/01/judge-no-defense-documents-for-boulder-county-serial-killer-scott-kimball/ (Downloaded, March 25, 2024)

https://www.justice.gov/usao-co/pr/dave-conner-assistant-us-attorney-and-career-prosecutor-dies-peacefully-home-after-15 (Downloaded, July 10, 2024)

Larsen, Jace. "Suspected Serial Killer Could Get Plea Bargain." December 11, 2008. https://www.9news.com/article/news/investigations/suspected-serial-killer-could-get-plea-bargain/73-341335589 (Downloaded, July 4, 2024)

Meek, Esther (2003). *Longing to Know: The Philosophy of Knowledge for Ordinary People.* Brazos Press.

Payne, David. *Somebody Somewhere.* (February 7, 2018) S1 Episode 3. "A Man Named Kimball." Rainstream Media.

Personal Journal, provided to authors Kevin Vaughan and Sara Burnett with consent of FBI OPA, PIO, and K. Wright from Denver FBI on September 14, 2010.

*Rocky Mountain News.* May 16, 2008.

Rowling, J.K. (2005). *Harry Potter and the Half Blood Prince.* Bloomsbury.

"Serial Killer Scott Kimball on his life of crime." *48 Hours.* (Updated on: June 16, 2024/1:07 AM EDT/CBS News) https://www.cbsnews.com/news/serial-killers-life-of-crime/

"Serial Murder: Multi-Disciplinary Perspectives for Investigators." https://www.fbi.gov/stats-services/publications/serial-murder

Smith, Jordan Michael (2021) "The Snitch." *The Atavist.* No. 115. (Downloaded, June 29, 2024)

State of Colorado, County of Boulder v. Scott Lee Kimball. Warrant for Arrest Upon Affidavit. 2009-CR-0001626 (Signed, October 5, 2009. Received, July 26, 2024.)

U.S. District Court, State and District of Colorado. Application and Affidavit for Search Warrant, Search of Toshiba laptop and Dell computer tower, Case 07SW-05116 (Signed, June 1, 2007. Received, July 3, 2024.)

UNITED STATES OF AMERICA, Plaintiff - Appellee, No. 09-1245 (D. Colorado) (D.C. No. 1:07-CR-00249-MSK-1) v. SCOTT KIMBALL, Defendant - Appellate Case: 09-1245 Document: 01018349505 (Date Filed, January 15, 2010. Downloaded, July 17, 2024.)

Vaughan, Kevin. "Serial killer Kimball investigated in 2004 unsolved murder." September 14, 2010. https://www.denverpost.com/2010/09/14/serial-killer-kimball-investigated-in-2004-unsolved-murder (Updated September 21, 2018. Downloaded July 23, 2024.)

www.ingramcontent.com/pod-product-compliance
Lightning Source LLC
Chambersburg PA
CBHW020531030426
42337CB00013B/810